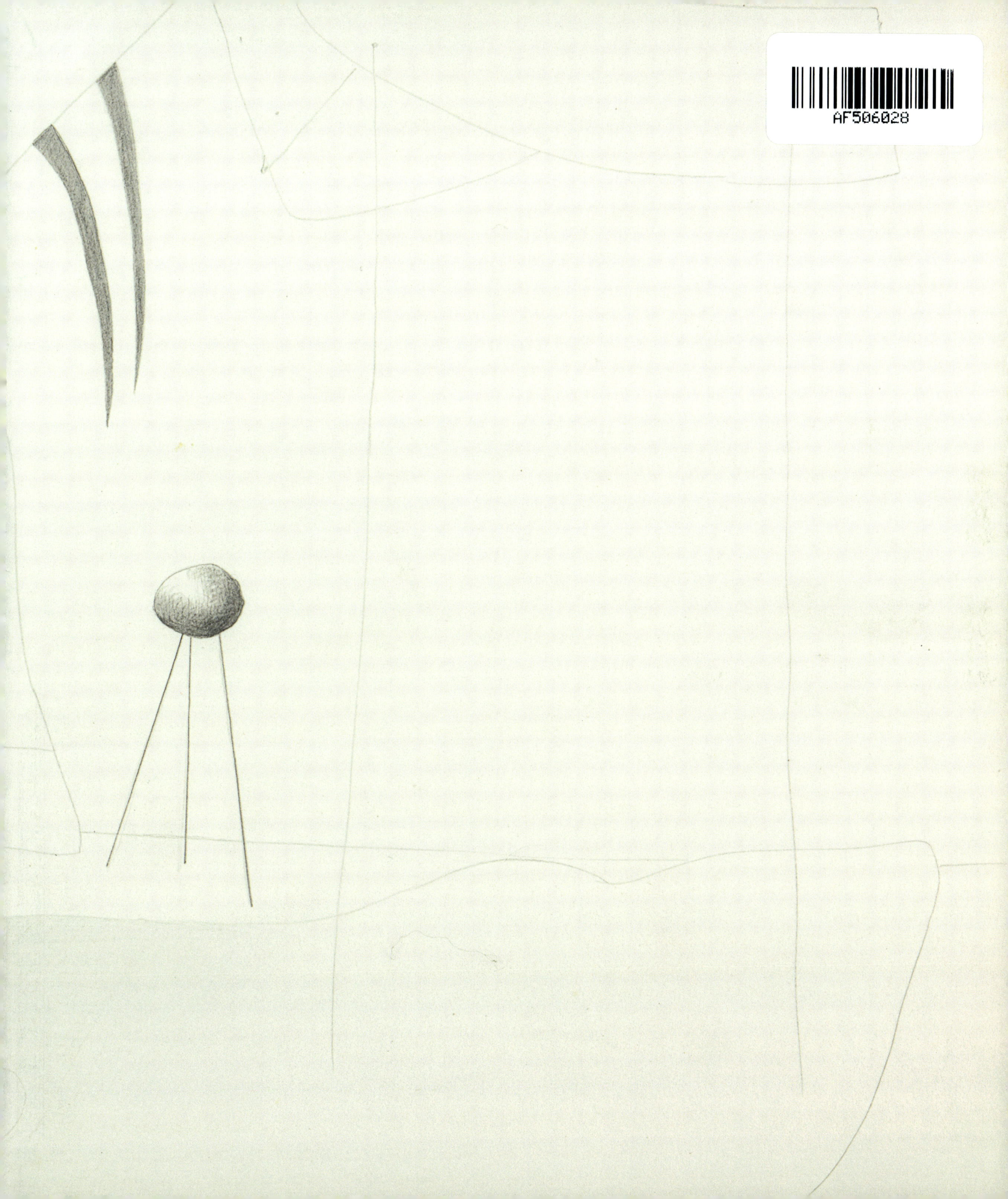
AF506028

Charles Howard

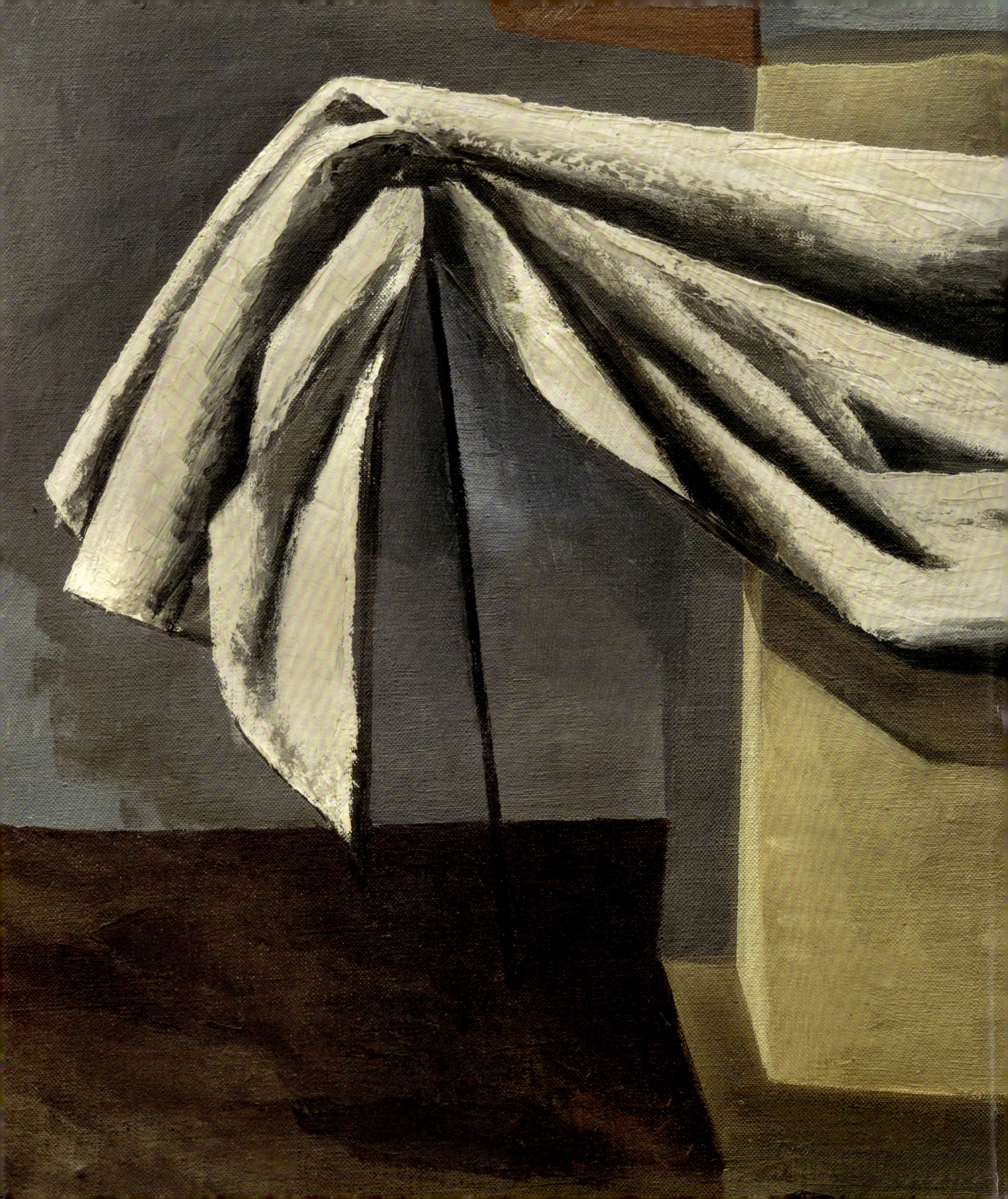

Charles Howard

A MARGIN OF CHAOS

Apsara DiQuinzio

with contributions by
Robert Gober and Lauren Kroiz

University of California,
Berkeley Art Museum and
Pacific Film Archive

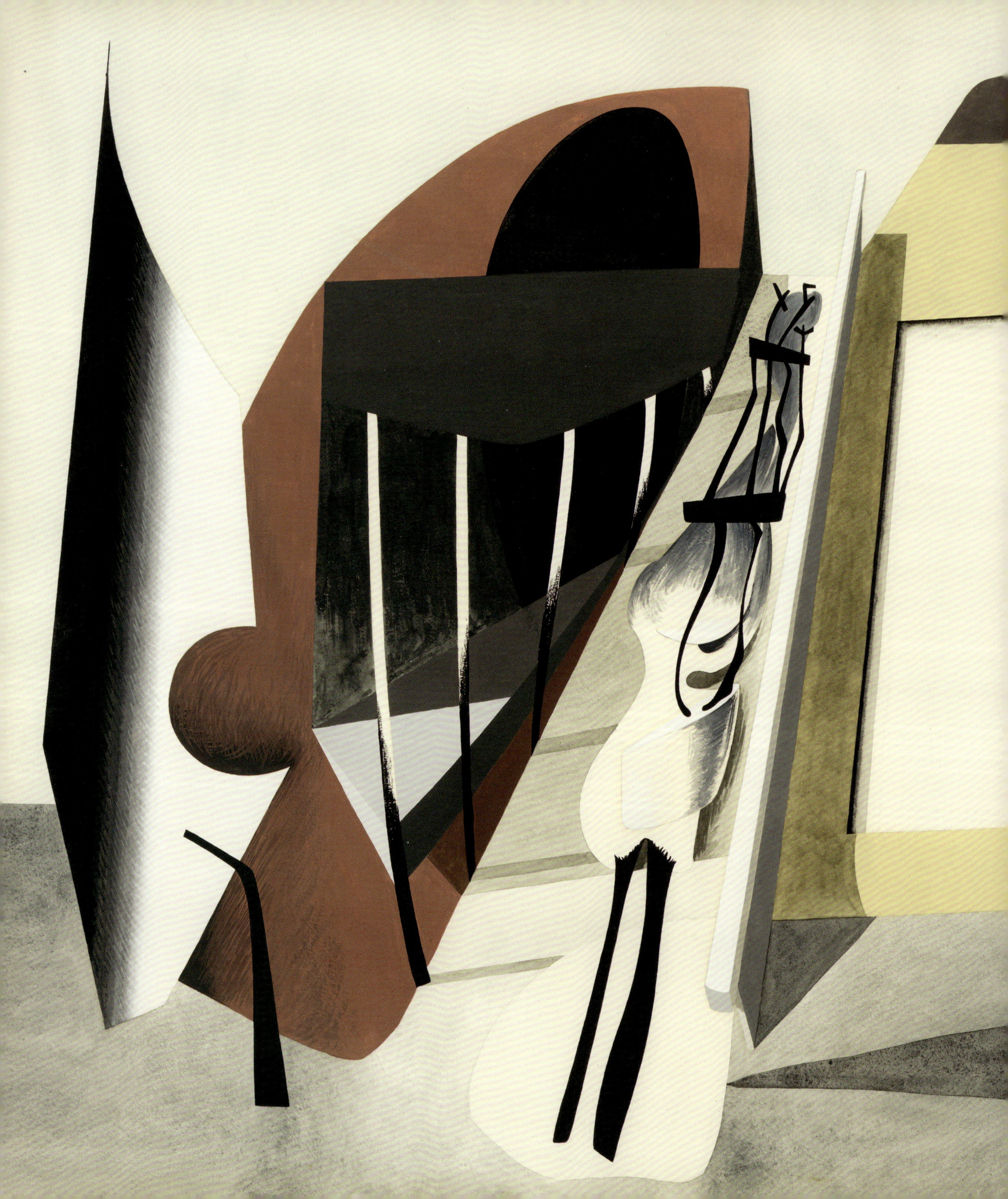

Contents

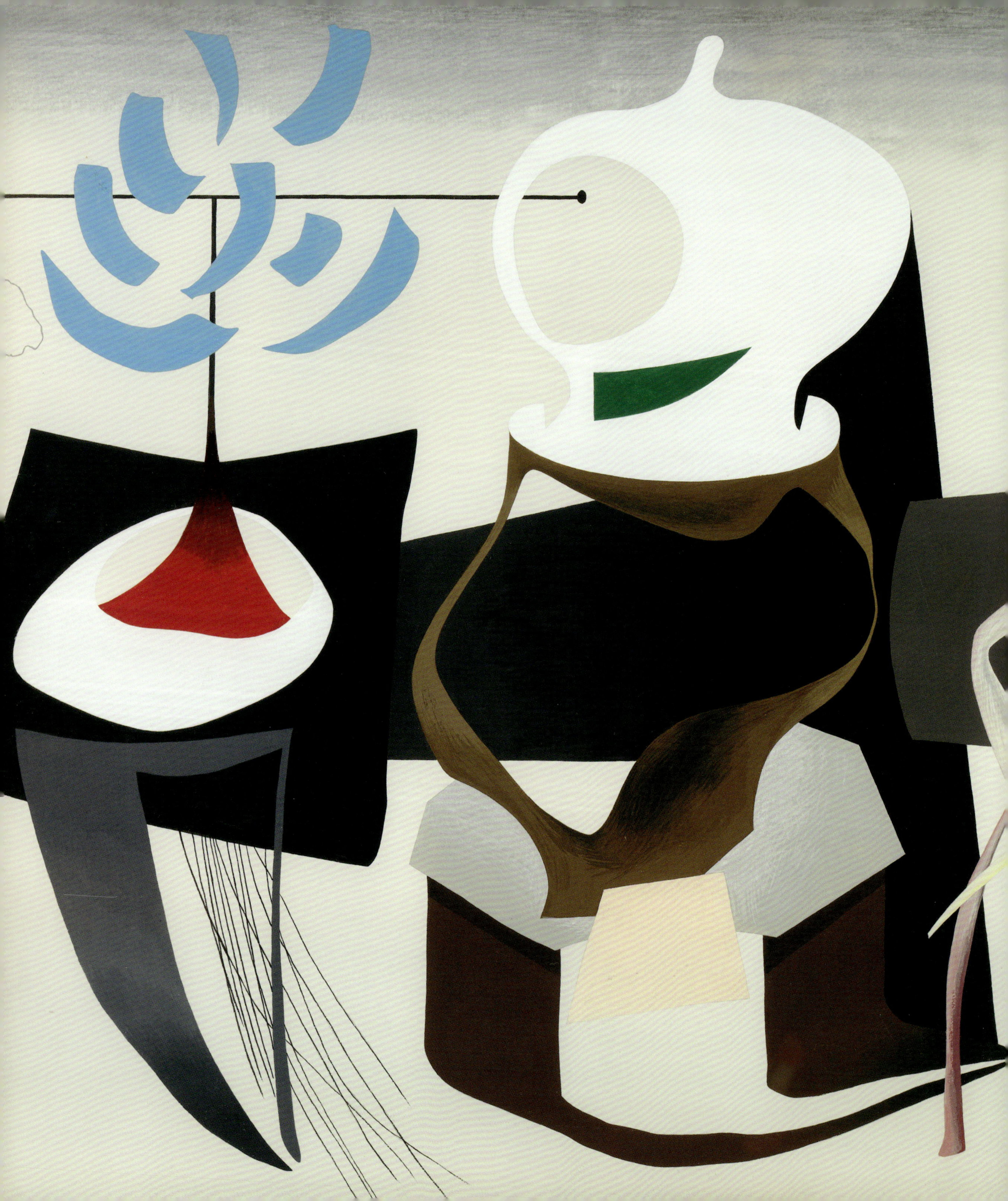

Director's Foreword

Berkeley has produced a remarkable number of extraordinary artists. Among these, Charles Houghton Howard (1899–1978) stands out for the intensely original character of his art and for his engagement with, and influence upon, an international coterie of artists. He was involved with many of the key avant-garde movements of the mid-twentieth century, including Surrealism and abstraction, and he was active not only in the San Francisco Bay Area but also in New York and London, where his milieu included artists and collectors such as Alexander Calder, Henry Moore, and Peggy Guggenheim, among many other leading figures of the day. Howard showed at notable galleries such as the Julien Levy Gallery and Art of This Century and was accorded a retrospective at the California Palace of the Legion of Honor (now part of the Fine Arts Museums of San Francisco) in 1946. Yet despite these distinguished achievements, he is little remembered today. *Charles Howard: A Margin of Chaos* aims to redress this glaring lacuna in the history of mid-century modern art and in our audience's awareness of one of Berkeley's greatest artistic masters.

It is especially gratifying and appropriate for the University of California, Berkeley Art Museum and Pacific Film Archive (BAMPFA) to organize this groundbreaking exhibition given the Howard family's nearly unparalleled significance to the artistic legacy of our community. Charles Howard was the son of John Galen Howard, supervising architect of UC Berkeley, who is responsible for the elegant, classical character of so many buildings on campus. Charles's four siblings were all artists or architects who collectively helped to shape the cosmopolitan yet idiosyncratic quality of Bay Area cultural history.

Charles Howard: A Margin of Chaos is the result of the dedicated research and scholarship of BAMPFA Curator of Modern and Contemporary Art and Phyllis C. Wattis MATRIX Curator Apsara DiQuinzio. She has scoured collections and archives throughout the United States and abroad to assemble the best possible survey of this remarkable artist's work. We are grateful for her diligence, insight, and connoisseur's eye. This exhibition could not have happened without the dedicated support of Curatorial Assistant Valerie Moon, who also wrote the illuminating chronology in this catalogue. I join Apsara in thanking Val and the many other members of BAMPFA's staff (listed on page 9) who have contributed so much to the success of this exhibition.

We would also like to thank Galen Howard Hilgard, the niece of Charles Howard and the daughter of Adaline Kent and Robert Boardman Howard, for her tremendous generosity throughout the process of organizing the exhibition. We are enormously grateful to the Terra Foundation for American Art for their magnanimous backing of this project. Gratitude is also due to the Michael Rosenfeld Gallery, LLC, Bonham's, Claire and Dan Carlevaro, and Robert and Daphne Bransten for their support. In addition we thank the many institutions, private collectors, and galleries across the United States listed on page 120 for lending their artworks; without their participation this exhibition would not have been possible.

Finally, our greatest debt of gratitude is to Charles Howard, whose work continues to amaze and inspire. We are thrilled to be mounting this long overdue exhibition.

Lawrence Rinder
Director, BAMPFA

Acknowledgments

The idea to survey the career of Charles Houghton Howard (1899–1978), who is mostly unknown to contemporary audiences, began with conversations I had with BAMPFA Director Lawrence Rinder, a passionate champion of artists whose work may reside beyond mainstream purviews. I thank him for his belief in the importance of undertaking projects of this kind, which open new avenues onto the histories of art and culture in the United States and beyond.

I first learned about Charles Howard in 2009 while working with Vincent Fecteau on the exhibition *Not New Work: Vincent Fecteau Selects* at the San Francisco Museum of Modern Art (SFMOMA). Howard's *Banner* (1934) was among the artworks he chose to present; he was drawn to its small scale, dark palette, and mysterious subject: architectonic forms ambiguously hovering in space in an indeterminate setting. It is Fecteau's discerning eye and questioning of received canons that planted the seed for this project. Upon beginning research for the exhibition I learned that Robert Gober had included Howard's work in two exhibitions: *The Meat Wagon,* which he curated at the Menil Collection in Houston in 2005, and his retrospective at the Schaulager in Switzerland in 2007. In both shows Gober included a dozen highly original drawings that Howard had made for his friend and supporter, the curator and art critic Douglas MacAgy, when MacAgy was hospitalized with a bad case of tuberculosis. That Howard's most recent advocates should be these two esteemed artists demonstrates how his work continues to be relevant today.

It was during the process of organizing *Not New Work* that I met Galen Howard Hilgard, Charles Howard's niece, who generously gifted *Banner* to SFMOMA as a result of that exhibition. Galen's continued generosity has been a benchmark and an inspiration for this undertaking; thanks to her, BAMPFA now owns a significant selection of work by Howard. It is because of her faithful and committed stewardship of Howard's legacy over many years that this show was possible. I am enormously grateful for the many hours she has spent with me plying through the Howard family's archives and excavating old letters and memorabilia. Her daughters Galen Rohrs Roll, Adaline J. Hilgard, and Julia Hilgard Ritter (and their extended families) have also been instrumental in realizing this project; I'd particularly like to thank Galen Roll for her generous hospitality throughout the process.

Charles Howard's art is represented in museums and private collections across the United States. I would like to join Larry in thanking the many lenders to this exhibition, listed on page 120. Several New York galleries have also been advocates of Howard's, namely Hirschl & Adler Galleries, who presented an exhibition of the artist's work in 1993. I'd especially like to acknowledge Tom Parker and Anne Gibson, who helped connect me with numerous exhibition lenders. The Michael Rosenfeld Gallery, LLC, also generously assisted in facilitating inquiries and lending key works; thanks are due to Michael Rosenfeld, Halley K. Harrisburg, and Zachary Ross. Additionally, the Jonathan Boos Gallery provided a helping hand. Several individuals were instrumental in helping us locate various works that sold at auction over the years: Kathy Wong and Sarah Nelson at Bonhams; Jennifer Biederbeck at Sotheby's; and Clara Goldman at Christie's. I also extend deep appreciation to the Terra Foundation for American Art for the generous grant they awarded the exhibition.

I've consulted the archives of myriad institutions throughout the process of preparing this exhibition, and I would like to acknowledge the many individuals who helped facilitate my research: Veronica Roberts and Meredith Sutton at the Blanton Museum of Art, The University of Texas at Austin; Alexander S. C. "Sandy" Rower, Lily Lyons, and Susan Braeuer Dam at the Calder Foundation, New York; Julian Cox, Lauren Palmor, and Colleen Terry at the Fine Arts Museums of San Francisco; Fariba Bogzaran at the Lucid Art Foundation, Inverness, California; Michelle White and Toby Kamps at the Menil Collection, Houston; Ian Alteveer, Carson Woś, and Allison Rudnick at The Metropolitan Museum of Art, New York; Christina Linden, Meredith Patute, and Anna Bunting at the Oakland Museum of California; Silvio Ruffert Veronese at the Peggy Guggenheim Collection, Venice; Peggy Huang at the Philadelphia Museum of Art; Jeff Gunderson at the San Francisco Art Institute; Gary Garrels, Robin Clark, Peggy Tran-Le, and Andrew Pierce at SFMOMA; Susan Davidson, Karole Vail, David Horowitz, Lidia Ferrara, and Tali Han at the Solomon R. Guggenheim Museum, New York; Pamela Sépulveda at the Whitechapel Gallery, London; and Dana Miller, Anita Duquette, and Claudia Gerbracht at the Whitney Museum of American Art, New York. Danielle O'Steen and Nick Hartigan assisted with research at the Archives of American Art (AAA) in Washington, DC, locating various documents, as did Marisa Bourgoin, Head of Reference Services at the AAA. I also extend thanks to Gina Bardi at the San Francisco Maritime National Historical Park Research Center, Alexandra Provence at Berkeley High School, and Sierra Gribble at the Berkeley Public Library.

I am grateful to my capable and resourceful team here at BAMPFA for their cooperation, collaboration, and enthusiastic support of this exhibition. Former Chief Curator Lucinda Barnes provided essential guidance in the project's early stages and laid the groundwork for its success. In the curatorial department I am enormously thankful for the exceptional organizational efforts of former Curatorial Associate Lauren O'Connell, who initially worked on this exhibition and set it on a smooth course. Curatorial Assistant Valerie Moon demonstrated her herculean project management skills after entering the process at a late stage, capably diving into every task with great aplomb and resourcefulness. Val has contributed greatly to all aspects of the exhibition and it is better for her commitment and careful oversight. The project also benefited from the able research and administrative assistance of interns Megan Alvarado Saggese, Paris Cotz, and Julie Turgeon. Head of Registration Lisa Calden and her team helped to facilitate loans and coordinate the conservation of many of Howard's works; I am thankful for Lisa's professionalism and expertise in countless ways. I also recognize registrars Pamela Pack and Tracy Jones, who helped organize transport of works in the exhibition. BAMPFA's industrious Chief Preparator Kelly Bennett and her exemplary team—Mike Meyers, Scott Orloff, Gary Bogus, and Laura Hansen—oversaw the installation, framing, and preparation of the overall exhibition. Director of Development Louise Gregory and her staff—especially Frances Pomperada, Karina Ryan, and Elizabeth Meyer—worked to secure funding for this exhibition. In our Communications Department I appreciate the contributions of Ann Wiens, A. J. Fox, Alex Harris, Nina Hufford, and Mary Kate Murphy. Sherry Goodman, Director of Education and Academic Relations, and her team conceived of and implemented the public programs relating to the exhibition.

I am deeply appreciative of those at Lucia|Marquand who, under the direction of Adrian Lucia, have helped to craft this original and thought-provoking catalogue—the first scholarly publication devoted entirely to Charles Howard. In particular, I would like to thank Ryan Polich, whose beautiful design brings Howard's work to vivid life, along with Melissa Duffes and Kestrel Rundle, who oversaw the book's editorial production. I was fortunate enough to work with Amanda Glesmann, who insightfully edited the texts and brought her invaluable perspective and expertise to many aspects of the catalogue. Furthermore, I am extremely grateful for the perceptive contributions of Robert Gober and art historian Lauren Kroiz, who have enhanced this volume with their thoughtful essays.

I have benefited from the intelligence of several individuals who have shared their ideas, lent an ear, and/or offered assistance along the way: Gwen Allen (who read an early draft of my essay), Adrienne Fish, Jeff Gunderson, Piers Secunda, Vincent Fecteau, Veronica Roberts, Michelle White, Rita Gonzalez, Lauren Kroiz, Ed Gilbert, Sally Woodbridge, Evelyn Hankins, and Sarah Roberts. Finally, Chris Bell was an enormous boost to this project—his encouragement, humor, and wit helped me every step of the way.

The Howard family was a remarkable Bay Area clan, each member talented and spirited. I have greatly enjoyed delving into their rich legacy that spans centuries, even reaching back to the first pilgrims to settle on this continent. I feel fortunate to have had a glimpse into their lives through the study of their endeavors; they were marvelous correspondents, and reading their letters in The Bancroft Library's and the family's collections has been enormously edifying, enriching my own understanding of world history in the process. Above all, I am profoundly appreciative of Charles Howard, our "absent friend," whose enigmatic work will continue to speak to us for centuries to come.

Apsara DiQuinzio

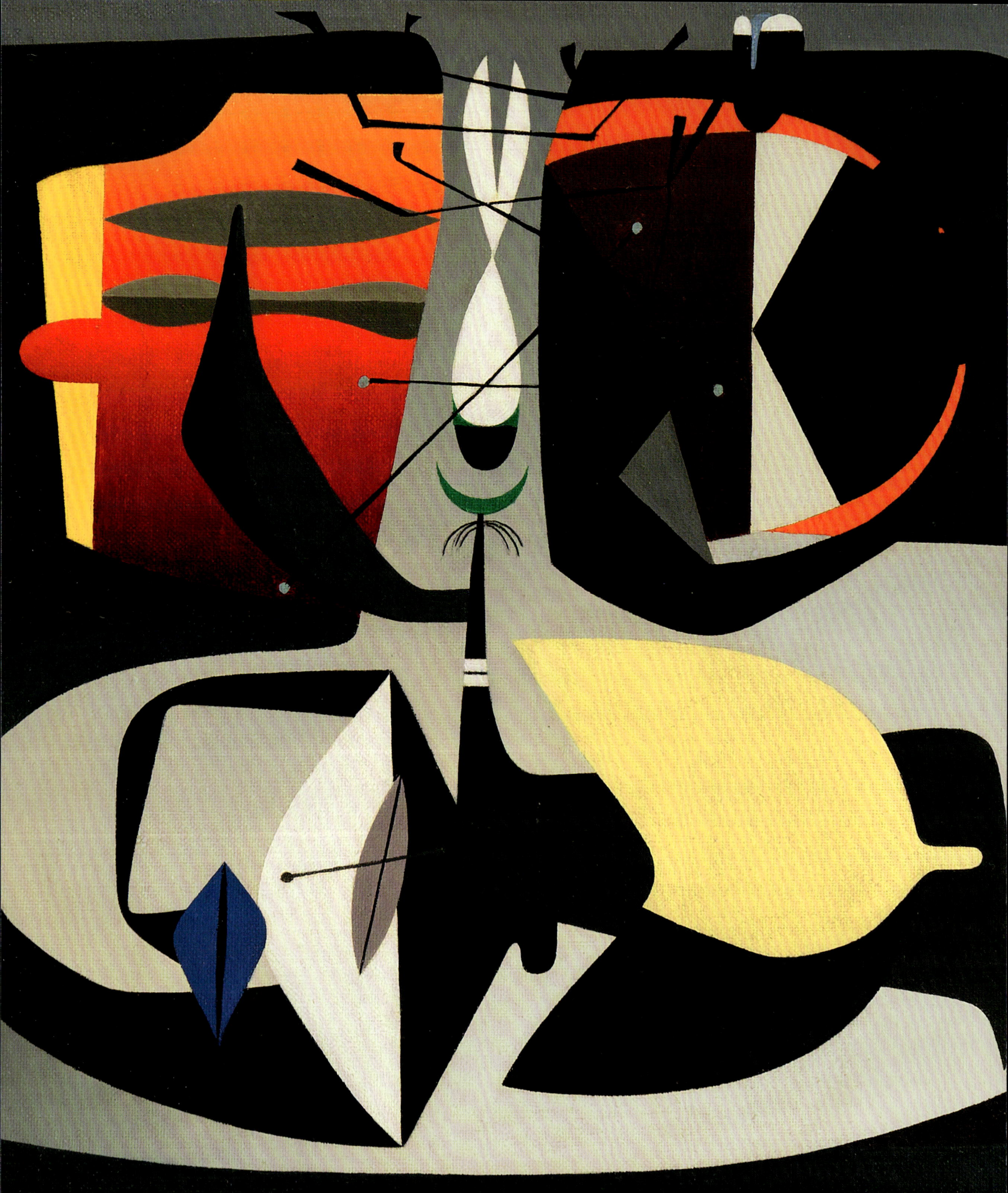

In and Around Margins

Apsara DiQuinzio

In his review of Charles Howard's 1946 retrospective at the California Palace of the Legion of Honor in San Francisco, the influential art and music critic Alfred Frankenstein, who would have a forty-five-year tenure at the *San Francisco Chronicle*, asserted: "Howard is what is often called a 'non-objective' painter, which means that you will not be able to relate any of the forms you see in his later pictures to forms you commonly see outside them. You either accept the 'non-objective' premise or you don't; if you do accept it, you are, I think, very likely to regard Howard as one of the most important artists now at work in the United States."[1] When this review was published, abstraction was a relatively new development in American art, and Howard was a leading exponent of the style. Forced to return to his native San Francisco Bay Area from London when World War II broke out, he had come to represent for many local artists a critical link between the abstract and surrealist movements in Europe. By the time of his retrospective at the Legion of Honor he had participated in a number of momentous exhibitions and artistic events, including Julien Levy's seminal 1932 exhibition *Surréalisme*, which introduced New York audiences to Surrealism, and the *International Surrealist Exhibition,* which was likewise a landmark event for London when it was held at the New Burlington Galleries in 1936. Moreover, Howard was included in many definitive group exhibitions in the United States, such as *The Americans* at the Museum of Modern Art (MoMA) and American heiress and arts patron Peggy Guggenheim's inaugural exhibition at her gallery Art of This Century, both presented in New York in 1942, and in 1944 he was featured in Sidney Janis's influential *Abstract and Surrealist Art in America.*

Given Howard's inclusion in such significant exhibitions and publications it is clear that Frankenstein's high regard for him was widely shared in mid twentieth-century art circles, yet today his name remains largely unknown. Over the decades he seems to have gradually disappeared from the primary narratives of the era, consigned to inchoate historical margins. When looking back at his work and life, a certain pattern emerges: despite his affiliation with many important art movements of his time, he tends to get lost in the conflicting accounts, categories, and geographies that circumscribe his oeuvre. Having never achieved the level of recognition of figures such as Joan Miró, Yves Tanguy, Alexander Calder, Ben Nicholson, or Isamu Noguchi—all artists he knew or exhibited with—he is often omitted, or gets edited out of, the abbreviated lists scholars compose relating to those periods, or he appears merely as a footnote in major art historical texts, which tend to privilege canonical artists. For instance, despite having known the protean English art historian Herbert Read—who likely advocated on Howard's behalf to Guggenheim, securing his inclusion in the program at her galleries in both London and New York—Howard is not mentioned in Read's definitive tome on European Modernism. And when in 1948 Read published the second edition of *Art Now: An Introduction to the Theory of Modern Painting and Sculpture,* Howard was represented only by a reproduction of his work on paper *Rumor* (1938), now presumed lost. (In the 1960 edition even that sole illustration disappeared.) Additionally, in Charles Harrison's *English Art and Modernism, 1900–1939*, he appears only in a footnote that lists the attendees of a meeting of British Surrealists in winter 1939–40.[2] Perhaps this oversight is due in part to the fact that Howard was American:

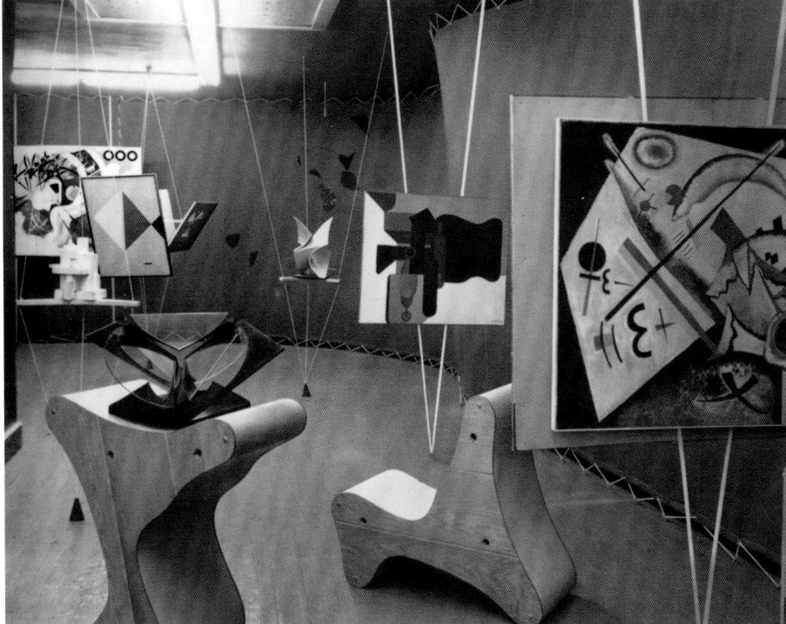

although he lived and worked in a European milieu, he did not necessarily fit into the British category. But given that he lived in England for more than thirty years, eventually becoming a citizen in 1963, he also tends to fall out of the American narratives (except in select studies of the 1940s), since he largely lived and worked outside the United States.[3]

Emblematic of Howard's historical conundrum is a widely reproduced installation photograph by Berenice Abbott of the Abstract and Cubist Gallery at the aforementioned Art of This Century (fig. 1). Despite the very oblique angle it is taken from we can make out just enough of Howard's painting *Prefiguration* (1940, also now lost) to be able to recognize it. Tilting downward in keeping with Frederick Kiesler's innovative installation design, which obviated the need for frames, it hangs in the background, to the left of a mobile by Calder. As if presaging the artist's subsequent historical elision, the picture privileges the better-known Kandinsky painting in the foreground, leaving Howard at the margins of our perceptual field, just beyond a clear frame of reference. This problematic has been reinforced by Howard's own eschewal of the many movements and groups that pervaded the arts during his time. Although he exhibited with surrealist artists from 1932 until 1940, he eventually discarded Surrealism for abstraction, preferring the idiosyncratic label "abstractionist." His resistance to categories and his insistence on stylistic independence in an era when group membership was often the passport for recognition, affording an artist an associative and established foundation from which to distinguish him or herself, necessarily

complicates the way we think of his work today. This exhibition and essay center on bringing the work of this unique and accomplished artist into historical focus, returning it to a field of understanding. For as Frankenstein articulates in his review: "Howard, it seems to me, accomplishes an extraordinary fusion of Surrealism and abstract art."[4]

EARLY LIFE AND THE HOWARD FAMILY

Charles Houghton Howard was born in 1899 to architect John Galen Howard (1864–1931) and artist Mary Robertson Bradbury Howard (1865–1963), who married in 1893 in Chicago and then moved to New York. The Howards were supportive and loving parents to their five children (fig. 2), all of whom would pursue creative professions like their parents: Henry Temple (1894–1967) was an architect; Robert Boardman (1896–1983) was a sculptor; John Langley (1902–1999) was a painter; and Janette (1905–1998) studied architecture until she married and started a family. John Galen Howard's father, a doctor, had initially disapproved of his son's desire to become an architect, and perhaps because of this John wholeheartedly encouraged his own children's artistic pursuits.[5]

In 1898, after he had established his own architecture firm in New York and worked for McKim, Mead & White for a time, John Galen Howard was hired by Phoebe Apperson Hearst to design the Hearst Memorial Mining Building at the University of California, Berkeley, in memory of her husband, mining magnate George Hearst. He and his partner Samuel Cauldwell also submitted a proposal to the Phoebe Hearst International Competition for the overall master plan for the campus that came in fourth place, but Howard nevertheless secured that project as well in 1901, when Hearst and University President Benjamin Ide Wheeler hired him to be the Supervising Architect for UC Berkeley after Émile Bénard (who initially had won the competition) left the post. The following year, when Charles Howard was about three years old, the Howard family resettled in Berkeley, moving from their home in Montclair, New Jersey, which John had built. The Howard family patriarch, who was also a poet, would remain Supervising Architect at the university until 1924, during which time he also became the first Dean of the Architecture Department. His designs, steeped in the Beaux-Arts tradition in which he was trained, still populate the campus. They include the Hearst Greek Theater, Doe Library, Boalt Hall, Wheeler Hall, Sather Gate, and Berkeley's famed campanile, Sather Tower (fig. 3), completed in 1914 and modeled on one he had seen in Venice.

Mary Robertson Bradbury Howard was a painter and pianist who studied art in Chicago and at the Art Students League of New York. When she was a young woman she had the unique opportunity to travel; while living in Paris for two years in the 1890s she worked various jobs, including a stint as manager of a clubhouse on the rue Vavin in the Latin Quarter. She first met John Galen Howard in New York, but it was in Paris that they got to know each other and became engaged. After they were married John enrolled at the École des Beaux-Arts in Paris at the behest of architect Charles McKim; Mary

once said she made a sketch a day while he was gone. Her style was primarily figurative and post-Impressionist; her charming watercolors reveal a lightness of touch, a strong sense of composition, and an ease with the brush (fig. 4). Mary, gregarious and outgoing, played an active role in cultivating her children's development in the arts and encouraged each of them to spend extended periods of time in Paris, a place that carried great importance for the family and to which they often returned.[6]

The Howards, known as "the first family of Bay Area Modernism," lived a bourgeois bohemian lifestyle and raised their children to be adventurous yet responsible. Their home in Berkeley was often the center of poetry and music gatherings.[7] Charles attended Berkeley High School, where he developed an interest in writing, becoming editor of the yearbook his senior year. Charles's sister Janette recalls that Charles was a "precocious child" who was almost sent to boarding school.[8] When he was sixteen he joined his brother Robert (then twenty) on a cross-country motorcycle expedition on which he rode "in the tandem"—a daring and adventurous thing to do even by today's standards (fig. 5). Upon reaching New York, Robert enrolled at the Art Students League and Charles returned to Berkeley on the train by himself.[9]

In the early 1900s the Howard family frequently spent their summers on the beach in an artist enclave in Carmel-by-the-Sea, California, eventually building a cabin there in 1903 that they called Copsey Court. Janette later described its decor: "a fishnet was hung on the ceiling and large starfish were stuffed into the net."[10] The family used to spend hours walking along the beach to Point Lobos, watching the groups

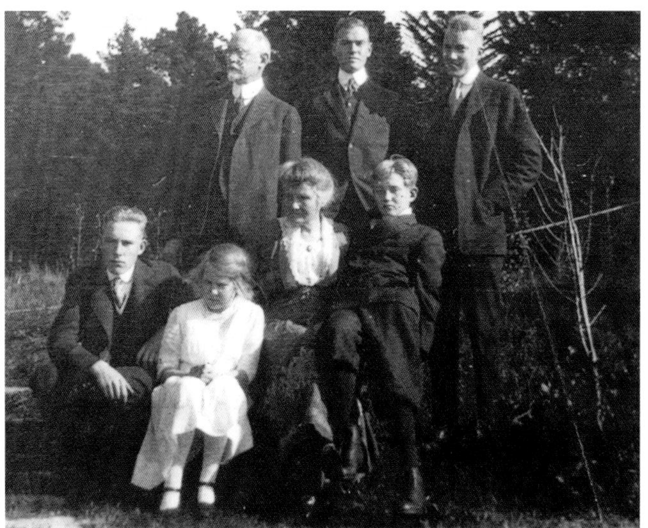

Fig. 2 The Howard family, n.d. Standing (from left): John Galen, Henry, and Robert. Seated (from left): Charles, Janette, Mary, and John Langley.

Fig. 3 Sather Tower, photographs of the First Unitarian Church and buildings on the University of California, Berkeley, campus, n.d.

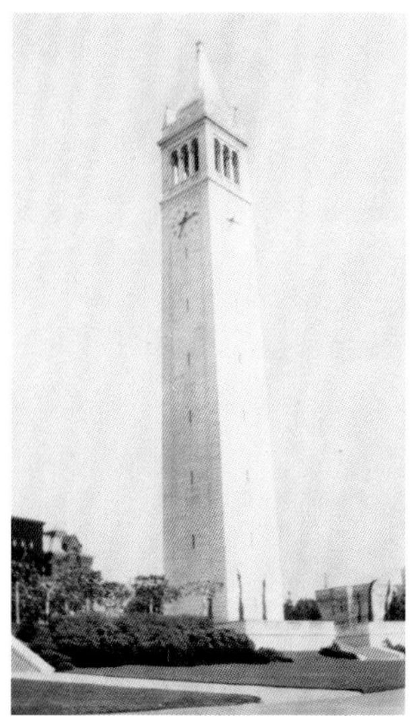

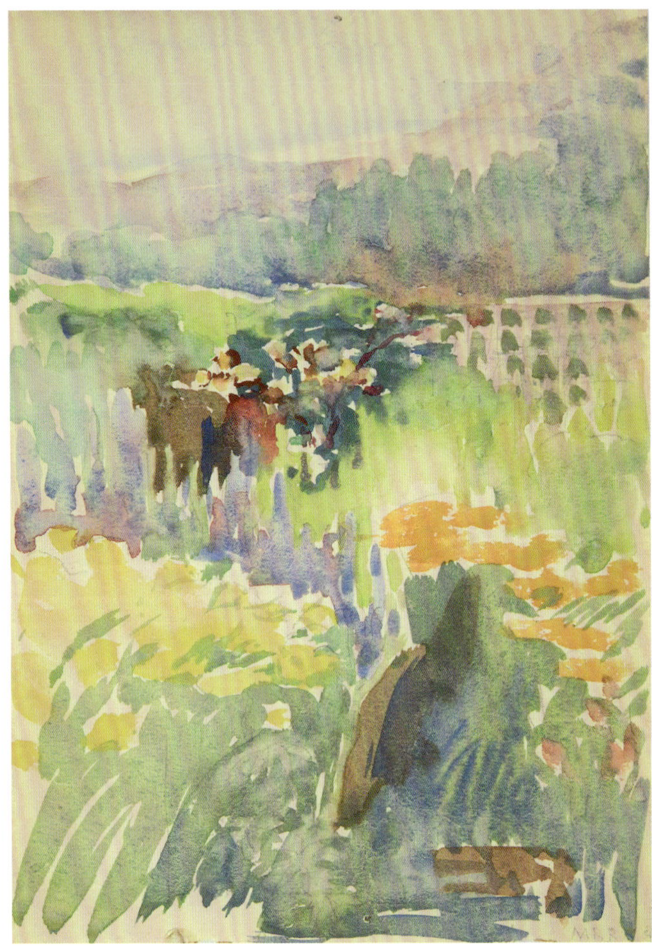

Fig. 4 Mary Robertson Bradbury Howard, *Untitled*, n.d. Watercolor on paper, 8 × 6 in. (20.3 × 15.2 cm).

Fig. 5 Charles Howard at the Russian River, Sonoma County, CA, n.d.

of Chinese fishermen who lived in the cliffs and sold their fish in town. Charles's early paintings would largely focus on beach scenes, with dismembered fish and feet featuring centrally in many compositions; fishing nets strewn about the rocks are also recurring motifs (plate 5).

After enrolling at UC Berkeley in 1917, Charles left to join the Students' Army Training Corps (SATC), an organization established to train reserve officers when the United States entered World War I. He returned to school after the war ended, in 1919, and graduated two years later with a degree in journalism, believing he would become a writer. Charles spent the summer before his final year of college in Paris, joining his mother, sister, and two elder brothers. Henry and Robert had been there since 1917, when they each joined the war effort in various capacities, and after being discharged they chose to stay.[11] Mary and Janette had arrived earlier that year (1920). In a letter to his father, Charles recounted that during the journey across the Atlantic on the USMS *Philadelphia* he had met an interesting woman, Mrs. Brewer, who worked for the *New York Tribune* and was on her way to meet a dancer named Isadora Duncan.[12] Charles enjoyed Paris immensely, absorbing its cultural sites, exploring the boulevards and alleys, and spending countless hours visiting museums and discussing the art he encountered with his family—his brother Robert in particular. Mary Howard recounted in a letter to her husband, "I do like the way [Charles] is taking in Paris—there is no rush or nervous anxiety to see 'everything' and get it all in to a short pace of time—but he thinks seriously over all he gets and plays around in the meantime, 'soaking in the atmosphere.'"[13]

In 1922, after briefly pursuing graduate studies in journalism at Harvard and Columbia universities, Charles returned to Europe, where he would live and travel for an extended period throughout France and Italy.[14] We learn in a letter written to his father from France in 1923 that he had begun experimenting with watercolor: "I've been doing some watercolors about the place and find it swell fun. I just swim around in the stuff and have no system at all but after the few that I've done I see a hell of a lot more than I ever did before and it is so engrossing in itself that I'm going to keep it up even if it is just to

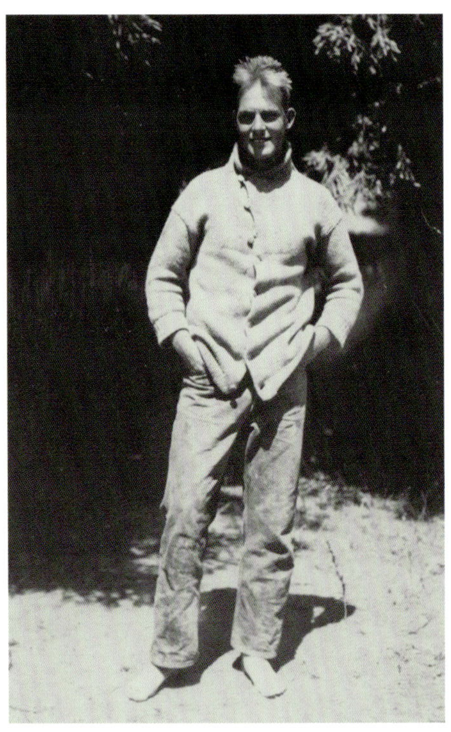

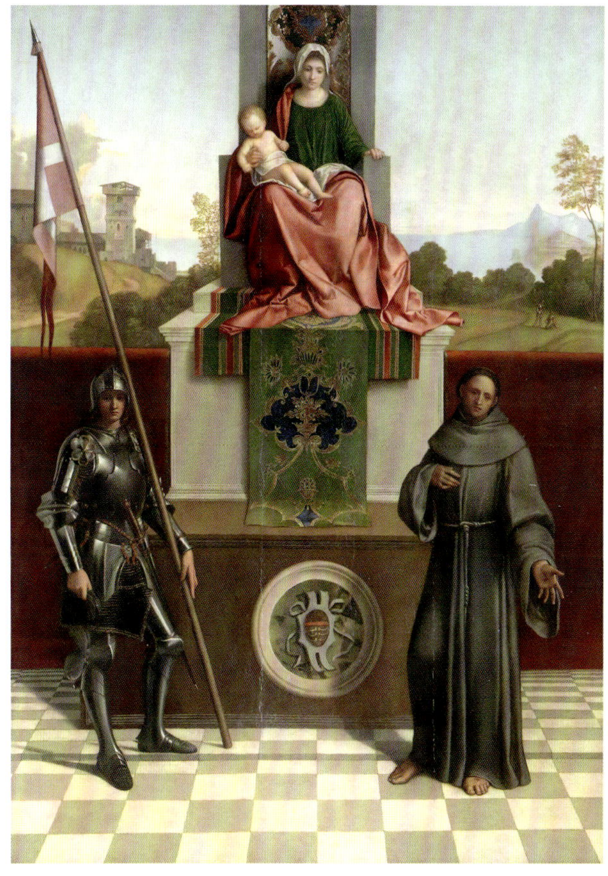

Fig. 6 Giorgione, *Madonna and Child Between St. Francis and St. Nicasius*, ca. 1503–4. Oil on panel, 78¾ × 59⅞ in. (200 × 152.4 cm). Cathedral of Castelfranco Veneto (Treviso), Italy

learn how a guy actually does get that kind of liquid color on paper and make it look like something. Here's another artist, Pop."[15] His experimentation with art underway, later that year Howard met the Iowa-born Regionalist Grant Wood, known today for paintings set in the Midwest such as *American Gothic* (1930). The two traveled around Italy together that summer, "during which time Wood preached the superiority of paint over words as a medium of self-expression."[16]

At some point during his travels that summer, Howard visited the town of Castelfranco, just north of Venice, and saw an altarpiece by the Italian painter Giorgione (1478–1510) titled *Madonna and Child Between St. Francis and St. Nicasius* (ca. 1503–4, fig. 6). He describes this momentous experience at length in his essay "What Concerns Me," reprinted on pages 57–59 of this volume. Given the significance of that encounter, the relevant passage is also quoted at length below:

> I looked at the picture for a quarter of an hour. I looked at nothing else. It may be that I thought of all the other pictures I had been looking at in Italy, when I had been spending time in galleries that should by all rights have been spent on something else, writing a novel, say. It may be that I ruminated on the somber, analytical, philosophical approach of the Florentine painters, and then [on] the free, warm, romantic fervor of Venice. I think it is fairly certain that I realized even in those few minutes that here, in this picture before me, was a combination of both these approaches, that here for once was a synthesis.
>
> Well, really I don't remember what I thought. I don't know what my state of mind was. I only know for sure that I was not a painter then, nor had I any idea of becoming one.
>
> After a while I simply got up and left. I went out of the church and down the street to the walled gate. When I was outside the town, on the road in the calm, sunlit air, with the trees and the fields, I had a quick and sudden reaction, and was violently ill.
>
> I cut the tour at once and hurried immediately back to Paris, to begin painting. I have been painting whenever I could ever since.[17]

Elements of the elusive Venetian's signature style filter throughout much of Howard's later work. Giorgione was unique in his time and became renowned for compositions that enshroud their subjects in mystery, such as his masterpiece *The Tempest* (ca. 1506–8, fig. 7). Howard would absorb this enigmatic quality in his own paintings, which he stated "are in fact all portraits of the same general subject, of the same idea, carried as far as I am able at the time." What this "obsessive subject" is Howard never discloses. But we can discern hints of it in his description of the Castelfranco altarpiece, in which he observes the importance of a stylistic synthesis. Similarly, in many of his own abstract paintings from the 1940s we notice a striking moment of synthesis that takes place in the center of the composition, where seemingly opposing forces, or styles, come together to produce a fleeting sense of balance and order. Notably, the Castelfranco altarpiece centers on a triangular arrangement of figures surrounding the Virgin Mary and the infant Jesus, placing it squarely within the *sacra conversazione* genre of Renaissance painting. This triadic structure is also evident in many of Howard's works, including *Trinity* (1941, plate 32) and *The Cage* (1938, plate 23), in which three amorphous figures define the composition. In earlier canvases

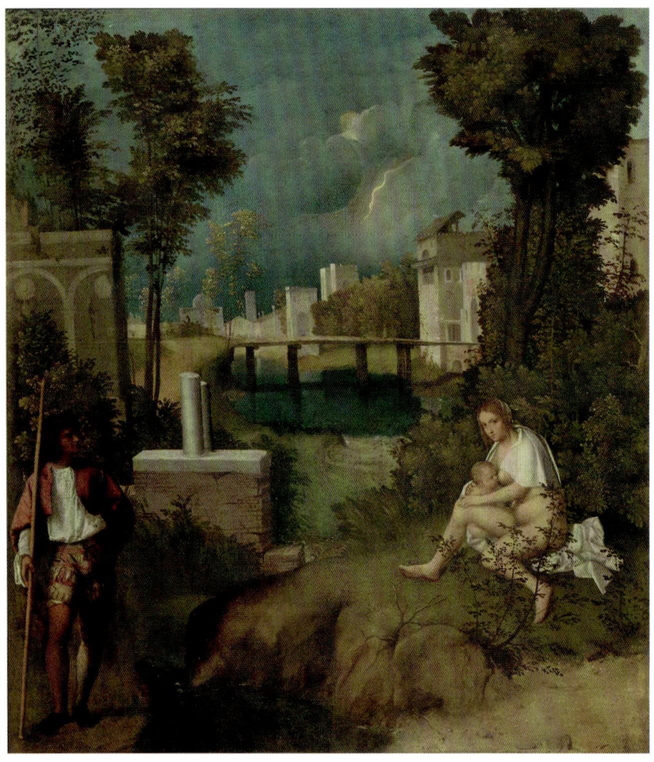

Fig. 7 Giorgione, *The Tempest*, ca. 1506–8. Oil on canvas, 32¼ × 28¾ in. (81.9 × 73 cm). Galleria dell'Accademia, Venice

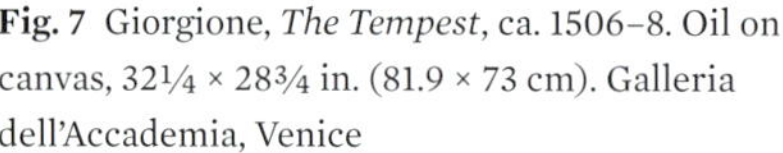

Fig. 8 View of the apartment of Hobart G. Erwin with decorative wall paintings by Charles Howard published in *Home & Field* magazine, 1932.

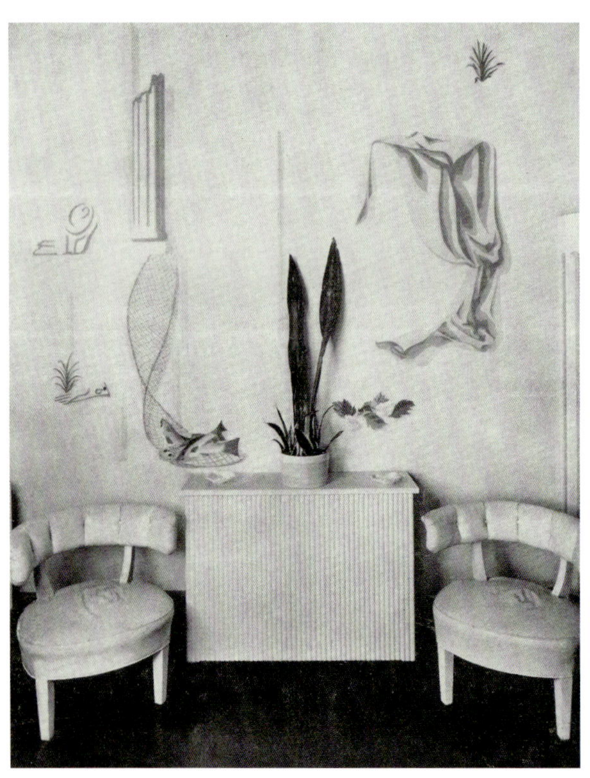

this arrangement is accompanied by landscapes undergoing processes of change or transformation, as in *Excavation* (1932, plate 7), *Grotto* (1932, plate 8), and *Banner* (1934, plate 12). The strong diagonal of the flagpole held by St. Nicasius in the Castelfranco altarpiece is echoed in these early Howard paintings as well; they feature curious pennants or banners that add dynamism to their surroundings—settings that often, as in the precariously counterbalanced architectonic forms that anchor *Banner*, seem to hover on the brink of collapse.

Upon returning from Europe Howard settled in New York, where he resided in Greenwich Village. He began working at the studio of Louis Bouché and Rudolph Guertler, teaching himself how to paint and practicing his new vocation. During the six or so years he painted murals for Bouché and Guertler he mainly executed site-specific works for private homes and clubs, including the Cosmopolitan Club in New York. Some of his designs appeared in magazines such as *Home & Field* (fig. 8) and *House Beautiful;* one even graced the cover of the September 1934 issue of *House and Garden.* These reproductions show his predilection for fragmented compositions and seascapes and his early focus on classical architectural subjects, such as fluted columns and balustrades, no doubt a lasting imprint of his father's training in the Beaux-Arts tradition. He also added these classical motifs to his drawings and works on canvas during the late 1920s and early 1930s, as seen in *1826 into 1926* (1927, plate 1) and *Untitled* (ca. 1927–29, plate 2).

Shortly after arriving in New York Howard joined Gertrude Vanderbilt Whitney's Studio Club (which in 1930 would become the Whitney Museum of American Art). His satirical drawings, his earliest artistic mode, were presented in numerous group shows there as well as in a solo exhibition in 1926 (see fig. 14). Other members of the Club during that time included Calder, with whom he briefly shared a studio in 1926, as well as Edward Hopper, Oscar Bluemner, Robert Henri, Charles Sheeler, and Howard's employer Bouché.[18] Calder's fanciful painting *Firemen's Dinner for Brancusi* (ca. 1926, fig. 9) is a remarkable record of the moment, made to commemorate Constantin Brancusi's third exhibition in the United States at the Brummer Gallery; in particular, it captures the merriment that ensued after the opening. In this painting many of the members of the Whitney Studio Club appear, including none other than Robert and Charles Howard, depicted spinning around the pole while Bouché stands at the table and Calder dances atop an adjacent one. Howard would later write that in this period New York was a place "where everything had seemed easy to paint, where you could go out into the street and in a couple of blocks get a dozen ideas. It was a stimulating place, like a cocktail. If you ran dry you simply went out-doors and there it was. You turned it on like a faucet."

Howard's aspirations to become a writer were realized to a certain extent when he wrote and illustrated the book *Design,* published in 1926 (fig. 10). It was one in a series of educational books for art students; others included *Animal Sketching* by Calder, *Constructive Anatomy* and *Bridgman's Life Drawing* by George B. Bridgman, and *Twelve Pictures in Color* by Jules Guerin. Bridgman, who was also the publisher of the series, taught figure and anatomy drawing for more than forty years at the Art Students League, where Howard's mother and brothers Robert and John Langley had studied (as had Calder). *Design,* which includes more than two hundred drawings by Howard, features a notable introduction in which Howard asserts that the elements of good design are rooted in notions of pattern, proportion, and profile. He emphasizes the importance of originality, writing, "Above all, in making a design, be original. This does not necessarily mean: be eccentric. It means: understand what your design will be used for; select an appropriate motif; then go ahead boldly with your design in the way that you would like to see it."[19] In his drawings for the book he creates a taxonomy of motifs—including various categories such as forms inspired by fish and shells, flowers and trees, birds, insects, and stars—in addition to charting a typology of design ranging from Greek, Oriental, and Egyptian to modern European (fig. 11). The book suggests that Howard's stylistic dexterity and range of knowledge were already apparent just a couple of years after he decided to become an artist. He would bring this proficiency to his later abstract canvases along with the striking precision that undergirds his clearly delineated sense of line, proportion, shape, and color.

In 1928, while Charles was still working for Bouché and Guertler, Mary Howard orchestrated an exhibition of her three artist sons—Robert, Charles, and John Langley—called *The Howard Brothers.* It was held at the Galerie Beaux-Arts in San Francisco, the first modern art gallery on the West Coast, founded and run by Beatrice Judd Ryan.[20] By this time the Howard brothers had begun to develop distinct styles, although

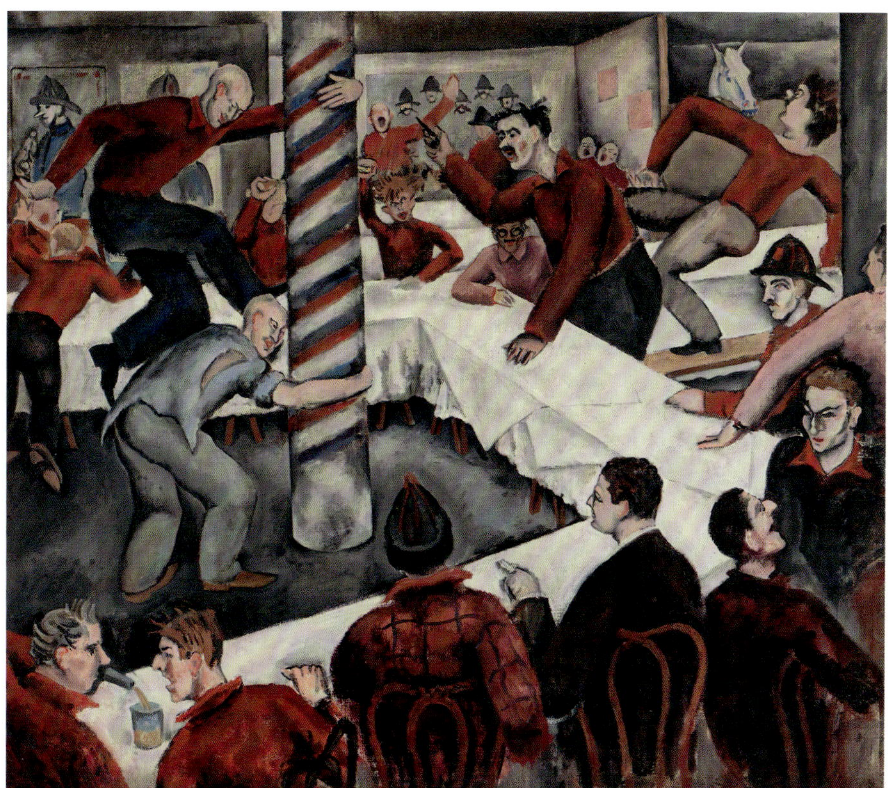

Fig. 9 Alexander Calder, *Firemen's Dinner for Brancusi*, ca. 1926. Oil on burlap, 36 × 42⅛ in. (91.4 × 107 cm). Whitney Museum of American Art, New York, gift of the artist

they were still in formative stages. A review in *The Argus* suggests that Charles was the most stylistically developed of the three at that point, describing him as "a satirist, full of good cheer and endowed with a biting wit, he chooses his people in the society of today and distorts them gracefully enough to take away whatever sermon-like spirit there might be in such subjects presented too seriously."[21] Charles made a drawing for the exhibition that appeared in *The Argus*. Entitled *The Brothers* (ca. 1928, fig. 12), it is a satirical reinterpretation of classic pastoral scenes from the history of art, such as Titian's *Pastoral Concert* (ca. 1509) or Édouard Manet's *Luncheon on the Grass* (1863), and it depicts Howard and his siblings with exaggerated bald heads and elongated limbs, reclining on a picnic blanket in their bathing suits. The drawing wryly recalls Marcel Duchamp's painting *The Chess Game* (1910, fig. 13), a reworking of the pastoral genre in which he pictures his brothers playing chess with their wives in a lush, green setting—perhaps, knowing the Duchamp work, Charles was wittily drawing a loose comparison between his own family and the better-known clan of artists.

In 1927, while preparing for the exhibition, Mary, who had just visited Charles in New York, wrote a long, detailed letter to Robert, who was in Egypt and wanted to hear about the work his brother was making. She described some of the other drawings that would be included in the show, writing of *Miss America* (now presumed lost):

It embodies *all* the spirit of the up-to-date girl, who in a bathing suit and visored cap stands on her acrobatic hands in the center, her feet high in the air—a vaudeville expression on her face, and the entourage, so cleverly and beautifully worked out. Consisting of Modern America from the flag of our country to latest radio wires and contrivances—neoclassical devices, etc., and a sort of framing of darkened sky with tiny white clouds. It gives one a jazzy stimulation that is astonishing—while the ensemble is a thing of beauty—but like all of Charles's work, *it must be seen*—it is quite impossible to describe.[22]

After the exhibition Mary wrote to Charles, who could not travel from New York to see it himself, that it had been a great success. "Public interest has been phenomenal," she proclaimed, adding "Ms. Ryan said attendance was greater than any other show she had had this year."[23]

The years that Howard lived in New York were marked by many personal challenges, despite that fact he found his artistic subjects easily. The Howard family letters indicate that he often struggled to make a living, finding mural commissions particularly difficult to come by during the Great Depression. In 1926 Howard married fellow artist Hester Miller. They often spent their summers in Woodstock, which in the late 1920s had developed a reputed artist colony where precisionist painters

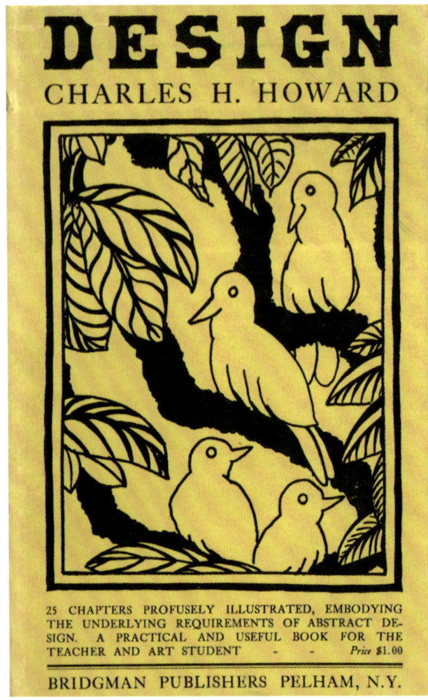

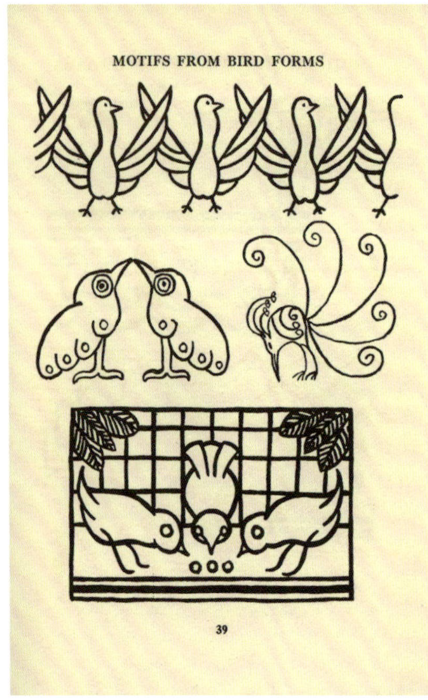

Fig. 10 Cover of *Design* by Charles Howard, 1926.

Fig. 11 Page from *Design* by Charles Howard, 1926.

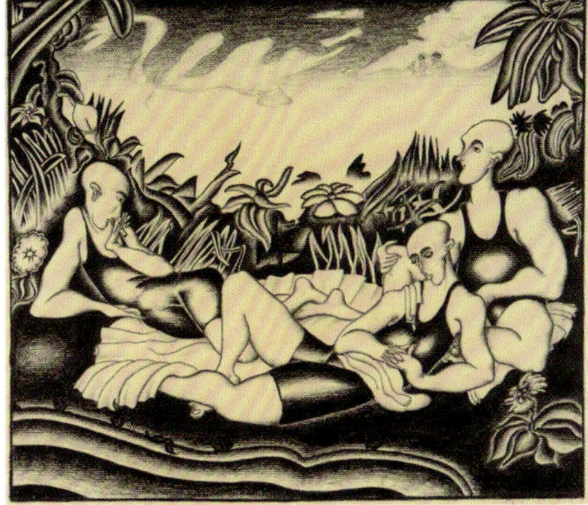

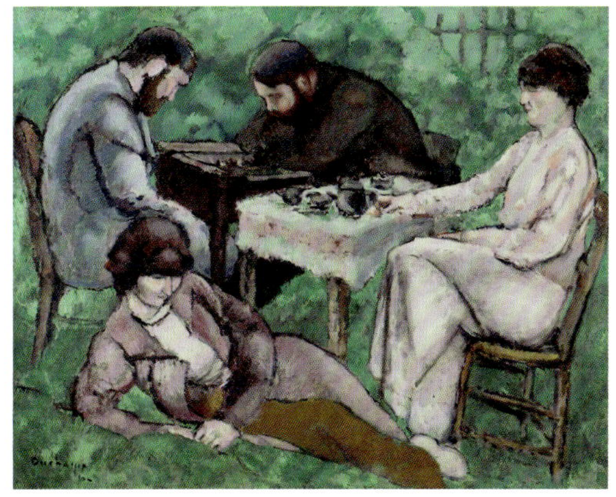

Fig. 12 Charles Howard, *The Brothers*, ca. 1928. Ink on paper, 10½ × 12¼ in. (26.7 × 31 cm). University of California, Berkeley Art Museum and Pacific Film Archive; Gift of Galen Howard Hilgard, in memory of her parents, Robert B. Howard and Adaline Kent

Fig. 13 Marcel Duchamp, *The Chess Game*, 1910. Oil on canvas, 44⅞ × 57¹¹⁄₁₆ in. (113 × 146.5 cm). Philadelphia Museum of Art, The Louise and Walter Arensberg Collection, 1950

Fig. 14 Charles Howard, *Untitled*, ca. 1925. Colored pencil and watercolor on paper, 18¾ × 15 in. (47.63 × 38.1 cm). University of California, Berkeley Art Museum and Pacific Film Archive; Gift of Galen Howard Hilgard, in memory of her parents, Robert B. Howard and Adaline Kent

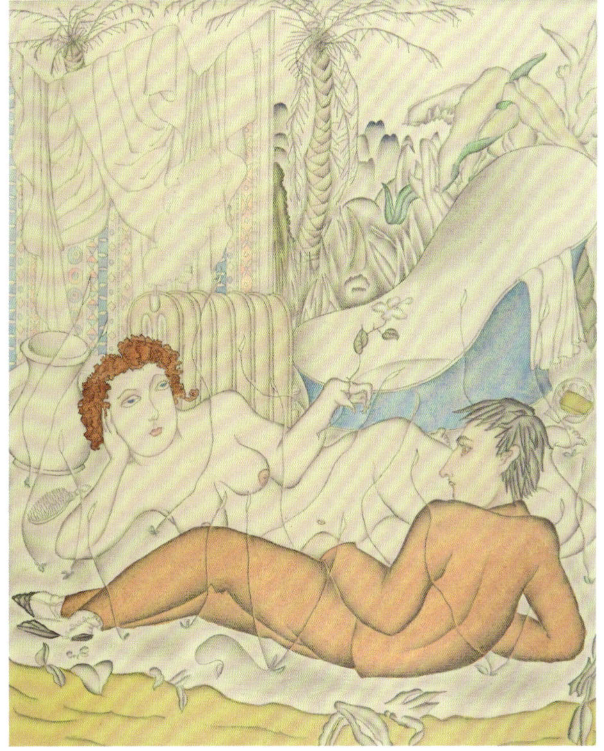

and members of the Ashcan School (another group involved with the Whitney Studio Club), such as George Ault, Robert Henri, and George Bellows, were known to work and frequent. In 1931, around the time that Charles's father died, Charles and Hester divorced. According to family letters, John Galen Howard's death affected Charles greatly.

SURREALISM AND ENGLAND

In 1933 Howard married English artist Madge Knight; the two would remain together until her death in 1974. Just before the couple left New York for London, Howard was in two significant exhibitions at the Julien Levy Gallery, which had opened its doors in 1931 and quickly became a leading venue for the avant-garde; artists such as Calder, Giacometti, Matta, Tanguy, and Gorky all got their start there.[24] The fourth exhibition at the gallery heralded the surrealist movement, introducing a wider American public to the painting, sculpture, photography, collage, drawing, and books of a style that purposefully evaded definition.[25] André Breton, the movement's founder, pointedly described Surrealism in terms of a synthesis of opposing states, writing, "I believe in the future resolution of two states (in appearance so contradictory), dream and reality, into a sort of absolute reality; Surréalité."[26] This idea of coalescence must have appealed to Howard, who was already attuned to the stylistic merging of Venetian and Florentine modes of painting, as witnessed in Giorgione's work. One of only three American artists in the show (along with Joseph Cornell and Man Ray), Howard contributed drawings to the exhibition, which also included works by Eugène Atgét, Herbert Bayer, Jean Cocteau, Max Ernst, László Moholy-Nagy, and, perhaps most memorably, Salvador Dalí, whose *The Persistence of Memory* (1931,

fig. 15) was widely reproduced in the many reviews the show generated.[27]

A year later, Levy gave Howard a solo exhibition—his first commercial gallery show in the United States. Bouché penned a brief essay for the exhibition brochure, for which Howard designed a humorous cover featuring a biomorphic form holding flags emblazoned with his name and the location of the show (fig. 16). The exhibition consisted of eleven paintings (including *Excavation* and *Grotto,* both completed in 1932) as well as watercolors and drawings. Bouché characterized the works as follows: "His figures, his human fragments, his stones, his wood, his flags are treated with a ruthlessness

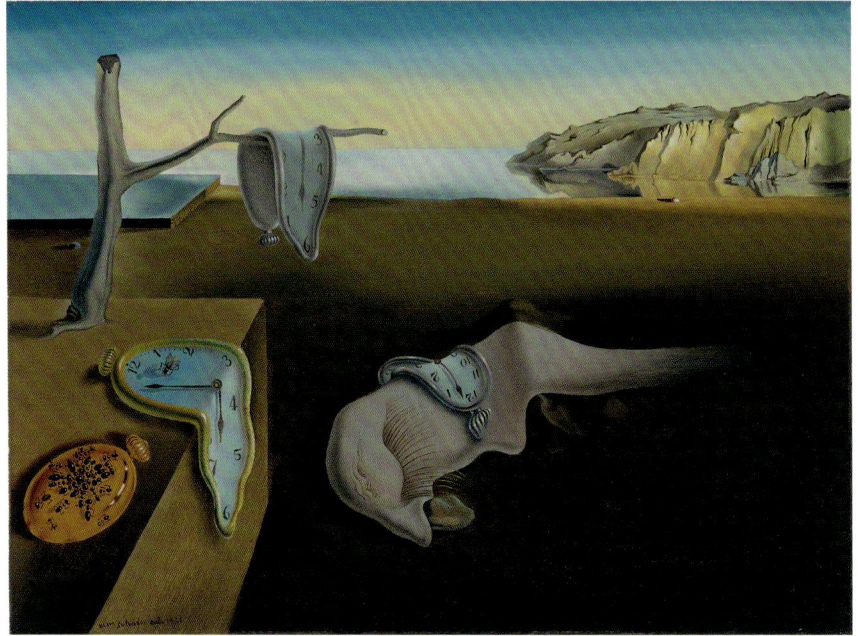

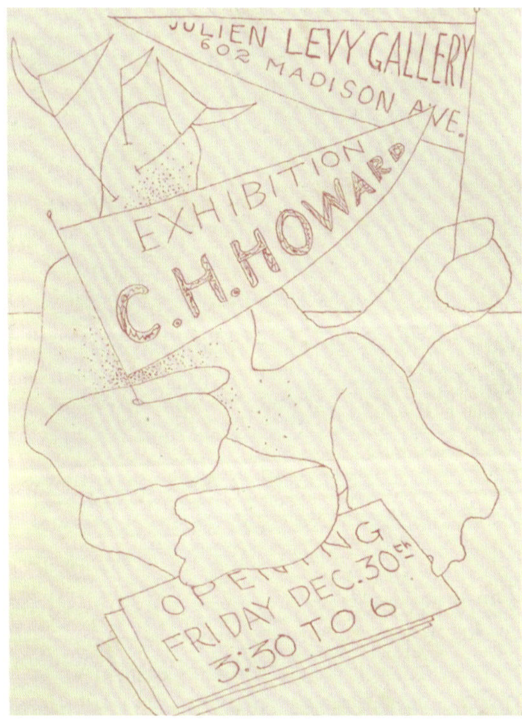

almost beyond imagination, yet always with a cold, clear ruthlessness controlledly [*sic*] dictated by the conceived rhythm of his design and his picture. These are no efforts to astound. They are too intense for that. They are the definitely logical transpositions of an artist handling his matter completely to suit his need."[28] Even as early as 1932 Bouché had identified what would become a salient attribute of Howard's work, pinpointing his imposition of logic and order into his furtive compositions.

Interestingly, however, when in 1936 Levy published his authoritative book *Surrealism*, Howard was omitted. Levy would later say that putting Howard in his *Surréalisme* show had been a misstep, explaining: "The inclusion of Charles Howard was a sanguine mistake, as he was only passingly surrealistic. One might say the same for Picasso, who had already renounced his short affiliation with the Surrealists."[29] Yet despite his later misgivings, one can understand Levy's initial thinking given that many of Howard's paintings and drawings from the 1930s (for instance the two *Untitled* drawings of 1931, plates 3, 4) possess unmistakable characteristics of Surrealism, including the depiction of psychologically charged scenes populated with figures and objects that do not conform to rational concerns or laws of science; an interest in absurd encounters; and a predilection for fragmented and biomorphic bodies. Moreover, in two untitled drawings, both from 1932 (plates 10, 11), Howard invokes the style of Italian artist Giorgio de Chirico, to whom Breton had laid claim in his treatise *Surrealism and Painting* (1928). One drawing features a still

life of fruits and vegetables set near the sea in an abandoned alleyway. Bright sunlight cast on the anonymous streetscape throws ominous shadows across the forms, recalling a signature attribute of de Chirico's dreamscapes. Howard's interest in the Italian artist resurfaces in later drawings from 1939; in *Elevation* (1939, plate 24) he inverts de Chirico's trademark colonnade on the left of the composition, tucking it under a rose-hued, conical structure. In *Hare Corner* (1939, plate 25) the colonnade appears upright again on the left in dramatic perspective. The composition echoes de Chirico's *Souvenir of Italy* (1913, fig. 17), which is reproduced in Levy's *Surrealism*. Howard replaces the reclining statue in de Chirico's composition, however, with his enigmatic "hare," which stretches off into the distance and down the alleyway as if it were a shadow. In these surrealist works from the late 1930s Howard assumes an increasingly abstract direction, with his figures becoming less and less identifiable.

Despite the overt surrealist qualities evident in much of Howard's work from this period, there *is* something true about Levy's statement: In contrast to that of other artists operating in a surrealist mode, Howard's work stands apart. These are not the wild, automatic meanderings of artists such as Ernst or André Masson, who would become emblematic of the movement. As Bouché noted, Howard's compositions possess a defining sense of logic and order. In a 1935 letter to critic Junius Cravens, Howard himself would characterize his work as distinct from the "illustrative" and "intellectual" mode of Surrealism, which he described as "strange but not mysterious." He added that in his paintings, "the objects (which are too abstract to be regarded literally as objects) as such become secondary, as I paint, and serve only as a point of departure. . . . That the natural problems of pure painting—unity, adjustment, poise, subtlety, style, grace, variety, quality, etc.—should be to me increasingly engrossing, as against objective delineation of subject, seems to me to exclude my work from Surrealism."[30]

And yet, just a year after writing this, Howard would renew his association with the movement as it took root in London.

Two years before Howard crafted this assessment of his work for Cravens, he struggled with the transition of relocating to England. He later wrote: "I suddenly found it impossible to make pictures. I could paint all right, but the picture eluded me. I sweated and rationalized, but the paintings remained blind, and only with considerable embarrassment would I force myself to finish them." Such an upheaval would have certainly been disruptive, but Howard quickly became acquainted with one of English Modernism's leading artists, Edward Wadsworth, who employed Howard to transfer a semi-abstract mural onto the wall of the De La Warr Pavilion in Bexhill-on-Sea, East Sussex (fig. 18), which upon its completion in 1935 was one of the first International Style buildings in England. Wadsworth, along with the artists Paul Nash, Henry Moore, Nicholson, and Barbara Hepworth, was a member of the group Unit One, which sought to create a new modern movement in Britain via the pairing of abstract form and psychological subject matter.[31] In the 1910s Wadsworth had also been associated with the English Vorticists, who introduced cubist and futurist fragmentation into the compositional plane and favored an all-over geometric abstraction. Having participated in Levy's exhibitions Howard must have been a welcome link between developing modernist movements in New York and those forming in England, particularly among artists who felt estranged from the wider art world at a time when Paris was still considered the epicenter of avant-garde developments.

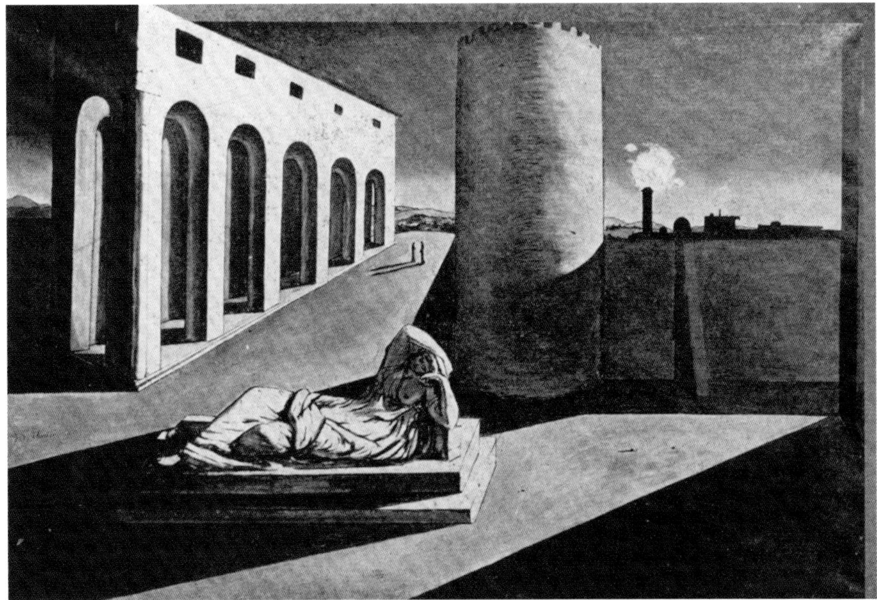

Fig. 17 Giorgio de Chirico, *Souvenir of Italy*, 1913.

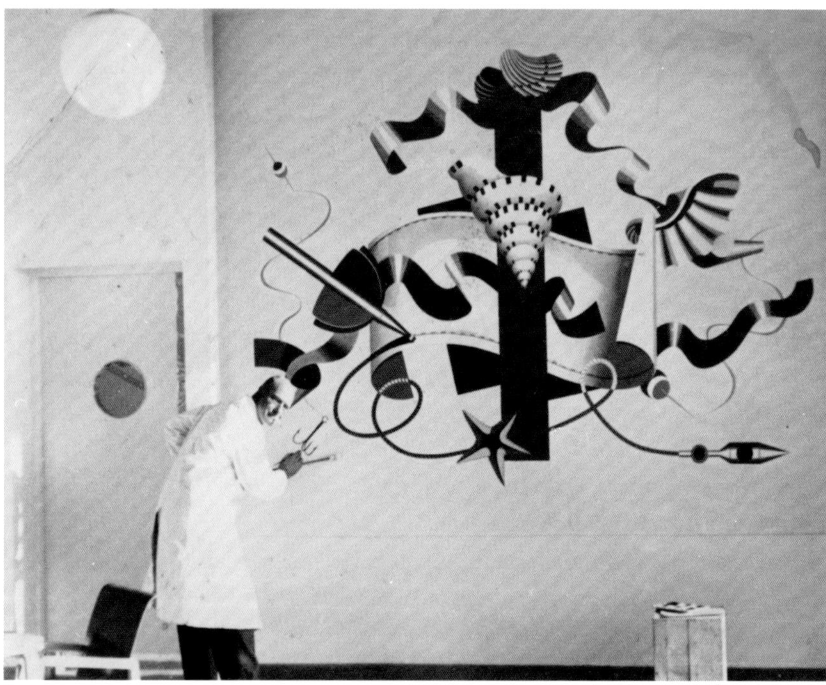

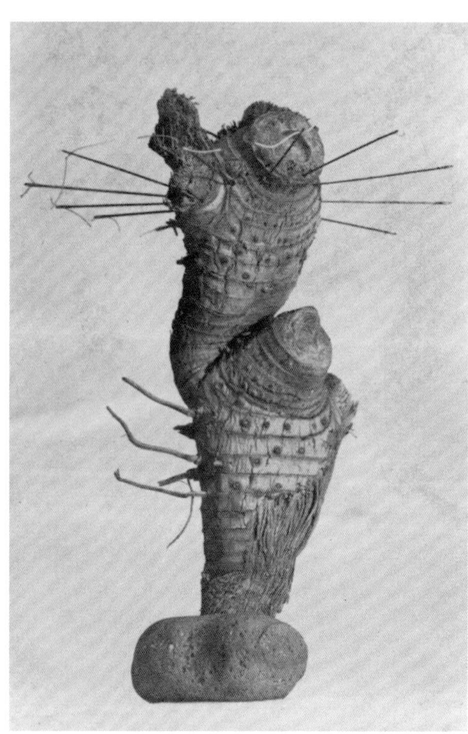

committee meetings). The exhibition, which "included over four hundred exhibits by some fifty-four artists drawn from fourteen nations," opened on June 11 at the New Burlington Galleries and attracted nearly 1,200 people on the first day.[32] During its month-long run the show welcomed twenty-three thousand visitors.[33] In addition to presenting the work of many English artists, it also included major figures of the movement, such as Arp, Dalí, Ernst, Duchamp, Magritte, Miró, and Meret Oppenheim, and generated a great deal of interest, much of it hostile, among the English public, who had not yet become acquainted with Surrealism. About Oppenheim's now famous fur-covered teacup, *Object* (1936), the *Evening News* declared, "Frankly, I don't see why a sense of world despair should make you want to construct a cup, saucer and spoon of rabbit fur. . . . It is not worth looking at. I don't mind it being meaningless, but it is horribly clumsy as well."[34] Howard was again one of three Americans included, the others being Calder and Man Ray.[35]

From 1936 until 1940, when he returned to the United States, Howard was associated with the English Surrealists. The group crystalized around the *International Surrealist Bulletin,* a journal established in London in 1936 that often featured the writings of leading member Herbert Read, who became the chief voice for Surrealism and abstraction in England.[36] In 1937, Howard and Madge Knight participated in the exhibition *Surrealist Objects & Poems* at the London Gallery. Howard contributed his only known sculptures to the

Unit One was short lived: The group dissolved in late 1934 and many of its members were later reabsorbed into the surrealist movement once it germinated in London in 1936 following the sensational *International Surrealist Exhibition* organized by Roland Penrose and Herbert Read with the participation of Breton (as well as others who attended the organizing

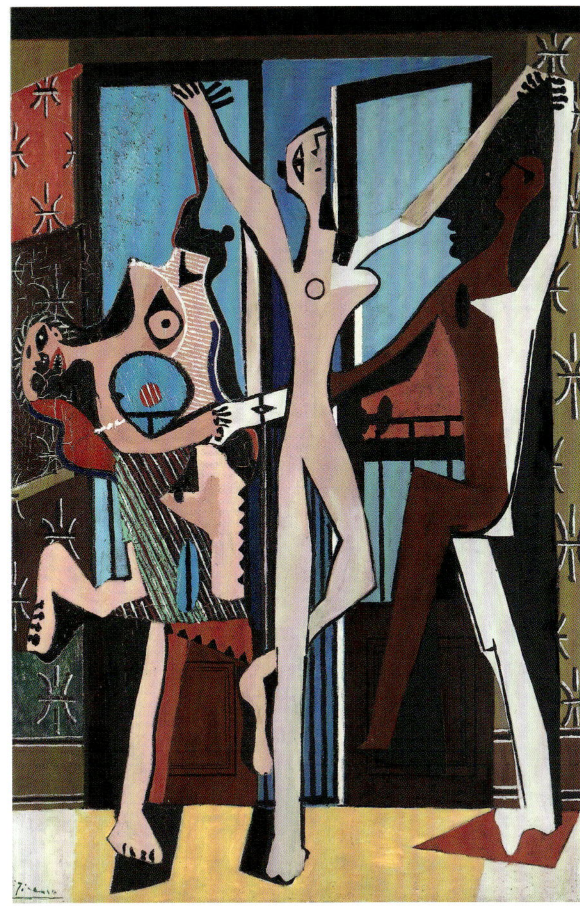

Fig. 20 Pablo Picasso, *The Three Dancers*, 1925. Oil on canvas, 84¾ × 55⅞ in. (215.4 × 142 cm). Tate Modern, London. Purchased with a special Grant-in-Aid and the Florence Fox Bequest with assistance from the Friends of the Tate Gallery and the Contemporary Art Society 1965

exhibition; one of the three works, *Inscrutable Object* (1937, presumed lost, fig. 19), was displayed in the "found objects" section and reproduced in the catalogue. An alluring abstract form, the sculpture consists of a stone upon which a bulbous piece of wood rests, with thorn-like sticks radiating outward at the top like a propeller. Art historian Michel Remy writes that it "peremptorily affirms that the object of our vision will forever remain foreign to us, since the object is neither more or less than the repository of our most secret desires."[37] This inscrutability is a predominant theme in Howard's work in general, which withholds its elusive subjects.

Howard's *The Sons Await Tradition* (plate 19) and *The Mother (Makes the Son) Plants the Seed* (plate 18), both from 1937, were painted at the peak of his surrealist mode, while he was still experimenting and moving fluidly between various abstract styles. In each of these pictures biomorphic, liquid forms predominate, recalling the work of Arp and Dalí. Howard admitted to quoting other artists, writing "I have welcomed the influence of other painters. I don't believe in pure originality, and in the elaboration of my work I have relied upon my own obsession. If that weren't strong enough to integrate its own expression, it seems to me it would be no use painting anyway."[38] The titles of these two paintings foreground the mother-child relationship espoused by Sigmund Freud, whose theories of unconscious desire were of great importance to the Surrealists. They perhaps also allude to Howard's own upbringing and to his relationship with his artistic mother and his architect father, who in his own work favored a more traditional neoclassical style.

In *The Cage* (1938, plate 23) Howard employs his favored "trinity" compositional structure, witnessed in Giorgione's altarpiece. Yet the work further refers to the triads that Picasso developed in his seminal paintings *The Three Musicians* (1921) and *The Three Dancers* (1925, fig. 20). As with Picasso's examples, in *The Cage* three figures seem to dance or play instruments in an indeterminate space, yet the sense of lyricism between Howard's bodies, which appear part human and part animal, is stronger, and the degree of abstraction is greater. Distant from a natural world order, these figures possess an inscrutability similar to that of his earlier sculpture. *The Cage*

is among the first of Howard's paintings in which the horizon line is abandoned and the setting is increasingly symbolic and interiorized.

Peggy Guggenheim, a polarizing figure among the English Surrealists, opened her first gallery in London, in 1938; she named it Guggenheim Jeune (a play on the name of the Parisian gallery Bernheim-Jeune) and enlisted Duchamp and later Read as her advisors. She inaugurated the gallery with an exhibition of Jean Cocteau works that ran concurrently with the *International Surrealism Exhibition* in Paris. Guggenheim Jeune quickly became an important catalyst for the London art scene, giving solo exhibitions to artists such as Wassily Kandinsky, Yves Tanguy, and Wolfgang Paalen. Howard was given a show there in April 1939, his second solo show in London (the first having been held at the Bloomsbury Gallery in 1935). Two years later Guggenheim traveled to San Francisco, where she visited Howard and purchased two paintings—*Prefiguration* (1940, fig. 21) and *Discovery* (1937)—from his exhibition at the Courvoisier Gallery. Those works would later be displayed in the Abstract and Cubist Gallery at her Art of This Century (fig. 22); the former was reproduced in the accompanying catalogue.

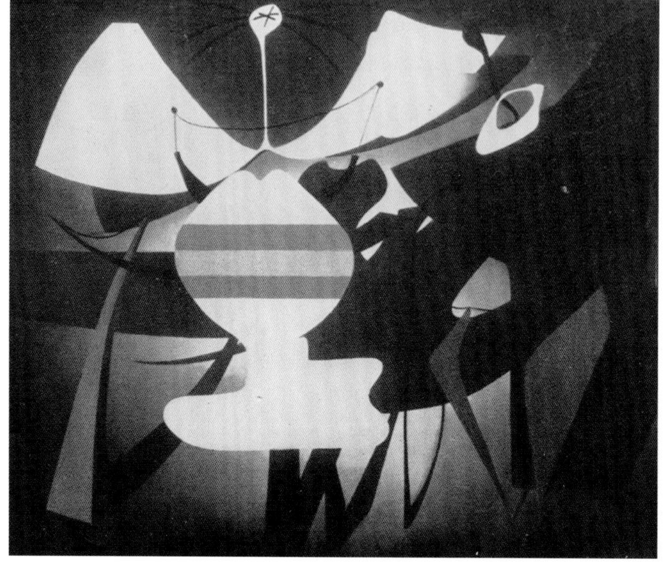

Fig. 21 Charles Howard, *Prefiguration*, 1940.

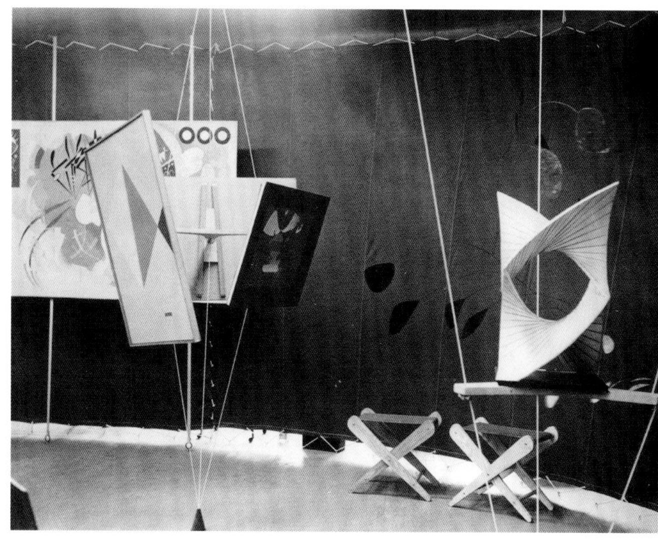

Fig. 22 South-facing installation view of the Abstract and Cubist Gallery, Art of This Century, New York, October 20, 1942. Photograph by Berenice Abbott.

SAN FRANCISCO DURING THE WAR

In summer 1940, after being recalled to the United States when World War II broke out, Charles Howard and Madge Knight moved to San Francisco.[39] They took an apartment at 91 Water Street, close to the California School of Fine Arts (CSFA; now the San Francisco Art Institute, SFAI) and the studios maintained by Robert Howard and his wife, the artist Adaline Kent, with whom they were close. Charles and Madge frequently spent evenings at Robert and Adaline's home, which was a gathering place for many other San Francisco artists who taught at CSFA. Reflecting on the rise of Surrealism in the 1930s, and the events leading up to the war, Howard wrote that it had been: "An anxious and vociferous period in our time. But however others solved the problem to their own satisfaction, painting as such had to remain the central point for me. I became an abstractionist. The way I understood it, what we needed, fundamentally and ideally, was order. And I thought also that these things, to be of good-will, should start at home. I set out to find them for myself, as a painter. Abstraction was order and logic, so I became, just like that, full of logic, an abstractionist."

Howard's growing concern about the war is perhaps most pronounced in *The Dove* (1939, plate 26), a work executed just before he returned to the United States. In this intimate, diminutive painting—a scale at which Howard excelled—he depicts two land masses connected by a white, wooden plank bridge upon which abstract forms, the largest of which walks on two squat, bird-like feet, cross carefully to the other side. As a symbol of peace, the dove alluded to in the title adds a particular weight to the composition, suggesting that the work may serve as a metaphorical depiction of safe passage to a distant shore. Howard once said that the titles of his paintings are "supplementary and allusive" rather than exacting and descriptive.[40] As this example suggests, that does not diminish their narrative power. *The Dove* also contains echoes of Giorgione's *The Tempest*: both compositions are divided into river banks connected by bridges, and the criss-crossing black lines in

Howard's painting also conjure the flash of the lightning bolt in Giorgione's dark and stormy sky (see fig. 7).

Along with the Howards, many artists active in the surrealist movement in London sought safety in the United States during the war. The Howards' friends, English artist Stanley William Hayter and his wife, the sculptor Helen Phillips, who was from the Bay Area, arrived in San Francisco the same year. Hayter was renowned for having established the influential print studio Atelier 17 in Paris in 1927. Historian Jeff Gunderson has observed: "Howard and Hayter arrived at a moment when San Francisco was hungry for the new directions in contemporary art it had encountered at the Golden Gate International Exposition, which had been held on Treasure Island in 1939–40. The pair served as key conduits for the European scene, helping to further [San Francisco Museum of Art (SFMA) director Grace McCann] Morley's (and later [curator Douglas] MacAgy's) designs on promoting the latest trends from the East Coast and abroad."[41] John Humphrey, a former curator at the San Francisco Museum of Modern Art (SFMOMA, as SFMA is now known), further recalled the significance of Howard's arrival and subsequent influence on the local art community in the 1940s, stating: "Charles Howard was a sophisticated mind who'd been for years exposed to the European situation in England as a painter and as a teacher. And during those war years, he was teaching at the Art Institute, and the range of his knowledge and his ability to communicate to the artist was tremendous."[42] Howard's arrival, along with that of others from Europe, galvanized the Bay Area art scene in the 1940s, prompting a renaissance for modernist abstraction. Howard's influence is particularly clear in the increasingly abstract work produced in the 1940s by his friend Clay Spohn, his brother Robert, and his sister-in-law Adaline Kent. In this period Kent and Robert Howard also began to embrace evocative titles reminiscent of those Charles assigned to his works, as with their sculptures *Presence* (1947, fig. 23) and *Semaphore* (1947, fig. 24).

Howard's abstraction is fully realized in *First War Winter* (plate 27), a painting he began in London in 1939 and finished in San Francisco in 1940. The composition's attenuated, elegant forms seem precariously connected, as if the kineticism of Calder's mobiles had been suddenly frozen in pictorial space. In this picture many of the hallmark characteristics of Howard's mature paintings become evident, including the luminous glow that emanates from the center of the composition, creating a theatrical sense of space and the illusion of a mysterious cavity. Clearly rendered, elegant lines define his proportionate geometric shapes, all of which seem to emblematize a world teetering on the brink of destruction. Almost immediately upon its completion *First War Winter* was exhibited at SFMA in the *San Francisco Art Association Annual* of 1940, where it won the Art Purchase Prize for that year and thus entered the museum's collection.

From about 1941 to 1945 Howard worked for the Marinship Shipyard in Sausalito, building liberty ships for the war effort, while Madge Knight worked at the graphic design firm of Walter Landor.[43] SFMA curator Douglas MacAgy, who became a great supporter of Howard's, later wrote that during this period Howard searched through "the scrap piles to find some accidental twist of metal that would relieve his mind for a moment of the oppression felt in the dominating presence of mechanically conceived forms. Often at night he would spend hours in the library seeking an antidote to the shapes of the day by means of illustrations in books on biology."[44] One such study found in Howard's notebooks details the wreckage of a car accident, offering an example of the kinds of metallic forms in which he found inspiration (fig. 25). In MacAgy's

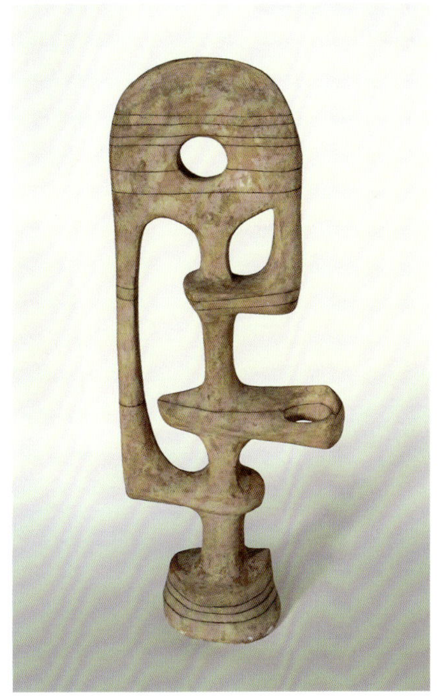

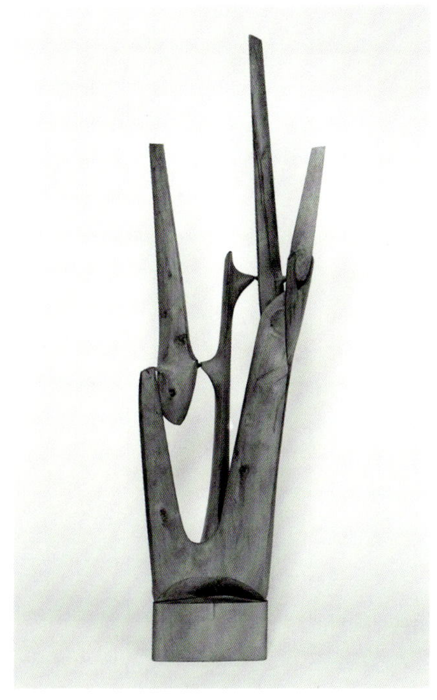

Fig. 23 Adaline Kent, *Presence*, 1947. Magnesite, 42¾ × 17¾ × 7¼ in. (108.6 × 45.1 × 18.4 cm). San Francisco Museum of Modern Art, gift of the Women's Board and the Membership Activities Board, acquired 1957

Fig. 24 Robert Howard, *Semaphore*, 1947. Pearwood, 44⅜ × 10⅛ × 13⅛ in. (112.7 × 25.7 × 33.3 cm). San Francisco Museum of Modern Art, gift of Mr. and Mrs. Brooks Walker, acquired 1978

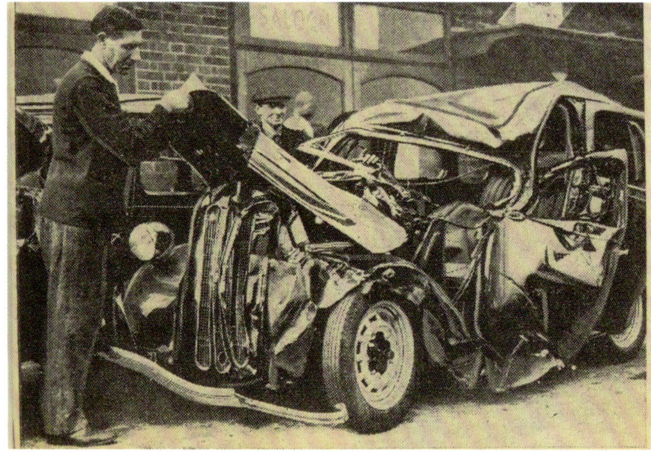

Fig. 25 Clipping from Charles Howard's notebooks, n.d.

Fig. 26 Man Ray, *Observatory Time—The Lovers*, 1936. Oil on canvas, 39⅜ × 98⅝ in. (100.1 × 250.4 cm). The Vera and Arturo Schwarz Collection of Dada and Surrealist Art in the Israel Museum, Jerusalem

statement we again see Howard striving to create a stylistic synthesis—now between the cold, metallic forms of the shipyard and the organic ones he discovered in science books.

Imagery inspired by ships or transatlantic voyages was nothing new to Howard's work and can be seen in earlier drawings such as *Untitled* from 1937 (plate 20), in which figures seem to descend from the sky to either enter or leave the gangway, hovering vertically in the center of the composition. Just to the left is a ship with a porthole, its anchor shown whipping high above the plank. In later works, such as *Prescience* (1942, plate 33), which is almost entirely abstract, the ship motifs become less clearly identifiable but are still apparent. We can recognize a seascape along the right side of the composition where an aperture, or porthole, gives way to a stark horizon line. In the interior, perhaps of a ship, an enigmatic event of some unknown organic nature unfolds: a lush, red amoebic form dominates the central foreground. Thin eyelash-like tendrils emanate from the crease where its two halves

appear joined like lips, and around it other dripping bodies assemble. The seductive red organism further recalls Man Ray's painting *Observatory Time—The Lovers* (1936, fig. 26), also included in Levy's *Surrealism,* in which photographer and model Lee Miller's lips float in the Parisian sky above an observatory. Despite his attempts to distance himself from the movement in the 1940s, in paintings such as *Prescience* and *First War Winter* Howard insinuates an ongoing application of surrealist motifs—in particular biomorphic and isomorphic forms.

While living in San Francisco, Howard also became the designing supervisor in the Art Section for the Works Progress Administration (WPA), making posters for the Oakland Defense Council that warned citizens about rolling blackouts and gas leaks (see page 54).[45] Under the auspices of the WPA he designed a series of murals for the Alameda Naval Air Station that ultimately were never executed because, as Robert Howard later recounted: "The commanding officer was changed and [the new one] didn't care for Charlie's designs. They were abstract and a little too much for [him], I guess."[46] One painting most likely created in preparation for an unrealized tapestry for the Officers' Recreational Building shows an airplane ascending through striations of color. Circular forms

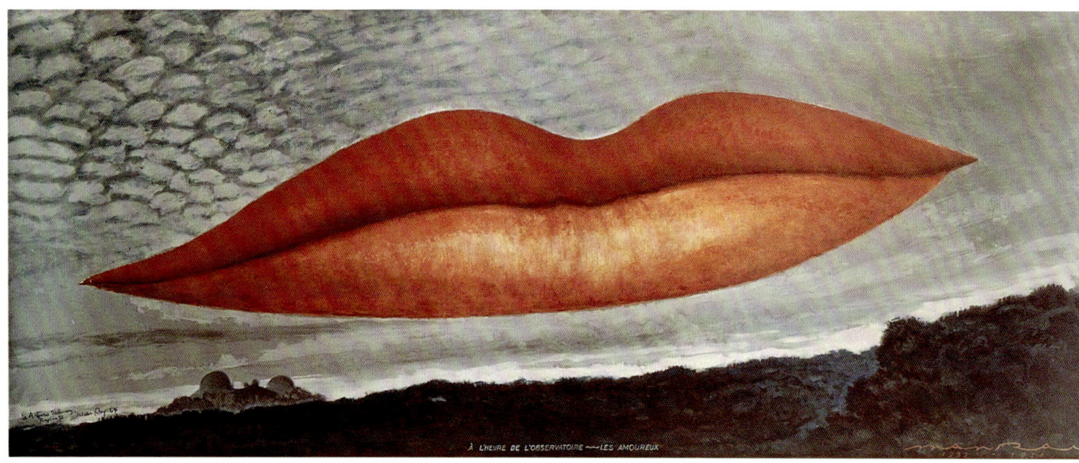

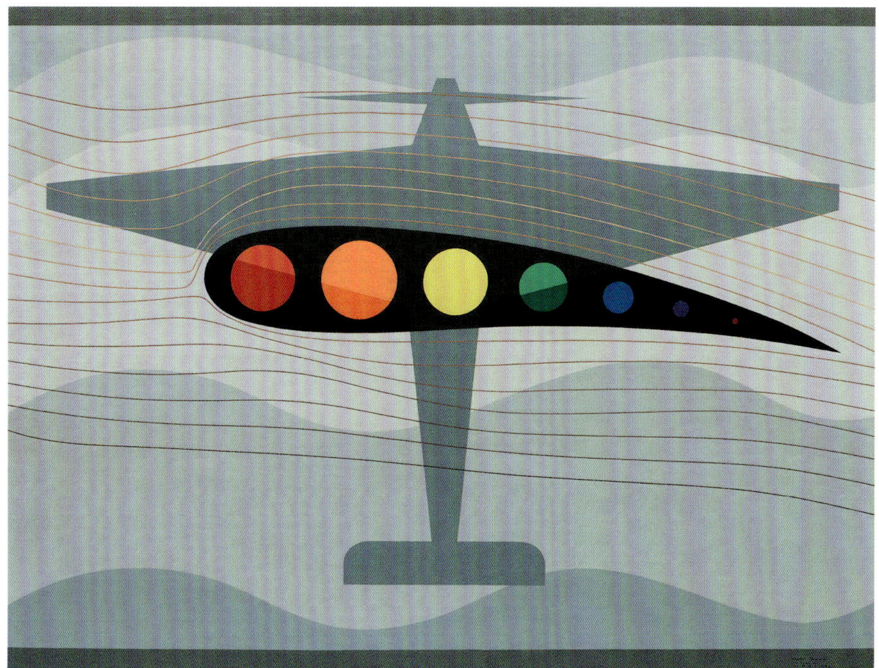

that resemble windows are superimposed on its silhouette, each aperture painted a different hue from the color spectrum (fig. 27). The composition's title, *Abstraction in Flight* (1942), is an apt descriptor for much of the work Howard produced from the late 1930s on.

Howard was in a spate of significant exhibitions in 1942, including his first solo show at an American museum, which took place at SFMA and featured a selection of his drawings. He would also participate in several notable group shows, including the inaugural presentation at Peggy Guggenheim's Art of This Century, as noted above, and *Artists for Victory* at the Metropolitan Museum of Art, New York, for which the museum made the uncustomary decision to turn over its galleries to the outside group Artists for Victory, Inc. During the exhibition, which was billed as a wartime celebration of contemporary American artists, forty-one purchase prizes were awarded, amounting to $51,000. Howard's *Prescience* received fifth place and subsequently entered the museum's collection.[47] Howard also participated in Dorothy Miller's *Americans 1942: 18 Artists from 9 States* (fig. 28), a similarly patriotic effort to promote American art. Heralded as the first in a series of exhibitions at MoMA to survey artists working and living in various cities across the nation, Miller's show aimed to highlight diverse art practices flourishing across the United States. In her foreword to the catalogue she wrote: "*Americans 1942* underscores the remarkable development of important art centers throughout the country in the past decade. The United

States Government art programs have had much to do with this development. With few exceptions the artists in this exhibition have been sponsored, at one time or another, by the Section of Fine Arts of the Public Buildings Administration of the WPA Art Program."[48] Howard, along with Knud Merrild, was by far the most stylistically abstract of the artists in the exhibition, with the others primarily reflecting figurative styles of American Regionalism. Other featured artists included recognizable names such as Morris Graves, Rico Lebrun, and Helen Lundeberg, as well as more unfamiliar ones like Darrel Austin, Emma Lu Davis, and Everett Spruce. The exhibition presented a substantial range of fifteen works by Howard, including *Hare Corner* (1939), *Presage* (1938), *The Cage* (1938), *Precinct* (1938), *Generation* (1940), and *Trinity* (1941). In his artist's statement for the catalogue Howard wrote: "Generally speaking the subject matter of the paintings is derived from everyday objects. A stone, a bird, a lamp post often serve as well as anything else. As the painter of the pictures, I operate as the dramatizing agent. The intention is to recall the shapes and relations of things which are common to all mankind. I consider that this is the object of all artists and that whatever else intervenes in a picture is merely arbitrary."[49]

It was nearly in tandem with Howard's most productive year that MacAgy had been hired as curator at SFMA, largely on the basis of a Picasso exhibition he had organized at the Cleveland Museum of Art that had deeply impressed SFMA director Morley. He arrived in San Francisco in 1941 with his equally visionary wife, Jermayne MacAgy (also from the Cleveland Museum of Art), who accepted a post at the Legion of Honor, where she would mount many inventive shows and eventually serve as acting director. It did not take long for Charles Howard and Madge Knight to become fast friends with the MacAgys, who were at the epicenter of artistic activity in San Francisco in the 1940s. In April 1942 Douglas MacAgy curated *Sawdust and Spangles: Arts from the Circus*, which was designed to uplift war-weary audiences. Howard and Madge Knight produced the poster for the exhibition (fig. 29) and contributed work, as did Robert Howard, Kent, and Spohn. The MacAgys would become two of Charles Howard's greatest advocates, continuing to champion his work even after they left San Francisco in the 1950s. Douglas MacAgy wrote several articles on Howard in the mid-1940s for journals such as *Circle, Magazine of Art*, and *Critique,* and in 1946, Jermayne (known as Jerry) curated Howard's largest and most exhaustive retrospective, for which Douglas penned a brochure essay. The couple also acquired two of Howard's paintings, *Dove Love* (1945, plate 37) and *The First Hypothesis* (1946, plate 41), which Jerry later bequeathed to the Menil Collection in Houston.[50]

In his essay, titled "A Margin of Chaos," Douglas MacAgy writes about Howard's work in relation to the concept of the abyss, which encompasses the uncontainable and the unknowable—the "archetype" of which, he avers, is "Chaos." Through the creative process, MacAgy suggests, Howard imposes a symmetry and structure that could otherwise be only fleetingly envisioned. In reference to Howard's *The Bride* (1942), MacAgy writes: "In spite of the vitality of these shapes, which are outlined sharply against the grey illumination beyond them, they appear to be arrested and still. Their hues have the peculiar lambency by which objects seem to become momentarily incandescent under a twilight sky. In the meeting of space with shape there is an effect which is analogous to that moment of hush which sometimes pervades a scene just before dawn, or just before darkness falls. It is a fleeting occasion of suspense, a time when one is on the verge of witnessing a cosmic change."[51] For MacAgy it is such moments on the cusp of epic metamorphosis—hovering in a zone he characterizes as the "margin of chaos"—that Howard captures in his paintings and drawings. MacAgy's reading is particularly apt for the paintings Howard made during World War II that convey the tenuousness of stability, and the precarity of world order, which, having witnessed two world wars, he experientially knew to hang in the balance between opposing forces of power.

Upon becoming director of CSFA in 1945, just as the GI Bill brought an influx of new students and funding, Douglas MacAgy immediately sought to modernize the school's curriculum by emphasizing abstraction. In a controversial move, he covered the school's Diego Rivera mural, suggesting that Rivera's figurative, social realist style was of the past.[52] He also sought to bring signatory modern voices to the Bay Area. For his first fall term MacAgy set about creating a visiting artist lecture program. Of the first four invited speakers—Man Ray, Dalí, Henry Miller, and Charles Howard—only Howard was able to participate.[53] MacAgy had hoped to hire him as a CSFA faculty member, however with the war by then over, Charles and Madge made their plans to return to England

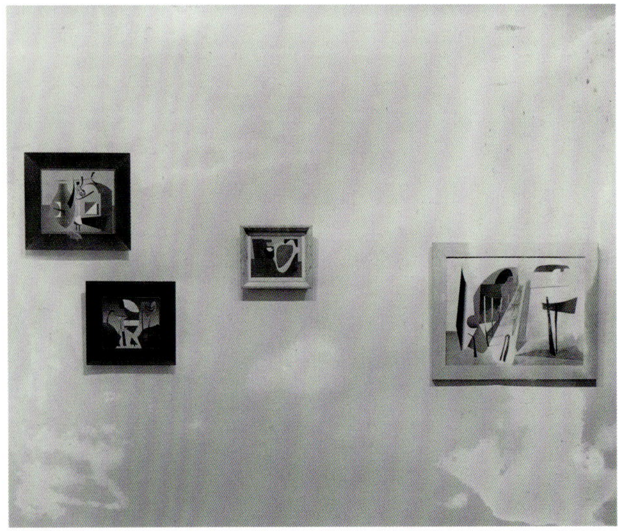

Fig. 28 Installation view of *Americans 1942: 18 Artists from 9 States,* The Museum of Modern Art, New York, January 21–March 8, 1942. The Museum of Modern Art Archives

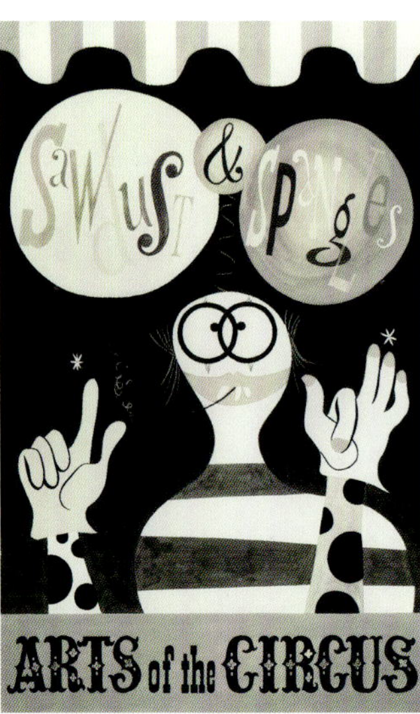

Fig. 29 Exhibition poster for *Sawdust and Spangles: Arts from the Circus,* San Francisco Museum of Art, April 14–May 10, 1942. SFMOMA Research Library

known. MacAgy settled for offering him a temporary teaching position, writing in a proposal to the School Committee of the San Francisco Art Association in fall 1945: "Problem: Charles Howard, the only artist in San Francisco with a reputation well established in this country and Europe, will leave San Francisco in several months. The school would gain considerable prestige through an association with Howard at this time. It is recommended that a limited group of local artists be assembled at the school for collaborative work instituted and presided over by Howard for a period of six weeks, beginning, say, November 6, and meeting twice a week."[54] Had Howard stayed in San Francisco, he most likely would have joined the school's prestigious faculty, which as of 1945 included Robert Howard, Spohn, Ansel Adams, David Park, Dorr Bothwell, Hassel Smith, and James McCray. Just a year later, MacAgy would hire painter Clyfford Still, who had a solo exhibition at SFMA in 1943, when MacAgy was still working at the museum. He also hired Mark Rothko (in the summers of 1947 and 1949) and Ad Reinhardt (in 1950); all three would prove to be crucial fomenters of Abstract Expressionism in the Bay Area.[55]

Charles Howard's six-year stay in San Francisco concluded with his capstone exhibition at the Legion of Honor organized by Jerry MacAgy. The show, Howard's largest, brought together forty-four paintings, thirty-two gouaches, and fourteen drawings made between 1925 and 1946.[56] As mentioned previously, the works were extolled by Alfred Frankenstein, who wrote in the *San Francisco Chronicle*:

> Howard's figuration, however, is accomplished with a mastery of shapes and their relationships quite unparalleled by Miró or anybody else. He went through rigorous discipline of the self-consciously abstract, and he has emerged from it with breath-taking virtuosity in line, in the arrangement of color and in the composition of shapes with reference to each other. The curves and rhythms and fluencies of his forms are wonderfully melodious in themselves, and the subtleties of his color, its modulations and transitions and contrasts, are simply incomparable. . . . They are all brought off, with surgical precision and clarity, and with a kind of classical aloofness and depth of resonance.[57]

This review is a significant indicator of the high esteem in which Howard was held in the Bay Area in the 1940s, and intimates the sense of loss the community would feel when he left.

RETURN TO ENGLAND

In summer 1946, after visiting New York for Howard's solo exhibition at the Nierendorf Gallery, Charles and Madge settled in England for good, as they had always expected to.[58] They first moved to the small village of Castle Camps, just southeast of Cambridge on the county borders of Suffolk and Essex. They maintained contact with family and friends from the United States, but travel between the two countries became infrequent. Charles and Adaline Kent often wrote to each other about political events, exhibitions they had seen, and books they were reading. In 1949 Charles wrote to her with his characteristic wit and humor:

> Have you read T. S. Eliot's notes towards the Definition of Culture? Doesn't make one very happy, but sure scrabbles the gravel in one's system. As balancer (not antidote) (and now you try to figure out why), (and his is a special kind of balance too, not two opposing beams but both on the same side—makes it go down faster and harder), I've been marveling at a lovely bookie that describes the measuring of the universe—boy, if there's one word (conception) that [Bertrand] Russell's bookie on History of Philosophy has taught me, is to eradicate that four-letterer: hope. Hope my arse (that's a four-letterer too, as is word: words my arse: let's draw it).[59]

Around 1950 Charles and Madge moved to Helions Bumpstead, a village less than an hour's drive from Castle Camps, where they would remain for the next twenty years. They adopted an increasingly quiet lifestyle in the countryside, enjoying traditional English pastimes such as gardening. Robert and Adaline and their two daughters, Ellen and Galen, visited them periodically over the years; other visitors included James Broughton, the filmmaker who owned Howard's painting *Bivouac* (1940, plate 28); Walter and Josephine Landor; and Douglas MacAgy, who brought his new wife, Betty Tillet, and a group from Dallas to England in 1961, after becoming Director of the Dallas Museum of Contemporary Art (now the Dallas Museum of Art).[60]

Perhaps the most incisive statement about Howard's work from the mid to late 1940s was written by the artist himself. Just before sailing for England in late June 1946 he and Madge had visited Connecticut to discuss a commission for the Container Corporation of America, a box company known for supporting the arts during the war by reproducing the work of American

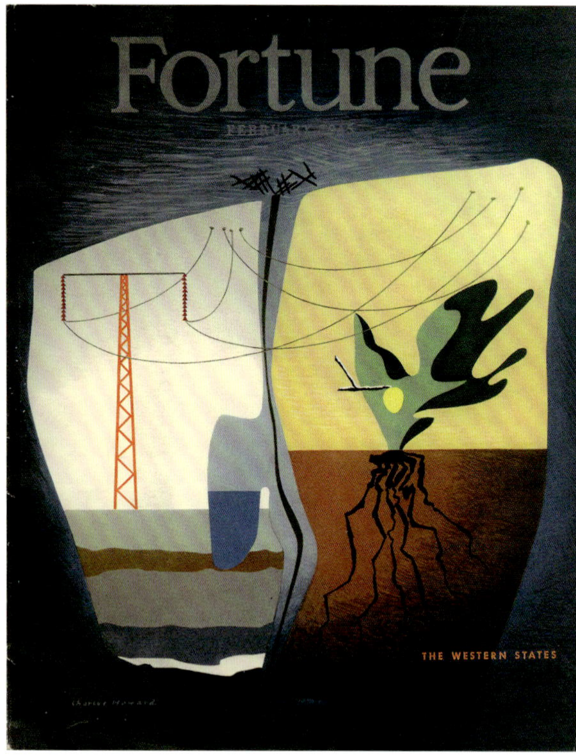

Fig. 30 Cover of *Fortune* magazine, February 1945.
Designed by Charles Howard

to the particular, but move from the particular to the general. You might even speak of them as portraiture, portraiture of ideas, plastic ideas rather than literary, objective or illustrative. They are, to use an unfortunately awkward word, ideographic.[62]

In this telling statement Howard identifies yet another category—the ideographic—that moves between figuration and abstraction, order and chaos, in an attempt to articulate a more complex, hybrid space that is unbounded by particular objective form. Expansive in its associative import, it is essentially symbolic of the artist's mind.

This ideographic style is evident in intimate works from the late 1940s, such as *The Aimant* (1949, plate 48), *The Cumulative Emblem* (1949, plate 50), and *The Ascending Aperture* (1949, plate 49). *Aimant* is a French word that translates as *magnet* (or *loving*) and thus is an apt metaphor to characterize the synthetic forces of abstraction, figuration, and surrealism that coalesce within the painting. As in his earlier work from the 1930s, in *The Aimant* a transformation takes place as the landscape moves from a subterranean cave up into a sunset sky. Abstract figures that bring to mind animals and insects appear to ascend (or to prepare to ascend) into a tunnel at the center of the composition, in which a green crescent moon and an ant-like, black-and-white shape hover. As in many other paintings of this time, Howard pictures these protagonists in a state of metamorphosis, balancing in space, as if suspended by opposing magnetic fields—the margin of chaos. Howard applies this particular hue of green to several pictures of the decade—most notably in *Dove Love* (plate 37) and *The Cage* (plate 23)—usually in the center of the composition. Interestingly, this forest green recalls the Virgin Mary's dress in Giorgione's *Madonna and Child Between St. Francis and St. Nicasius* as well as the banner that drapes beneath her, both in the center of the painting.

From the 1950s on Howard was in few exhibitions in either England or the United States. In New York he showed with the Howard Wise Gallery in 1963, most likely as a result of Douglas MacAgy's advocacy (the gallery had hired MacAgy as an advisor). In London he showed with the Hanover Gallery and McRoberts and Tunnard. When Howard was fifty-seven, in 1956, the Whitechapel Gallery in London accorded him a retrospective (his largest and most extensive exhibition in the city) after including him in the group exhibitions *Twentieth*

artists in its advertising.[61] Perhaps inspired by the cover for *Fortune* magazine that Howard had designed the previous year (fig. 30) for an issue on the Western States, the company had invited him to make a work about California. In a letter penned in 1947 to art critic Emily Genauer—who was planning to include the resulting gouache in a book she was writing for Doubleday on the year's best American paintings—Howard writes that *California* (1946, plate 39) was not intended to be an illustration, or a representation of the state per se, but rather an allusive conjuring of the geographic locality. The letter also reveals the extent to which Howard was then still wrestling with aesthetic categories, even abstraction. He pointedly writes:

I do not consider that all my pictures fall into [the abstract] category. Roughly and generally, abstraction by definition seems to me to be a type of simplification of objects in themselves entities—objective subject matter reduced to essentials for a purpose. This is in line with the observation that there is abstraction in all design, a reduction of representation. [That] action is centripetal, moving from the whole outside of an objective piece of subject-matter to its core. My pictures are the reverse of this process: they expand from a central essential centrifugally [*sic*]. They do not go through a process of abstracting from the general

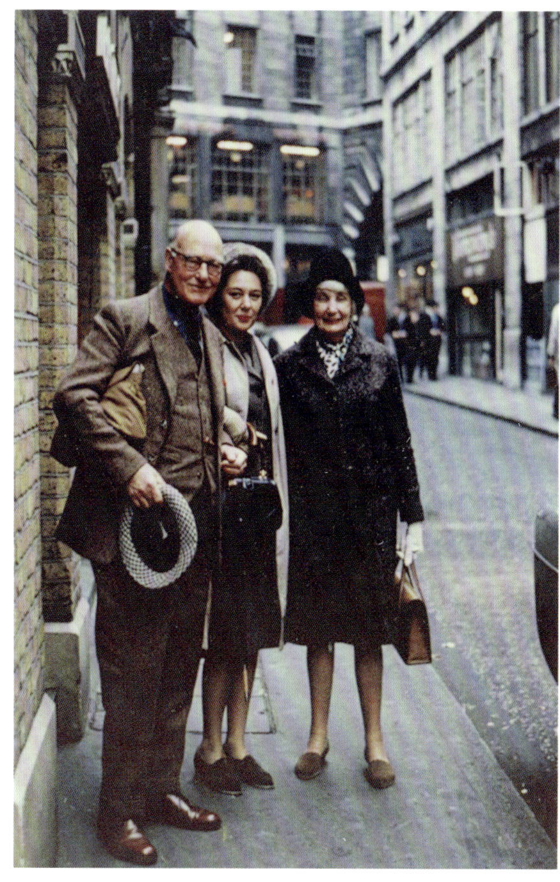

Century Form (1953) and *British Painting and Sculpture* (1954). The English art critic Basil Taylor contributed an essay for the exhibition catalogue that attempts to parse the relationship between Howard's work and various modes of abstraction, distinguishing him from moralistic abstract artists such as Piet Mondrian and Naum Gabo, who, as he explains, "believe in the order and spiritual effectiveness of an eternal geometry, who seek to reform human existence more or less radically through the poise, purity and impersonality of their constructions, who have maintained the Platonic ideal of a divine and immaterial harmony." Instead, he aligns Howard with artists such as Arp, Kandinsky, and Miró, quoting Kandinsky in his characterization of Howard's work: "It is not obvious geometrical configurations that will be the richest in possibilities, but hidden ones emerging unnoticed from the canvas and meant for the soul rather than the eye. The hidden construction may be composed of seemingly fortuitous shapes without apparent connection. But the absence of such a connection is proof of its inner presence. Outward loosening points to an internal merging."[63] Taylor also identifies the depiction of synthesis and balance as the distinguishing feature of Howard's compositions, writing that "his work declares very explicitly a balance between reasoned construction and free intuition."[64]

From the late 1950s until 1963 Howard commuted regularly between Suffolk and London to teach at the Camberwell School of Arts and Crafts (fig. 31). After Charles's teaching commitment ended he and Madge started to think about escaping the gray, wet weather of England by retiring to the warmer climes of southern France or Italy. They finally settled on Bagni di Lucca, known for its Roman baths, and found an old farmhouse perched on a hill near the Tuscan village Graniola. From about 1964 to 1970 they divided their time between Helions Bumpstead, where they spent their fall and winter, and Bagni di Lucca, where they went in the spring and through the summer, traversing the mountainous terrain of Europe in their Volkswagen bug. They permanently relocated to Bagni di Lucca in 1970. Howard would continue to paint in his studio until cataracts made that impossible. Both artists died at seventy-eight years of age, Madge in 1974 and Charles four years later. They are buried on a hill in Bagni di Lucca overlooking the rolling Tuscan landscape.

Howard's peaceful last years were a final transition in an evolving career in which he continued to define his vision and his place amid the interstices of various artistic categories. Despite the resistance to abstraction outlined in his letter to Genauer in 1947, his work from the mid-1950s assumed a more minimal and pared-down style. Around 1955 he began limiting his palette dramatically, emphasizing black and white with the occasional incorporation of dark earth tones and completely eliminating the illusion of depth. Like abstract expressionist artists working in the 1950s and 1960s, such as Franz Kline and Robert Motherwell, Howard adopted an all-over sense of abstraction that was more geometric than biomorphic. Gone was the sense of the ideographic—a melding of abstraction, figuration, and surrealism. We can still witness in these works, however, an attention to compositional balance achieved between curvilinear and rectilinear shapes and negative and positive space. In later works, such as *Painting (I)* (1962, plate 55), a central, vertical balancing agent like that found in his paintings from the 1940s, such as *The First Hypothesis,* is still present, along with his signature use of tendrils that protrude from ovular shapes, as seen in *Prescience* (1942). Yet as he moved in and around margins his forms became increasingly distilled and flattened, the margin of chaos progressively diminishing in the shift toward a quiet resolve.

Notes

1. Alfred Frankenstein, "Art Galleries," *San Francisco Chronicle*, May 12, 1946.

2. The individuals in attendance included Herbert Read, Mesens, Roland Penrose, Humphrey Jennings, Jacques Brunius, Ithell Colquhoun, Eileen Agar, Edith Rimmington, Stanley Hayter, A. C. Hester, Dr. Grace Pailthorpe, Reuben Mednikoff, John Banting, Gordon Onslow Ford, and Charles Howard. See Charles Harrison, *English Art and Modernism 1900–1939* (Bloomington, IN: Indiana University Press, 1981), 341n42.

3. As this essay will establish, Howard lived in England from 1933 until 1940, and then again from 1946 until 1970, when he retired to Italy.

4. Frankenstein, "Art Galleries."

5. Janette Howard Wallace, "Reminiscences of Janette Howard Wallace, Daughter of John Galen Howard and Mary Robertson Bradbury Howard" (unpublished manuscript, 1986), 4. BANC MSS 87/89 c. The Bancroft Library, University of California, Berkeley.

6. Ibid.

7. The Howards first lived at 2421 Ridge Road in Berkeley, in a house John Galen Howard designed and built in 1902–3 (it was later destroyed in the Great Fire of 1923). In 1912 they moved to another house John built at the intersection of Rose and Leroy streets on the property of Warren and Sadie Gregory, who were close family friends. For more on John Galen Howard see Sally Woodbridge's essay "Two Generations in Architecture: John Galen Howard and Henry Temple Howard," in *The Howards, First Family of Bay Area Modernism*, ed. Stacy Moss, exh. cat. (Oakland, CA: The Oakland Museum, 1988), 13–28.

8. Wallace, "Reminiscences," 40.

9. Ibid., 37.

10. Ibid., 31.

11. John Galen Howard joined the Red Cross in France in 1918 and then helped establish the American Expeditionary Force University in Beaune, France, before returning home in 1919. Henry became an ambulance driver in the French army, transporting the wounded in the battle of Chemin des Dames, and then joined the American army when the US entered the war. Robert became "a motorcycle dispatch rider for the American Field Service" in the final days of World War I. See Sally Woodbridge, "Two Generations in Architecture," in *The Howards*, ed. Moss, 24 and 27, and Stacey Moss, "Painters and Sculptors," in *The Howards*, ed. Moss, 34.

12. Many years later Charles and his father would see Isadora Duncan perform in New York together, and Charles once said he enjoyed her biography so much that he read it in one day. Letter from Charles Howard to John Galen Howard, May 24, 1920. John Galen Howard Papers, BANC MSS 67/35 c, Box 10:136. The Bancroft Library, University of California, Berkeley.

13. Letter from Mary Howard to John Galen Howard, June 4, 1920. John Galen Howard Papers, BANC MSS 67/35 c, Box 11: 148. The Bancroft Library, University of California, Berkeley.

14. The edition of *California Art Research* on Charles Howard published in 1936–37 asserts that he went to Europe in the summer of 1923 (see note 16); however, letters between the artist and his family suggest he left the previous summer, in 1922. This timing is supported by his passport, which was issued on July 11, 1922, and indicates a departure date of July 15, 1922. Additionally, records from Harvard University establish that he enrolled there in September 1921 and withdrew on January 30, 1922; at that point he likely enrolled at Columbia University for the spring semester in 1922, then departed for Europe that summer.

15. Letter from Charles Howard to John Galen Howard, June 23, 1923. John Galen Howard Papers, BANC MSS 67/35 c, Box 12:160. The Bancroft Library, University of California, Berkeley.

16. "Charles Houghton Howard," in *California Art Research: John Galen Howard, Robert Boardman Howard, Charles Houghton Howard, Adaline Kent, Jane Berlandina,* ed. Gene Hailey (San Francisco: Works Progress Administration California Art Research Project, vol. 17, 1936–37), 41. Although this study suggests that Howard met Grant Wood in 1924, I believe this actually occurred in summer 1923. In a letter to his father dated June 23, 1923, Howard indicates that he will be traveling to Italy after leaving France. When Howard returned from his travels remains unclear in the Howard family letters, however, so in that case I defer to the *California Art Research* study, which indicates that he moved to New York City in 1924.

17. This and other quotations by Howard in this essay come from his text "What Concerns Me," reprinted on pages 57–59 of this volume, unless otherwise noted. The unpublished typescript owned by the Howard family is the basis of that transcription. A slightly revised version of the text was published as "What Concerns Me," *Magazine of Art* 39, no. 2 (February 1946): 63–65.

18. Patterson Sims has identified the other members present as follows: "Clockwise about the table are seen Alexander Brook, Yasuo Kuniyoshi, an orating Louis Bouché, a leaping Calder, Niles Spencer, Walt Kuhn, an unidentified figure, Donald Greason, another unidentified figure, Edmund Duffy, Art Young, and, on the pole, the athletic artist-brothers Robert and Charles Howard." The Romanian Brancusi himself is likely seated in the middle with his back to the viewer, wearing a cossack hat. Calder briefly shared a studio with Charles Howard and had been included along with most of the others in the March 1926 Whitney Studio Club Annual Exhibition. Patterson Sims, *Alexander Calder: A Concentration of Works from the Permanent Collection of the Whitney Museum of American Art* (New York: Whitney Museum of American Art, 1981), 14.

19. Charles H. Howard, *Design* (Pelham, NY: Bridgman Publishers, 1926), 9.

20. Paul J. Karlstrom, ed. *On the Edge of America: California Modernist Art, 1900–1950,* (Berkeley: University of California Press, 1996), 279.

21. Jehanne Bietry Salinger, "In the San Francisco Galleries," *The Argus* 3, no. 1 (April 1928): 5.

22. Letter from Mary Howard to Robert Howard, October 10, 1927. John Galen Howard Papers, BANC MSS 67/35 c, Box 13: 175. The Bancroft Library, University of California, Berkeley. Emphasis in original.

23. Letter from Mary Howard to Charles Howard, April 6, 1928. John Galen Howard Papers, BANC MSS 67/35 c, Box 13:175. The Bancroft Library, University of California, Berkeley.

24. Ingrid Schaffner and Lisa Jacobs, eds. *Julien Levy: Portrait of an Art Gallery* (Cambridge, MA: MIT Press, 1998), 45.

25. The first exhibition of Surrealism in the United States occurred at the Wadsworth Atheneum Museum of Art in Hartford, CT, in 1931, just two months before Levy's exhibition would open in January 1932. *Newer Super-Realism* was organized by the Wadsworth's director, Chick Austin, who was a friend of Levy's. The two men frequently shared exhibitions between their spaces.

26. André Breton quoted in *Surrealism,* ed. Julien Levy (New York: The Black Sun Press, 1936), 9.

27. Other artists included in this seminal exhibition—adapted by Levy for his gallery in New York after it had been presented at the Wadsworth Atheneum under the title *Newer Super-Realism*—were Jacques-André Boiffard, George Platt Lynes, Roger Parry, Pablo Picasso, Pierre Roy, Maurice Tabard, Umbo, and Jean Viollier. The film program featured Fernand Léger's *Ballet Mécanique*, Jay Leyda's *A Bronx Morning*, and Man Ray's *L'Étoile de Mer*. Charles Howard was not included at the Wadsworth and appeared only in Levy's exhibition. See note 24 above and the chronology in *Julien Levy*, ed. Schaffner and Jacobs, 173–74.

28. Louis Bouché, brochure text for *Paintings by Charles Howard*, Julien Levy Gallery, New York, December 30, 1932–January 25, 1933.

29. Julien Levy, *Memoir of an Art Gallery* (New York: Putnam, 1977), 82.

30. "Charles Houghton Howard," *California Art Research*, 48.

31. Upon the group's formation in 1933, the complete list of members in Unit One included: Henry Moore, Barbara Hepworth, Paul Nash, Ben Nicholson, John Armstrong, John Bigge, Edward Burra, Frances Hodgkins, Edward Wadsworth, Wells Coates. Soon after the group was founded Hodgkins resigned and Tristram Hillier joined. For more on the membership on Unit One see Harrison, *English Art and Modernism*, 231–53.

32. Ibid., 309.

33. Michel Remy, *Surrealism in Britain* (Brookfield, VT: Ashgate Publishing Company, 1999), 78.

34. "Surrealist Art Is Clumsy as Well as Meaningless," *Evening News*, June 12, 1936.

35. The catalogue indicates that Howard contributed one painting to the exhibition, entitled *Entities Undergoing Treatment* (date unknown, presumed lost).

36. See Remy, *Surrealism in Britain*.

37. Ibid., 119.

38. Charles Howard, artist statement in *Americans 1942: 18 Artists from 9 States*, ed. Dorothy C. Miller, exh. cat. (New York: The Museum of Modern Art, 1942), 75.

39. Charles and Madge Knight Howard sailed from Galway, Ireland, on the USS *George Washington* on July 2, 1940; Charles was forty-one and Madge was forty-four years old. Passenger Lists of Vessels Arriving at New York, New York, 1897–1957. Microfilm Publication T715, 8,892 rolls. Records of the Immigration and Naturalization Service. National Archives at Washington, DC.

40. Howard in Miller, *Americans 1942*, 76.

41. Jeff Gunderson, "A Combination of Accidents: The San Francisco Art Scene in the 1940s," in *San Francisco Museum of Modern Art: 75 Years of Looking Forward*, ed. Janet Bishop, Corey Keller, and Sarah Roberts, exh. cat. (San Francisco: San Francisco Museum of Modern Art, 2009), 135.

42. "Oral history interview with John Humphrey, conducted by Paul Karlstrom, 1974 June 25," Archives of American Art, Smithsonian Institution. http://www.aaa.si.edu/collections/interviews /oral-history-interview-john-humphrey-12413.

43. Galen Howard Hilgard, conversation with the author, August 18, 2016. Hilgard is Charles Howard's niece and the daughter of Adaline Kent and Robert Howard.

44. Douglas MacAgy, "Introduction," in *Charles Howard, Retrospective Exhibition 1925–1946*, ed. Jermayne MacAgy, exh. cat. (San Francisco: California Palace of the Legion of Honor, 1946), 112.

45. See the "Biographical Note" in *Charles Howard*, ed. Bryan Robertson, exh. cat. (London: Whitechapel Art Gallery, 1956), 6.

46. "Oral history interview with Robert Boardman Howard, conducted by Mary Fuller McChesney, 1964 Sept. 16," Archives of American Art, Smithsonian Institution. http://www.aaa.si.edu /collections/interviews/oral-history-interview -robert-boardman-howard-13247.

47. Active from 1942 to 1946, the organization Artists for Victory, Inc. was run by artists who desired to assist in the war effort by using their artistic abilities. See A. Hyatt Mayor, "The Artists for Victory Exhibition," in *Artists for Victory*, ed. Mayor, exh. cat. (New York: Metropolitan Museum of Art, 1942), 141.

48. Miller, *Americans 1942*, 9.

49. Ibid., 75–76.

50. After Jerry and Douglas MacAgy divorced in 1954, Jerry moved to Texas and became director at Contemporary Art Association of Houston, where she would meet Dominique de Menil. They became close friends and de Menil considered her among her closest advisors; de Menil would later hire Jerry to found the Art History Department at the University of St. Thomas in Houston.

51. Douglas MacAgy, "A Margin of Chaos," *Circle* 10 (Summer 1948): 42.

52. Jeff Gunderson, conversation with the author, August 26, 2016. Gunderson is Librarian and Archivist at the San Francisco Art Institute.

53. Letters between MacAgy and the artists in the Archives of the San Francisco Art Institute indicate that Man Ray, Salvador Dalí, and Henry Miller were not able to travel at that time, leaving Charles Howard to stand as the sole voice of modernism. San Francisco Art Institute records from that period are sparse and do not indicate what Howard lectured about; it is presumed that he did indeed deliver the lecture since he was in San Francisco and able to do so.

54. Douglas MacAgy, proposal submitted to the School Committee of the San Francisco Art Association, fall 1945. Archives of the San Francisco Art Institute.

55. Rothko lived at Robert Howard and Adaline Kent's San Francisco home at 2500 Leavenworth Street (just around the corner from CSFA) when he taught at the school, since they and their daughters went to Kentfield during the summers. Adaline's father was William Kent, a US Congressman, philanthropist, and founder of Muir Woods. Kentfield was named after William's father, Albert Emmet Kent, who bought the land from James Ross in 1871.

56. The locations of many of the works included in this 1946 exhibition are unknown today.

57. Frankenstein, "Art Galleries."

58. Galen Howard Hilgard remembers that Charles and Madge lived out of orange crates in their San Francisco apartment, suggesting that they never fully settled and did not intend to stay once the war ended. Hilgard, conversation with the author, August 18, 2016.

59. Letter from Charles Howard to Adaline Kent, March 16, 1949. Collection of Galen Howard Hilgard.

60. MacAgy would later assume the post of Deputy Chairman of the National Endowment of the Arts and eventually become curator of the Hirshhorn Museum and Sculpture Garden in Washington, DC; he died of a heart attack in 1973, shortly after assuming the latter post. See David R. Beasley, *Douglas MacAgy and the Foundations of Modern Art Curatorship* (Simcoe, Ontario: Davus Publishing, 1998), 78.

61. Letter from Charles Howard and Madge Knight to Robert Howard and Adaline Kent, June 3, 1946. Collection of Galen Howard Hilgard.

62. Letter from Charles Howard to Emily Genauer, July 1, 1947. Emily Genauer papers, ca. 1920s–1990s. Archives of American Art, Smithsonian Institution.

63. Basil Taylor, "Introduction" in *Charles Howard*, ed. Robertson, 8–9.

64. Ibid., 9.

To the Absent Friend

Robert Gober

I have always been drawn to the work of unknown or underappreciated artists. Maybe it is the thrill of authenticity, when an artist works beautifully without acclaim or recognition from this transient world.

This was not exactly the case for Charles Howard, but for years he was unknown to me. Or at least his drawings were. His paintings, biomorphic abstractions, rang a vague visual bell. I have always meant to ask the painter Lari Pittman if Howard's work holds any special resonance or influence for him. But I usually hesitate to ask another artist a question like that because influence is strange; it doesn't necessarily bubble up or rain down from other art or artists.

I got to know Howard's strange drawings in 2004 when Matthew Drutt, then chief curator at the Menil Collection in Houston, invited me to create an exhibition from the Menil's unique, diverse holdings. An exhibition that would hew, as closely as I could make it, to the spirit of the Menil's founders, John and Dominique de Menil. An exhibition that brought me to their graves to describe my project and ask their permission.

The Howard drawings that are in the Menil's collection, which I was proud to include in my eventual exhibition, *The Meat Wagon*, came from the estate of Jermayne MacAgy, an unsung visionary of the curatorial world. She and her husband, Douglas MacAgy (fig. 1), who was also a curator, were close friends of Howard's.

In 1944 Douglas MacAgy was admitted to the Alum Rock Sanitarium in San Jose, California, with what seemed to be a hopeless case of tuberculosis. For fifty-four days, every day that MacAgy was a patient there, Charles Howard sent him a drawing. They are drawn in a straightforward manner with black ink on inexpensive sheets of business-size paper, folded in thirds to fit their envelopes. Each one is inspired. Aside from the bravura use of modest means, the drawings speak volumes about art as communication in a difficult world, when life is short and fellow feeling really matters. They are surreal and indignant and original. A nose with a large mucus drip. We have all experienced this, but have I ever seen it depicted in art so plainly and provocatively? Or the view, I think, from inside of one's own head as your hand moves to feed—what? a miniature turkey or chicken?—on a spoon into your mouth. Each drawing is singular, bizarre, and touching.

An experimental treatment of the antibiotic streptomycin proved unexpectedly successful. Douglas MacAgy lived. And, thankfully, so do the drawings, which are also intimate letters; the first one inscribed, "To the absent friend, 12/31/44."

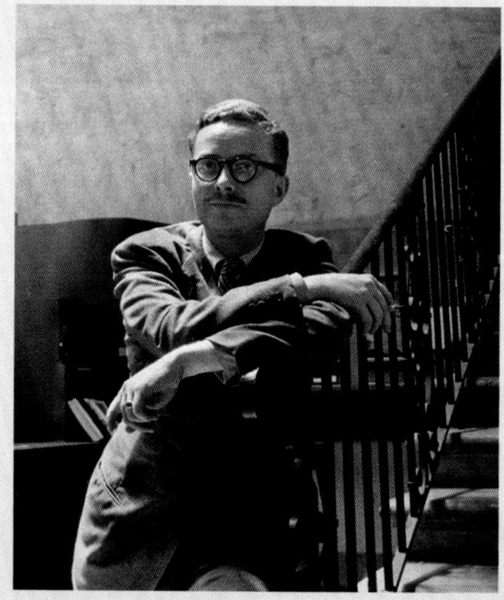

Fig. 1 Douglas MacAgy, n.d.

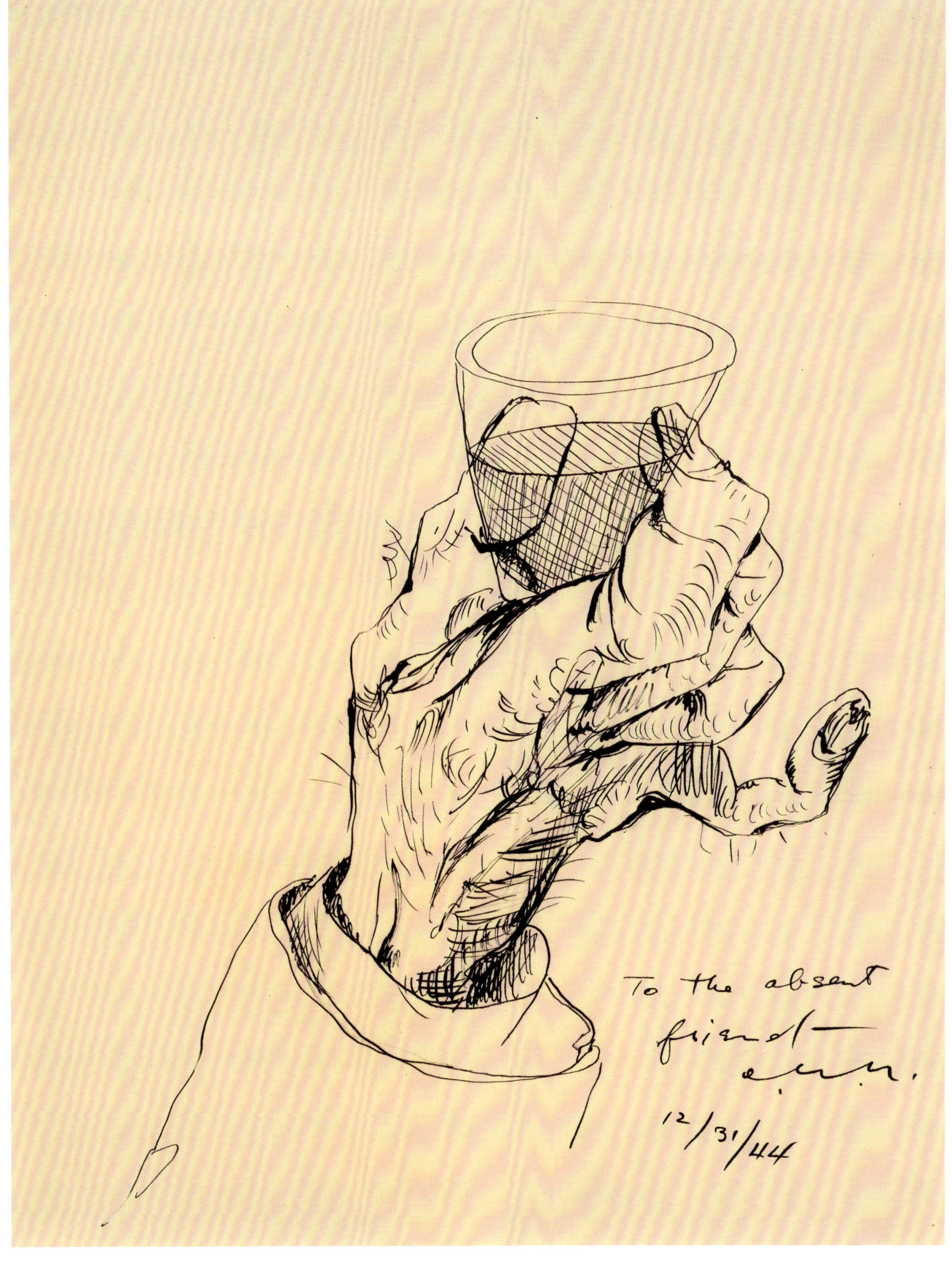

To the absent
friend —
e.m.m.
12/31/44

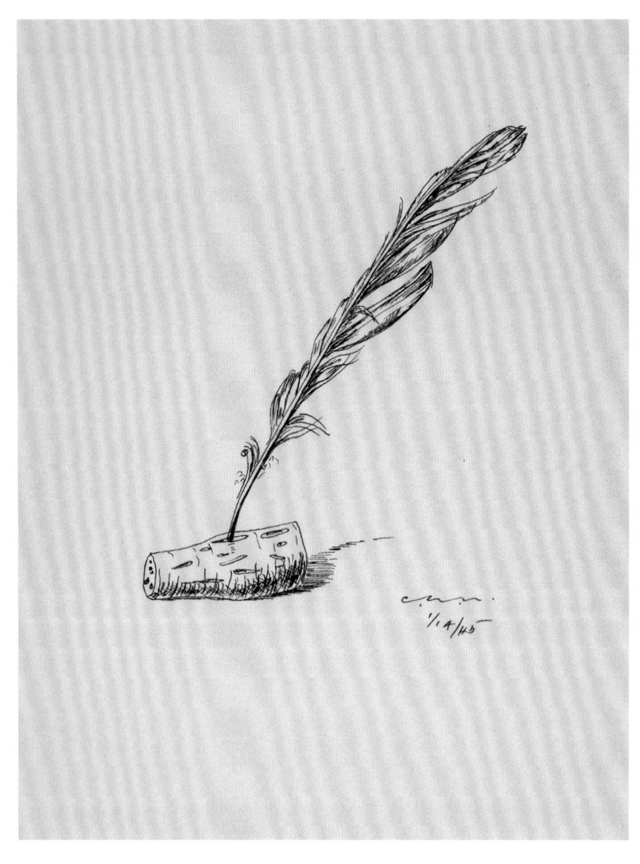

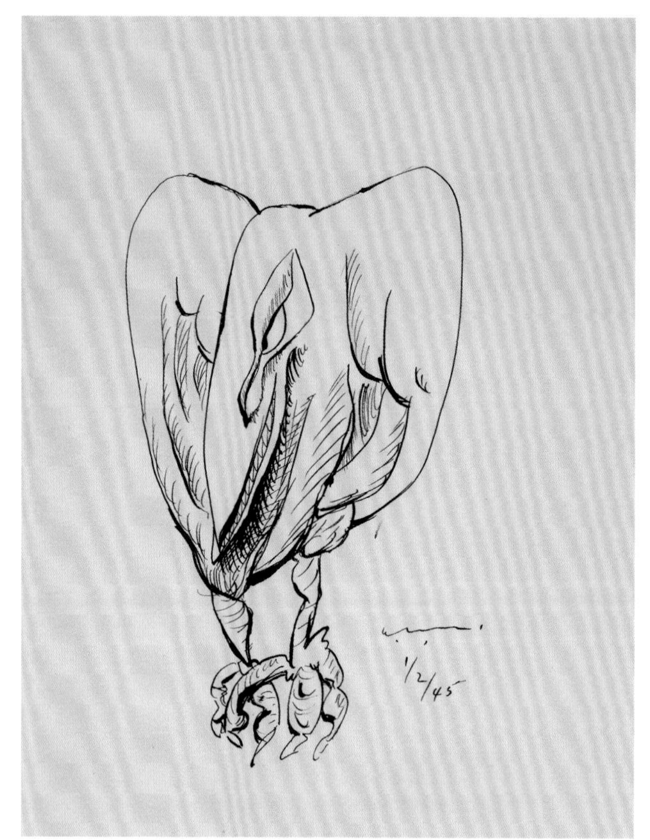

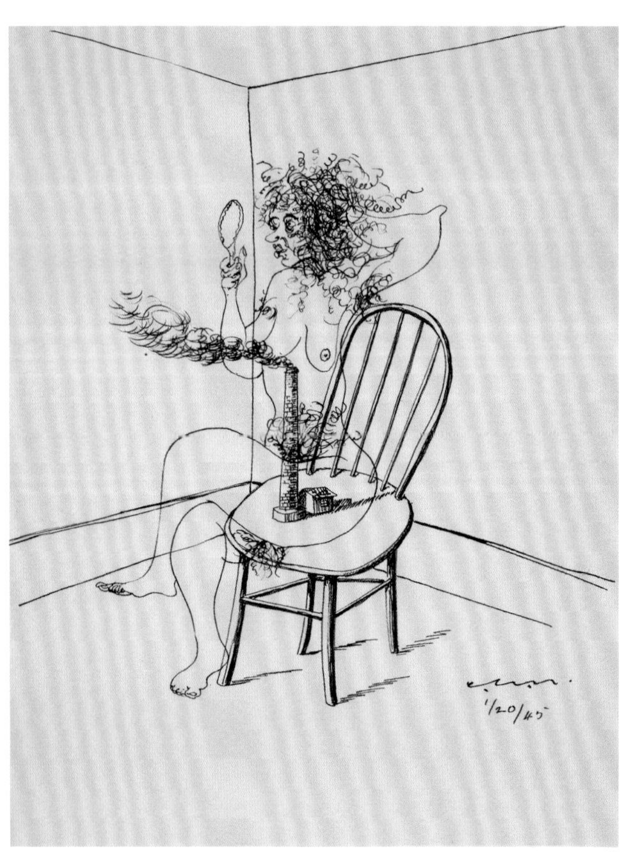

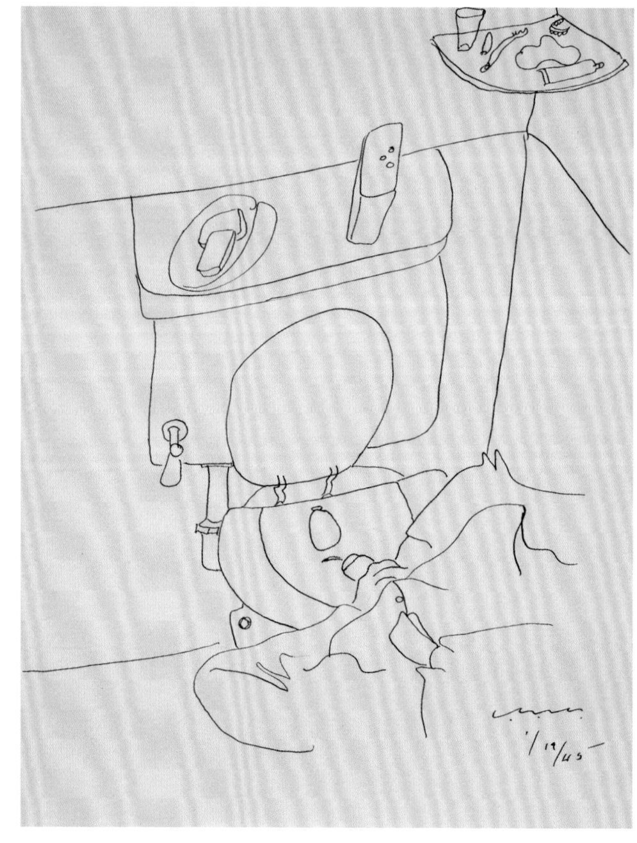

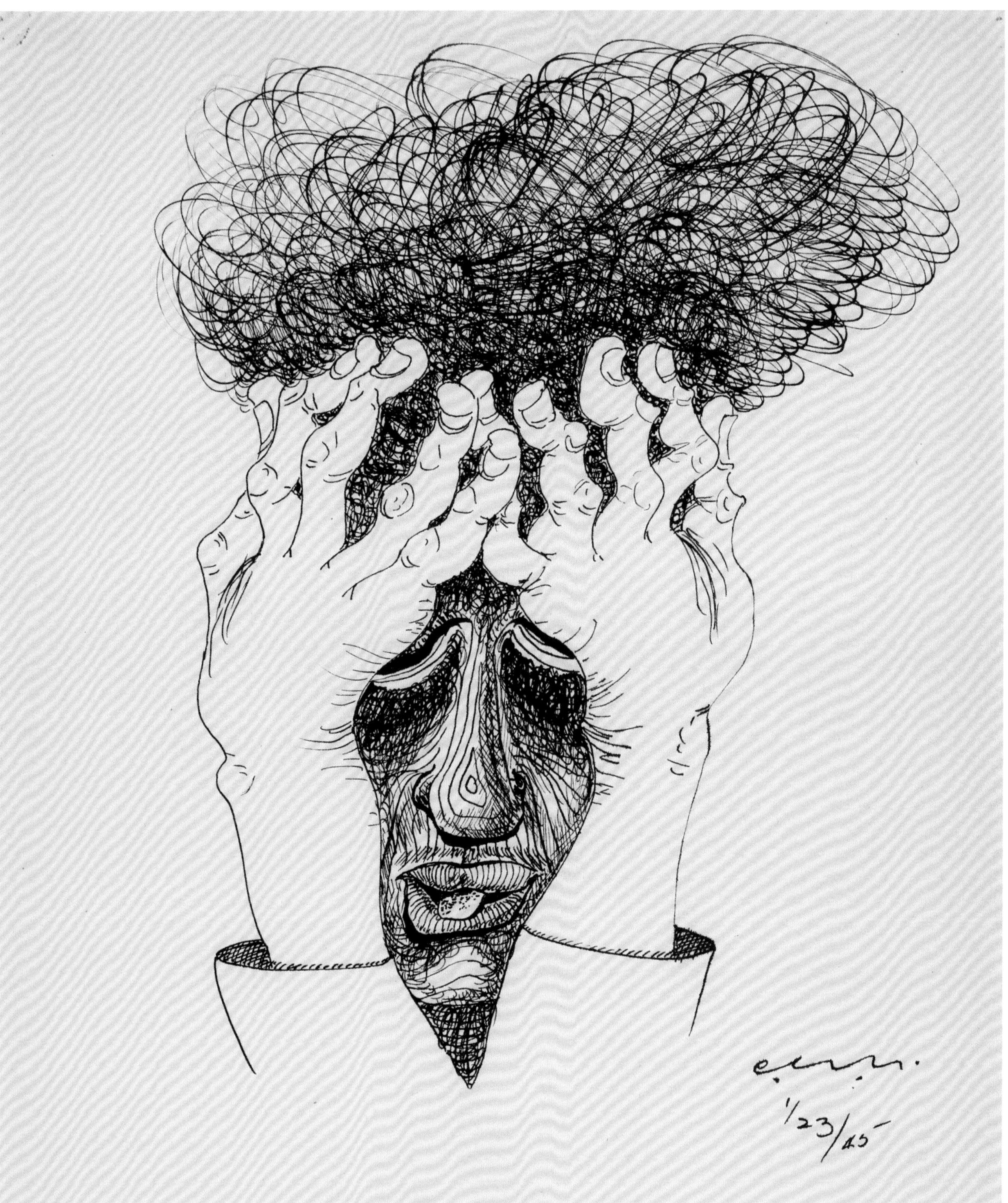

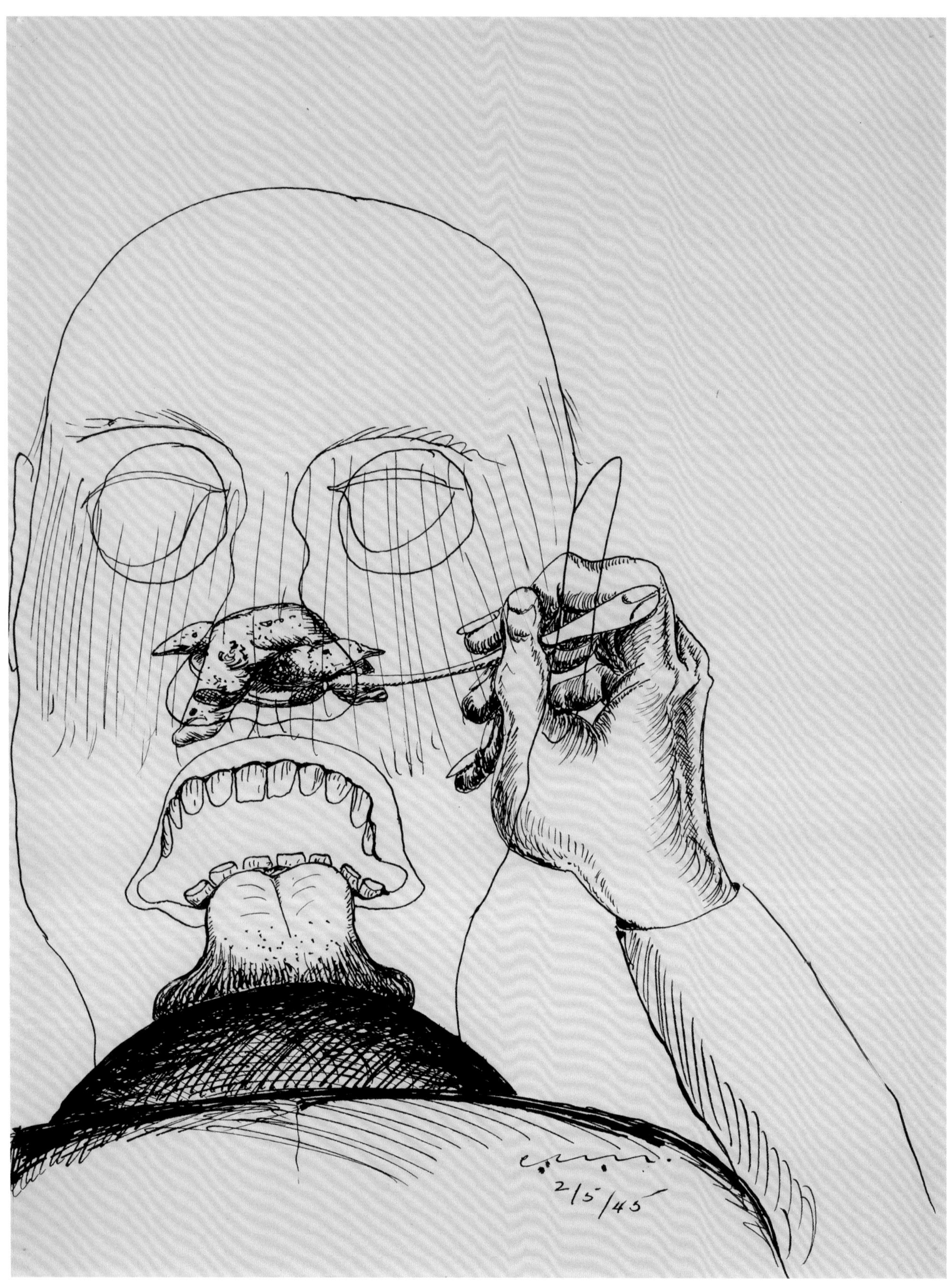
2/5/45

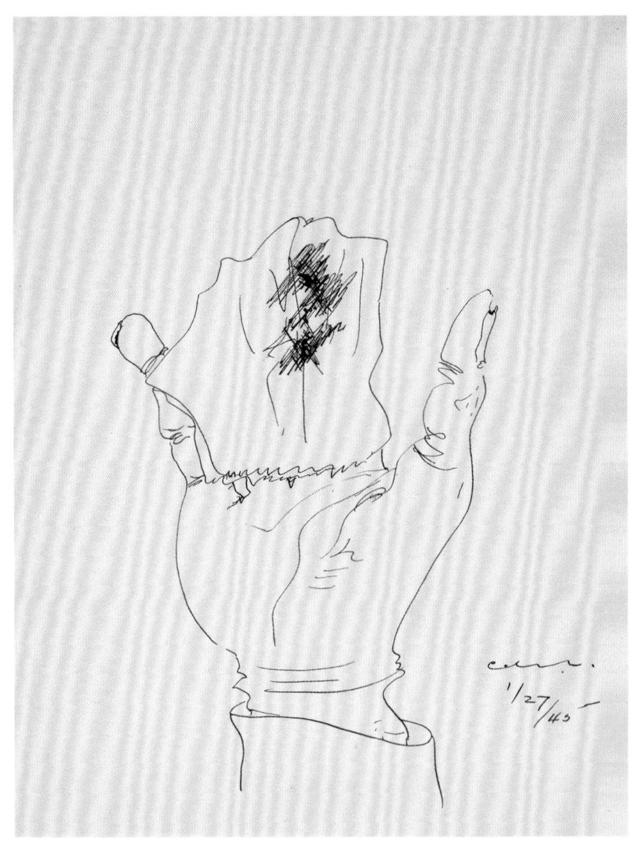
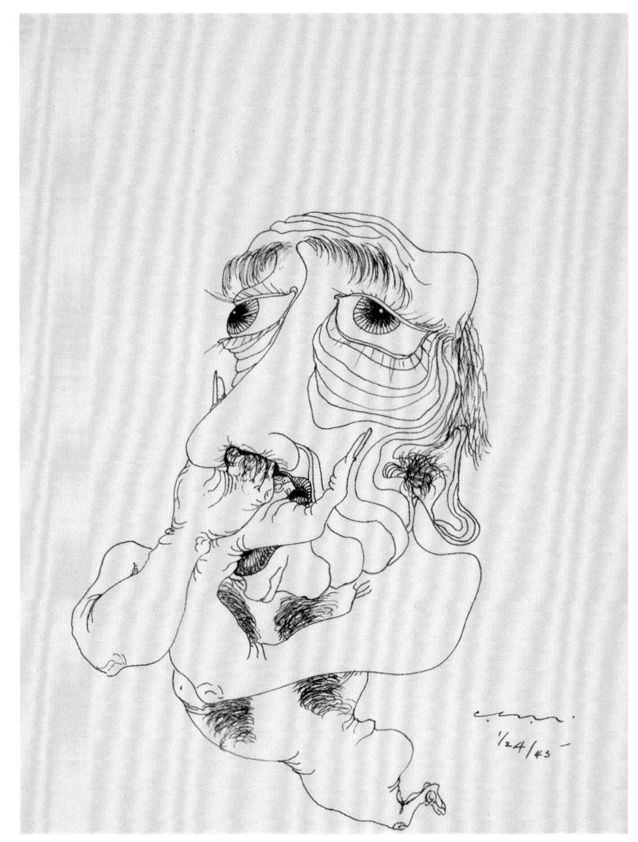
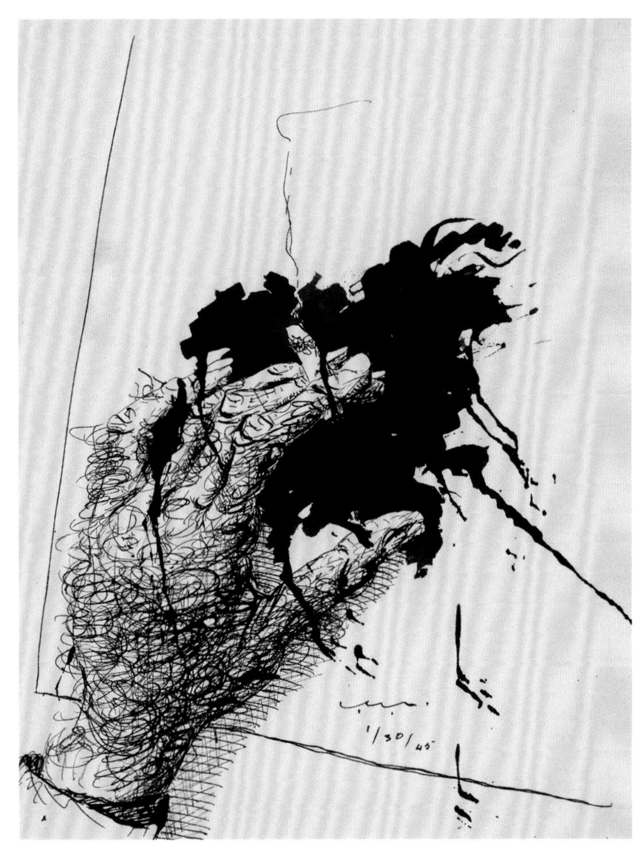
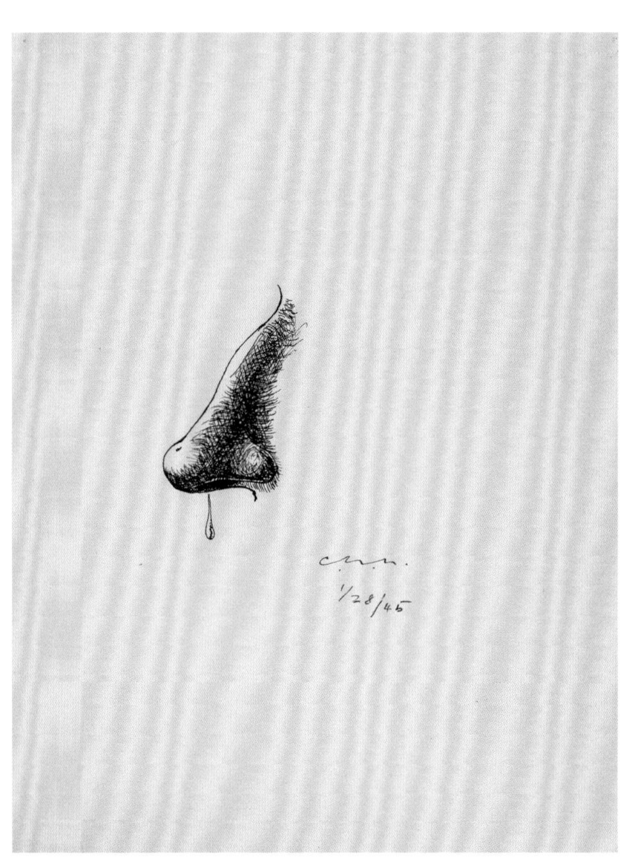

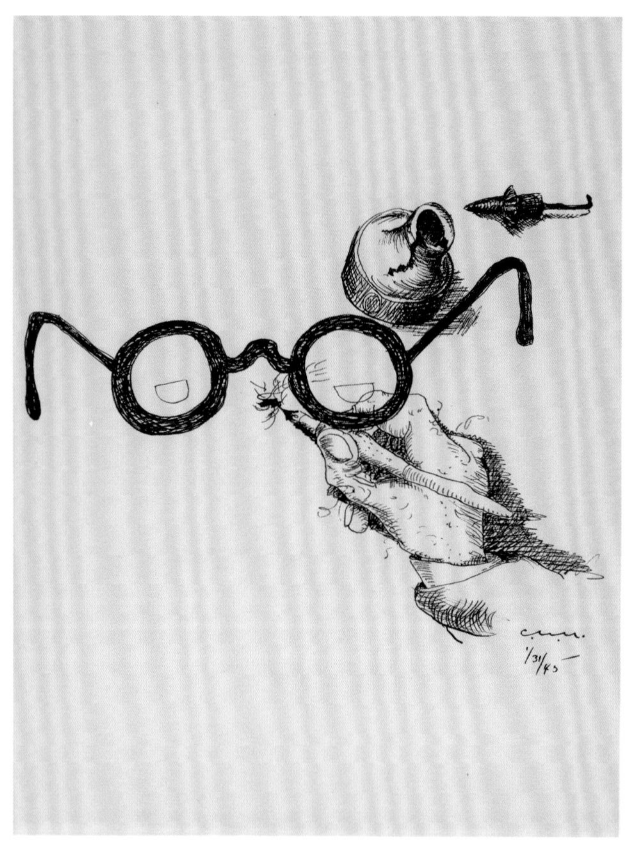

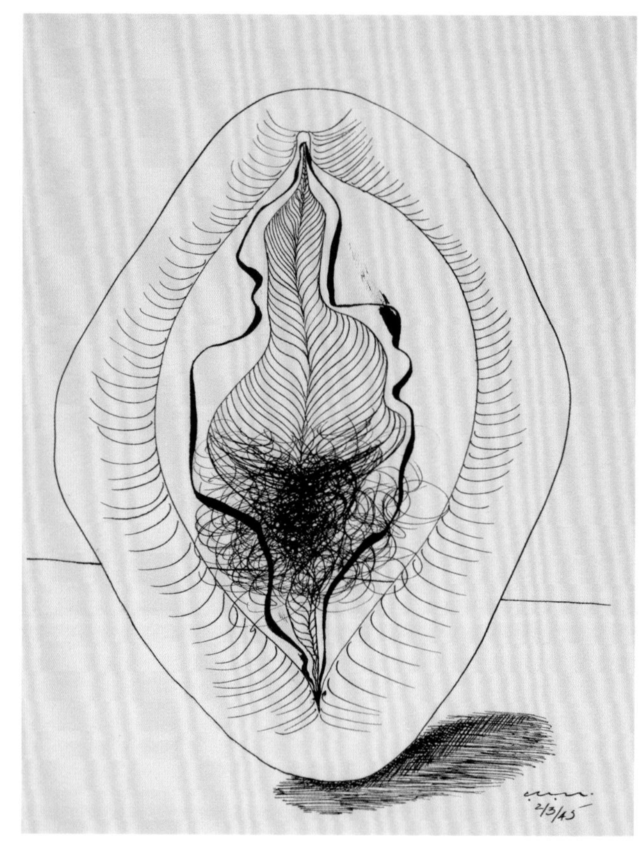

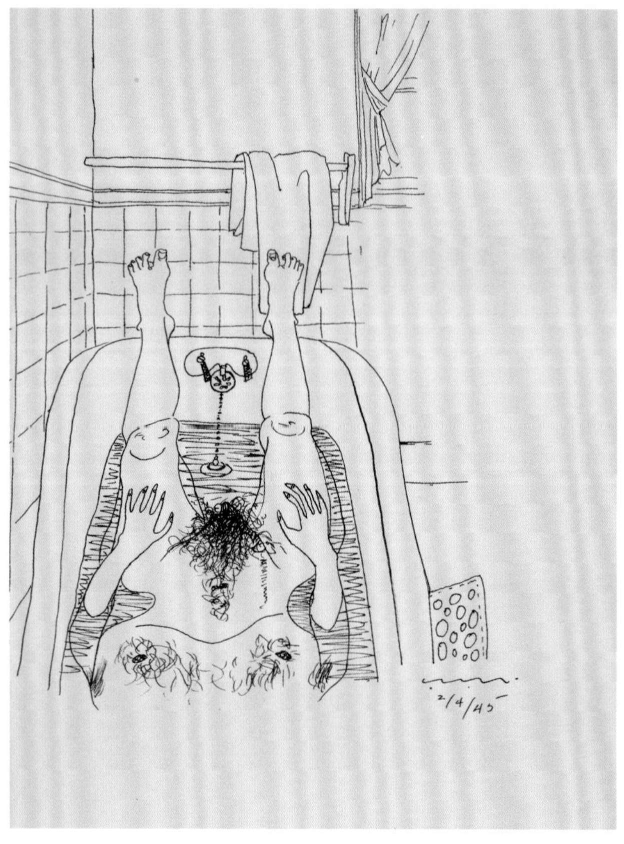

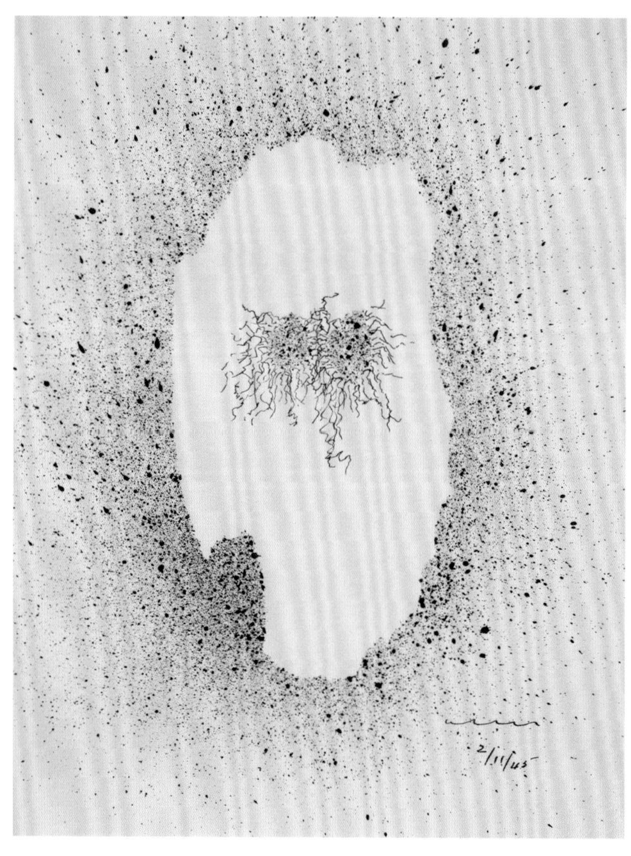

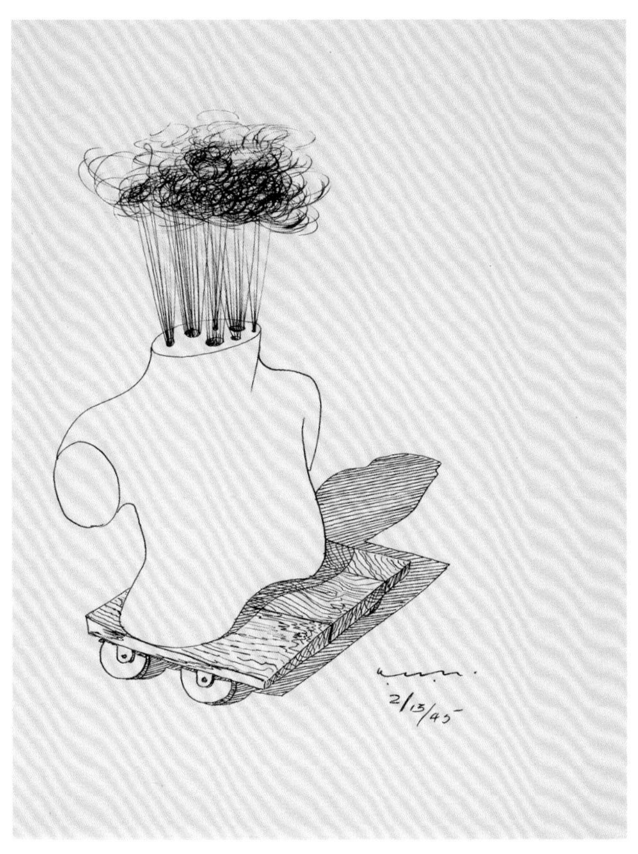

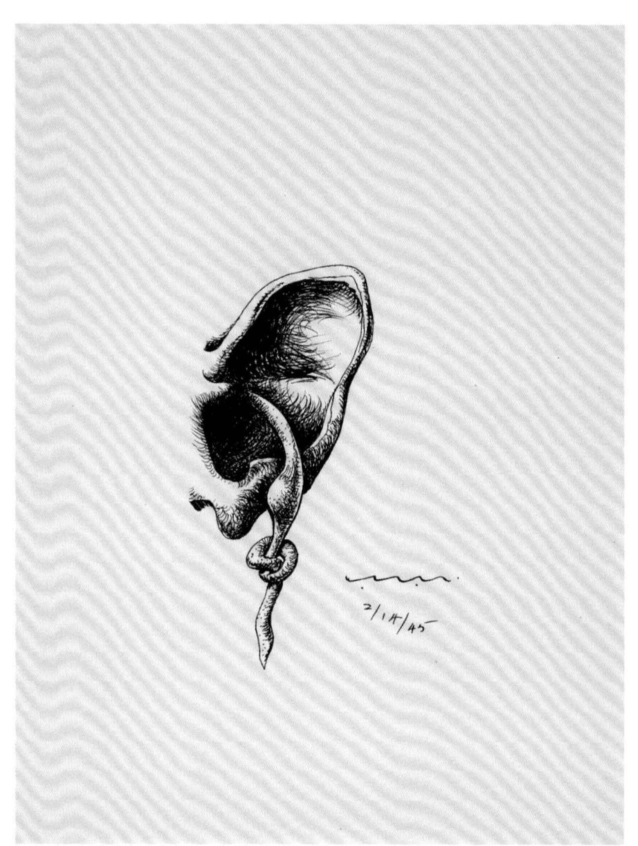

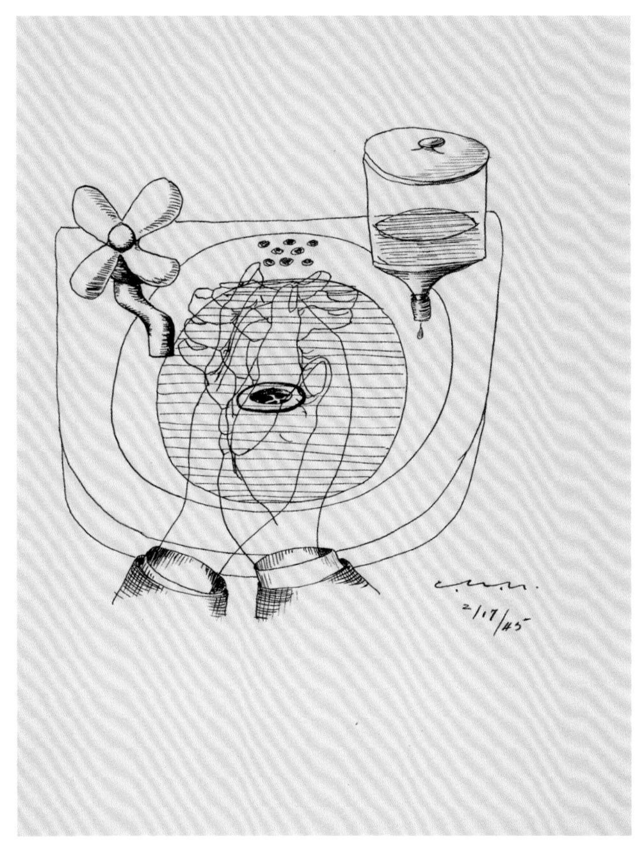

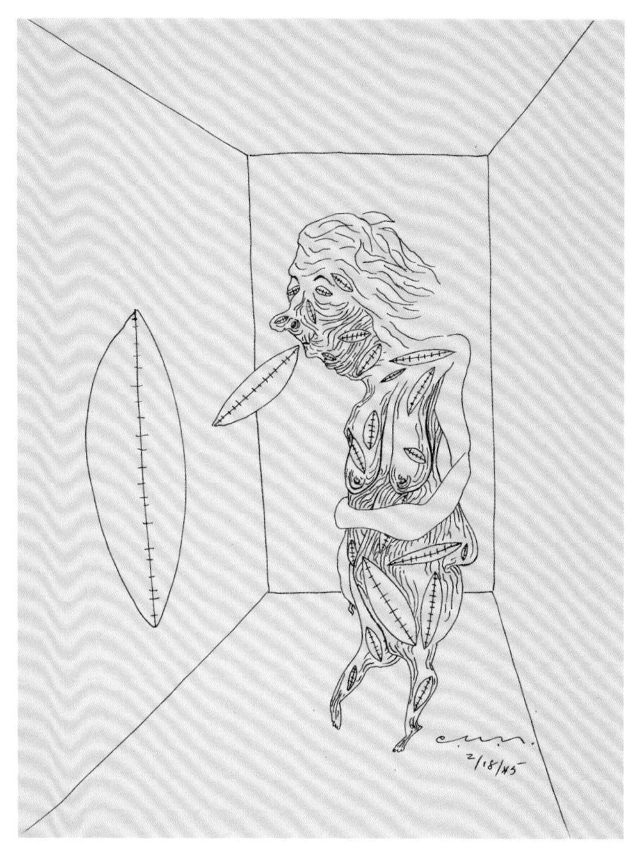

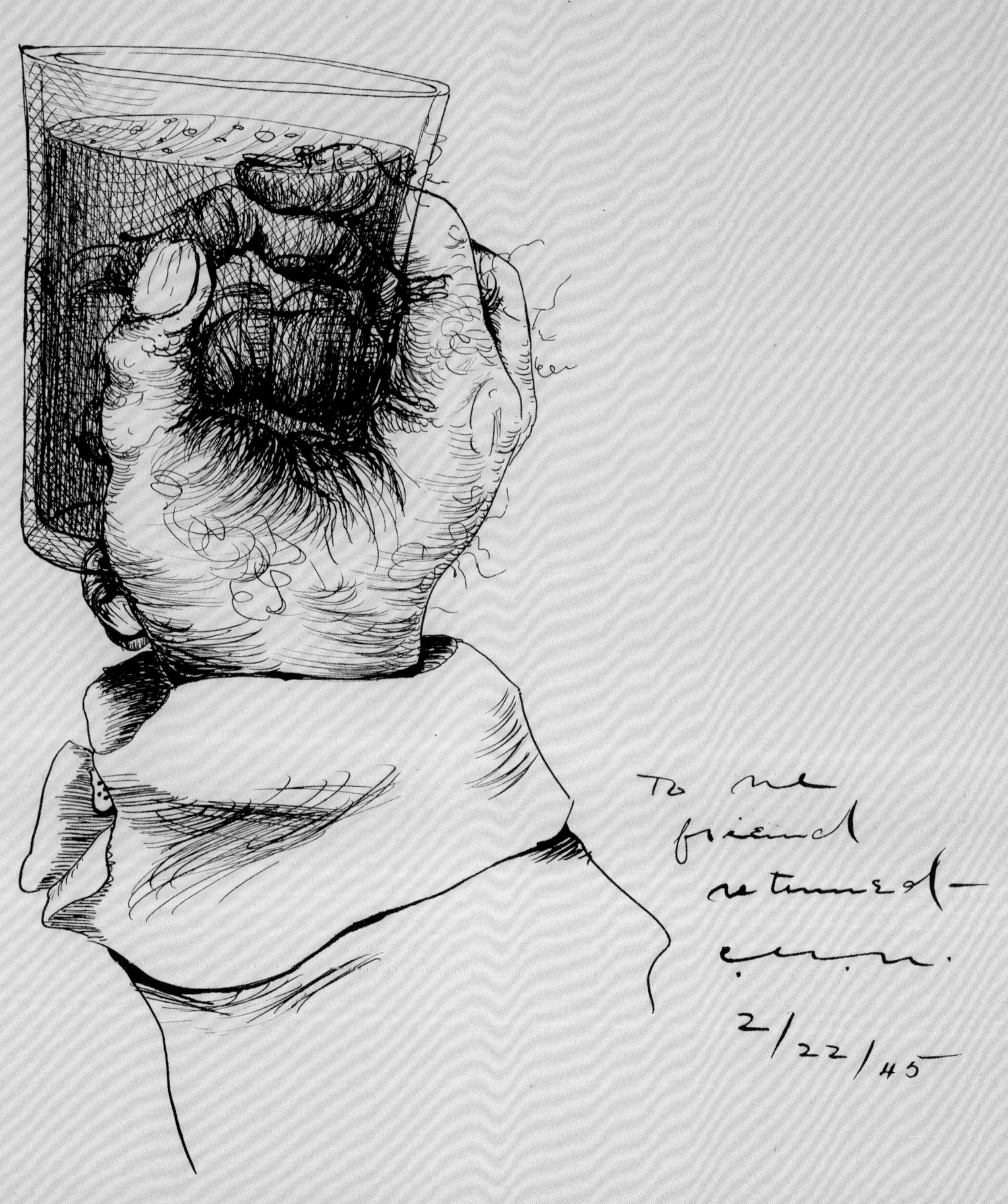

To my
friend
returned —
[signature]
2/22/45

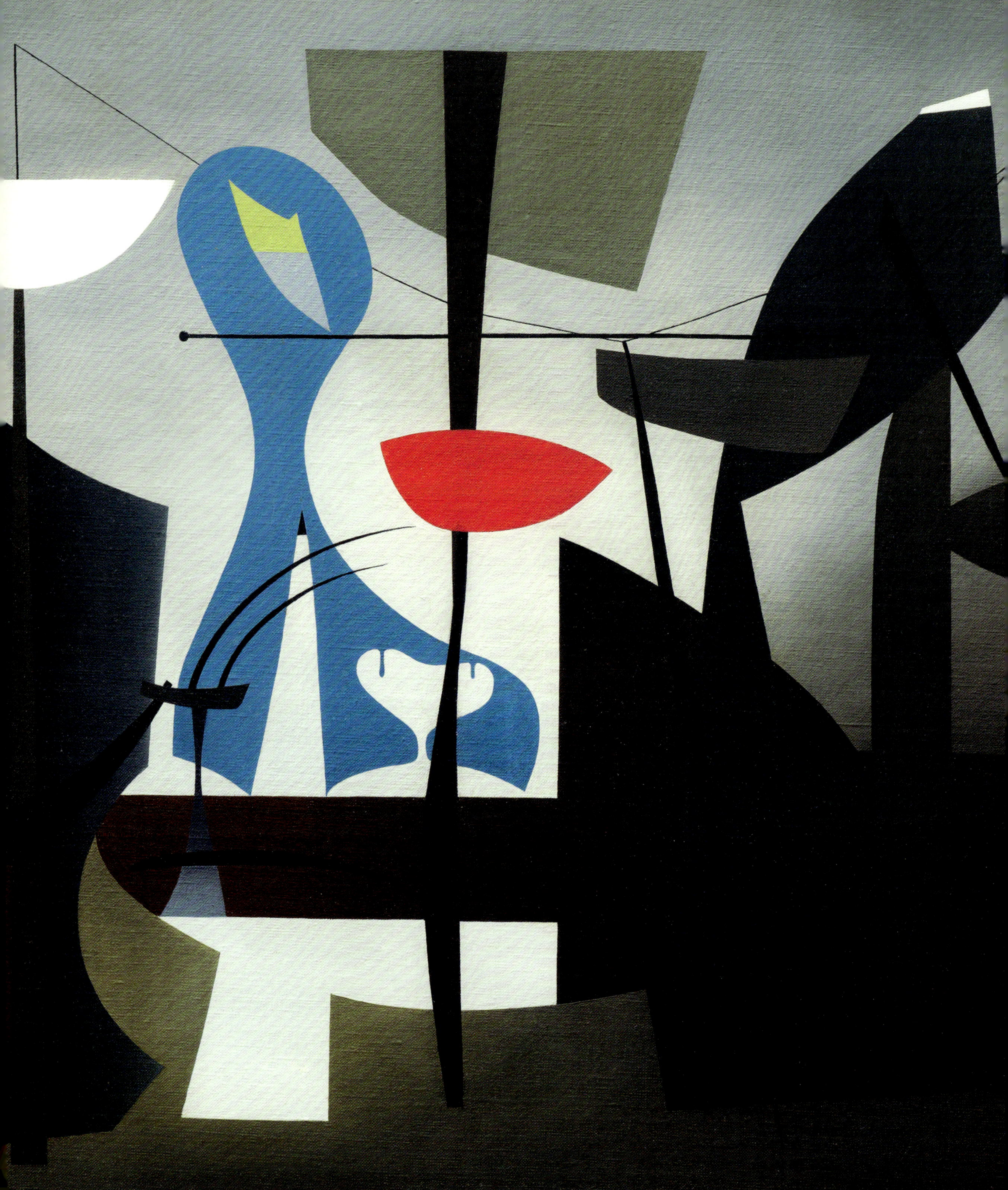

Charles Howard

INTERMEDIATE GENIUS

Lauren Kroiz

> Cannot we have geometric as well as organic sensibil-
> ity? The history of art proves that we can, abundantly.
> One may, of course, question the relative values of
> these two sensibili[ties], but that they both have a
> natural existence is not to be denied.
>
> — Herbert Read, 1936[1]

With these words English writer and critic Herbert Read attempted to schematize the world of modern art that Charles Houghton Howard (1899–1978) confronted upon deciding to become a painter. Placing his moment within a longer history, Read argued that the quickly shifting avant-gardes by which the interwar period is often defined were not the only or the most productive ways to frame the contemporary artistic land-scape. He points out that individual artists of the 1930s had arrived at differing "extremes," citing the work of German Surrealist Max Ernst and English geometric abstractionist Ben Nicholson and describing them as representatives of "wings" that seemed "incapable of touching one another." Read himself threw his critical enthusiasm alternatingly behind Surrealism and abstraction, especially in the early 1930s. In *Art Now: An Introduction to the Theory of Modern Painting and Sculpture* (1933) he points to the distance between the two styles but urges audiences to focus on the fact that "the space between them is occupied by an unbroken series" of artists that do not belong to either school.[2] He cites and illustrates work by a couple of the most famous artists of his day (and ours), Pablo Picasso and Henry Moore, as "intermediate artists." Although this description might suggest a kind of middling quality or

contribution, Read assures readers that these artists are actu-ally "among those most evidently in possession of a fertile and powerful genius," their in-between status an indication that they have avoided the doctrinal attitudes associated with any school.[3] Yet even as deviation from established styles suggests originality it also, in retrospect, tends to expose artists who work outside or on the margins of recognized movements to the risk of becoming lost from historical narratives, which are so often propelled by categorization and classification.

Studying Howard, who has slipped in and out of the canon, in the space between the categories of Surrealism and abstraction reveals him to be an artist with a distinctive formal vocabulary. Exploring Howard's work and its recep-tion in a sustained way opens new avenues through which to understand the relations between European and American Modernism and different artistic media of the 1930s and 1940s — Howard's most productive era. Read's illustrations in the 1948 edition of *Art Now* include Howard's *Rumor* (1938, fig. 5) alongside Max Ernst's *Zoomorphic Couple* (1933, fig. 1), Nicholson's *1935 (white relief)* (1935, fig. 3), Picasso's *Female Bather with Raised Arms* (1929, fig. 2), and Moore's *Composition* (1931, fig. 4). Howard's painting shares the biomorphic forms of Picasso and Moore, yet his dark, floating forms towering high above a low horizon line suggest both the psychological unease of Ernst and the clearly delineated geometries of Nicholson. Yet unlike the four other artists, who are mentioned in Read's text, Howard was not featured in the earlier or later printings of the book, which attempts to define the central currents of contemporaneous Modernism. Howard's genius can be found between the dominant schools of abstraction and Surrealism, in an intermediate zone where it has passed through the cracks in the art world and the history of Modernism.

Raised in Berkeley among a family of artists and architects, Howard spent his early career in New York. In 1933 he married and moved to London with his second wife, English painter Madge Knight, who was also the child of an artist—painter Adam Knight. There Howard quickly joined the divided European avant-garde of the late 1930s, which was awash in competing schools of abstraction, Surrealism, Expressionism, and realism, among other aesthetic agendas of the age. In mid-1940, as war broke out across Europe, Charles Howard and Madge Knight became part of an avant-garde exodus to the United States, returning to San Francisco from 1940 to 1946. Although Howard spent most of his career near London, his family and friends championed his work in San Francisco and he experienced acclaim as a conduit to the latest in European painting. He worked across professions, employed as a decorator, a shipbuilder, and a poster designer in addition to painting. Howard and his artwork likewise moved across avant-garde centers, traveling between San Francisco, New York, and London.

One of Howard's most avid champions in San Francisco was Douglas MacAgy, a curator and director of the California School of Fine Arts (CSFA, now the San Francisco Art Institute) from 1945 to 1950. MacAgy often praised Howard's work specifically for its unique ability to envision the spaces between extremes. In his paintings the abyss of chaos and the unity of the cosmos seem to alternate, according to MacAgy,

almost as a kind of optical illusion.[4] Howard himself repeatedly emphasized his use of "allusive" titles in order to suggest "epic" and "totemic" understandings that originated in his own emotions but transcended individual reactions through a rigorous process of preparatory drawing and planning.[5] Trained as a journalist at the University of California, Berkeley, he turned to painting to find a mode of expression that transcended language. As MacAgy wrote, "at face value the words have a way of blocking our insight."[6] Howard's ambiguous visual forms move beyond fixed categories or personal thoughts and feelings to envision the space between universal binaries.

Ill-fitting words often classify and shape our understanding of Howard's allusive forms. In 1951 the Museum of Modern Art (MoMA), New York, included Howard's *Trinity* (1941, plate 32) in the landmark exhibition *Abstract Painting and Sculpture in America*, classifying his work as "Expressionist Biomorphic" along with that of artists such as Arshile Gorky, Jackson Pollock, and Mark Rothko.[7] Howard's painting, however, stands out for its hard, distinct edges, which suggest that it might as well be classified with that of the "Expressionist Geometric" group. Indeed, the novel appearance of Howard's work is often described with a kind of shorthand that points to various styles. English critic Lawrence Alloway, for instance, once wrote: "Out of Helion and Miró he makes a Calderish world of hard curved surfaces."[8] Although words may fail to explain Howard's paintings, the artist's movement among professions, countries, and artistic groups resulted in a remarkably consistent personal style that links the uncanny psychological

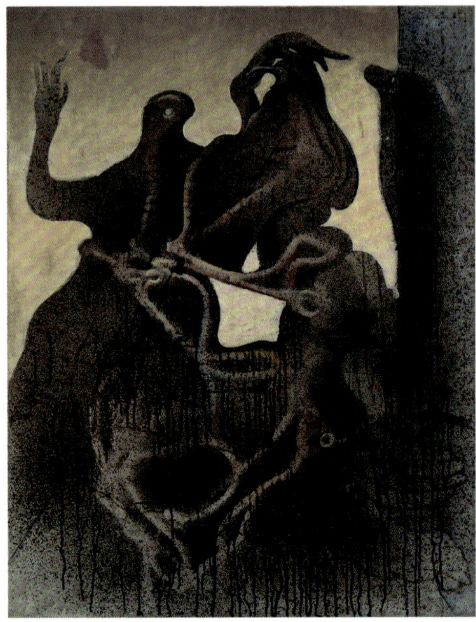

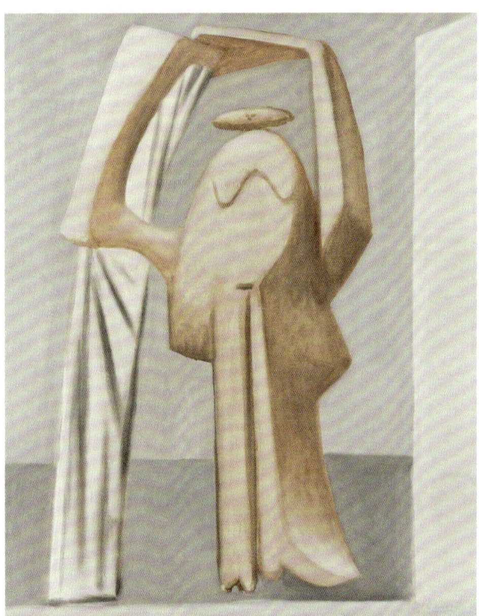

Fig. 1 Max Ernst, *Zoomorphic Couple*, 1933. Oil on canvas, 36¼ × 28⅞ in. (92.1 × 73.4 cm). The Solomon R. Guggenheim Foundation, Peggy Guggenheim Collection, Venice, 1976

Fig. 2 Pablo Picasso, *Female Bather with Raised Arms*, 1929. Oil on canvas, 28 × 23 in. (71.1 × 58.4 cm). Phoenix Art Museum, gift of the Allen-Bradley Company of Milwaukee

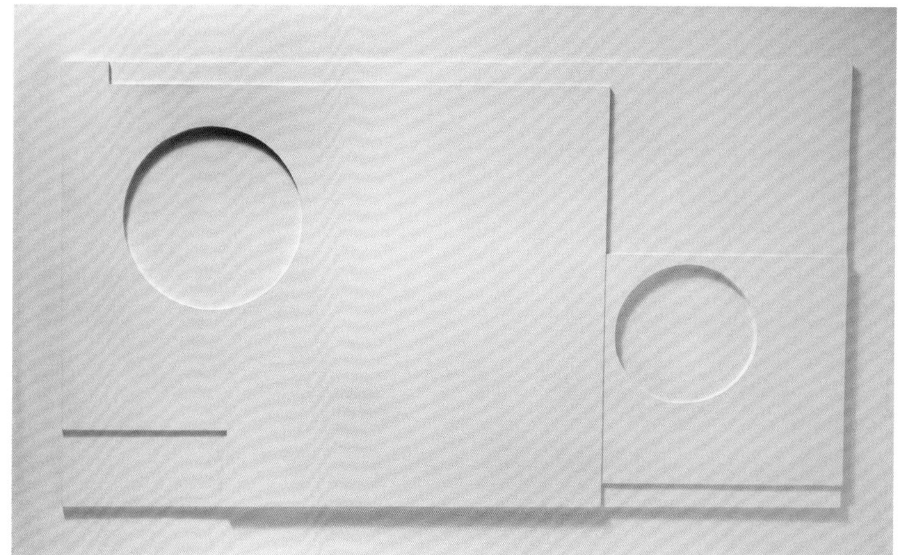

qualities of an organic Surrealism with the logic of geometric abstraction.

Howard decided to become a painter on a trip to Europe in the mid-1920s during which he met and traveled with Iowan artist Grant Wood. Howard later recalled Wood's repeated attempts to convince him of painting's superiority over verbal forms of self-expression.[9] As discussed in detail elsewhere in this volume, the specific origin moment for Howard's conversion to painting, however, occurred during a visit to Castelfranco, a small town in Northern Italy, where he encountered a work by the Renaissance artist Giorgione (1478–1510) titled *Madonna and Child Between St. Francis and St. Nicasius* (ca. 1503–4, see page 15) that shifted his outlook. He studied the image intently for about fifteen minutes, considering the ways it united "the somber, analytical, philosophical approach of the Florentine painters, and then of the free, warm, romantic fervor of Venice." Although few scholars of the Italian Renaissance would associate Giorgione with Florence, here, crucially, Howard praised the painting for operating not as a "combination" of varied approaches but as a novel "synthesis." After seeing the altarpiece, Howard left the church, walked outside and down the street, and became "violently ill." He stopped his tour, decamped to Paris, and began painting. Howard's turn to visual art derived from a subconsciously motivated bodily reaction and a logical formal analysis of a specific artwork's success as a kind of stylistic intermediary.

Howard returned to the United States in 1924, settled in New York's artistic center, Greenwich Village, and began to draw and paint. Despite his lack of training he found a job in the decorating studios of Louis Bouché and Rudolph Guertler,

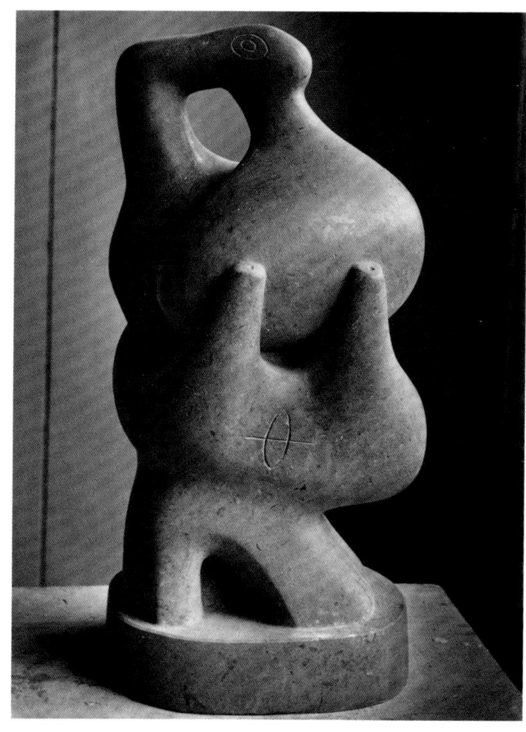

who were particularly well known in the era for their murals. Working as an artist and decorator simultaneously, in 1926, at the age of twenty-five, Howard mounted a solo exhibition of drawings at the Whitney Studio Club, a central venue for modern American art in New York. Although many of these drawings are now lost or destroyed, others that Howard presented alongside works by his brothers in exhibitions in Berkeley and San Francisco in 1927 and 1928 give clues to their subject matter. A review in the *San Francisco Chronicle* praised his satirical

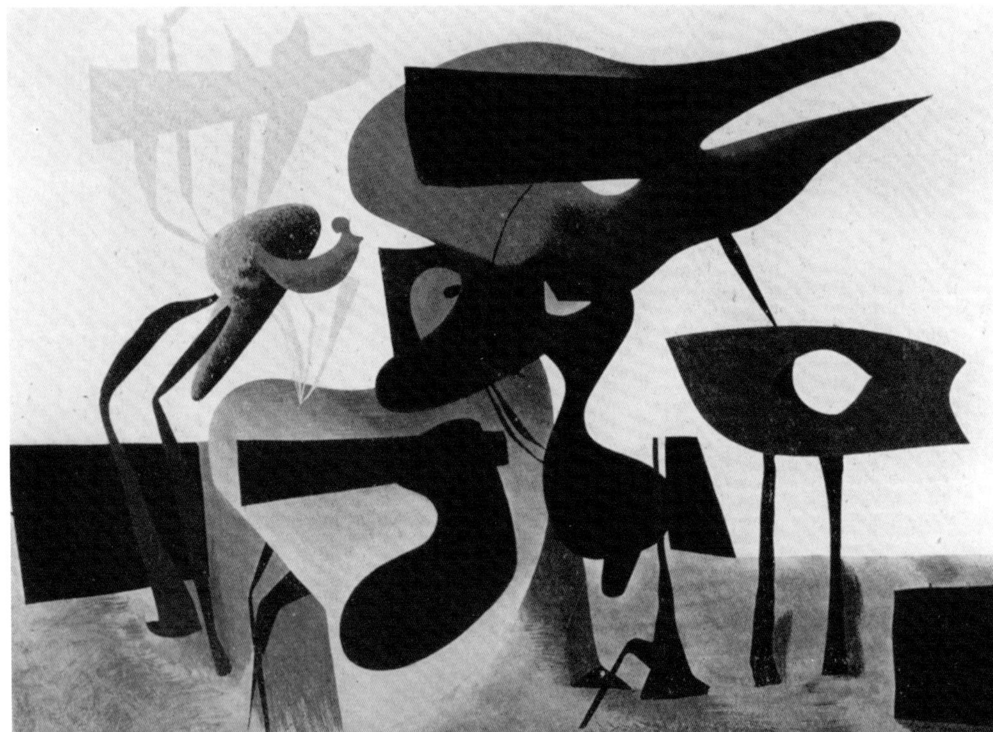

take on American mechanization, describing in detail a drawing titled *Miss America* that depicts a female acrobat against "an American flag and mechanical devices suggestive of steam fittings, electrical fixtures, and other angular objects."[10] *1826 into 1926* (plate 1), an early watercolor by Howard in which decorative architectural forms play across a faceted space, also suggests both the skill the artist had quickly acquired in the unforgiving graphite medium and the ways he combined art and decoration through an attention to distinctive forms.

In the early 1930s Howard shifted from satirical drawings and studies of architectural elements to an increasingly symbolic abstraction. For example, *Untitled*, 1931 (plate 5) deploys marine forms, nets, and shells along with a blocky foot that is reminiscent of Picasso's series of bathers and female acrobats of the period. In Howard's gouache the beige shape, suggestive of a leg and foot, comes unmoored from its female referent. Instead it lies in a landscape (suggested by the horizon line bisecting the blue sky and brown ground of the image) that is at once crowded and empty. Howard creates distinctive textures—wood grain at center right and woven netting at lower left—that root the shapes as objects even as their forms remain ambiguous. For example, the elongated brown rectangle with a black spot seen in the lower center of *Untitled* recurs in another painting of 1931, *Untitled Abstract Landscape* (plate 6). The repetition, complete with circle and dark slashing lines

at center and end, suggests that the form has a specific meaning. Is it a fish, a distinct piece of driftwood, or something else entirely? How are viewers to understand the subtle variations? Do Howard's forms suggest seaside memories, a narrative of his transatlantic and cross-coastal travels, or some more elemental relations between the natural and the man-made?

The central form in *Untitled Abstract Landscape* adds further complications. Curving architecture sprouts out of another flat landscape whose horizon is delimited by a single straight line. Here the structure, rendered with textures of brick, brown rock or earth, and carved stone, both casts a shadow and seems to be surrounded by a mysteriously generated moat of shadow. The stone architectural detail gives way to an irregular organic line that continues the arch, but without unity, in the center of the composition. Blue pennants pop irregularly across the center of the scene. Unfurled and alert as if in a strong wind, their forms resemble maritime signal flags reduced to shades of blue. Howard's ambiguous architectural forms and flags recall the compositions of Giorgio de Chirico, a self-proclaimed metaphysical painter whose work from the period around World War I deeply influenced Surrealists across Europe. In Howard's hands the structure and flags do not securely suggest the process of construction or ruin but rather an odd stasis in between.

In the early 1930s Howard's reputation as a leader in New York's burgeoning surrealist movement was established and solidified through exhibitions at Julien Levy's gallery of modern art. His paintings and period reviews of them underscore the extent to which his understanding of and association with currents of Surrealism began in that city. After moving to London in 1933 Howard and Madge Knight participated avidly in the rapidly expanding field of English modern art, one led by the loosely affiliated group Unit One and buoyed by numerous artists who had fled continental Europe as war became imminent.[11] Howard continued his loose affiliation with Surrealism, participating in the noted *International Surrealist Exhibition* (1936) and in *Surrealist Objects & Poems* (1937), yet he also began to combine his early organic forms with harder-edged geometric abstraction. He later wrote that when he first moved to London he found that although he could still paint it was suddenly "impossible to make pictures." After much deliberation he realized the problem derived from leaving New York, which had been "a stimulating place, like a cocktail." Although Howard averred that he could have continued painting there with joy and ease, he considered it ultimately fortunate that he had not. The "simple accident of displacement" enabled him to find "the existence of a far richer ore." Howard had been voluntarily displaced once already, when he moved from his childhood home in the San Francisco Bay Area to New York, but in his second chosen exile, to London, he found new pictures that deepened his relationship with the European avant-garde.

Banner (plate 12) dates from Howard's first London year, 1934. The painting resembles the heavily textured gouaches he created in New York, with a similar space of brown ground and blue sky that becomes bleaker with darker washes. Two blocky, rectilinear forms tower on the painting's right, casting long shadows. One red pennant flies erect from the light beige tower at center, while the heavy drapery of a sagging white banner in the foreground obscures much of the structures. Propped across two precariously slanting, thin sticks, the banner overtakes the composition with sagging, dark folds. Howard seems to have painted a literal white flag of defeated pictures across his tableau. Perhaps *Banner* dates from around the brief period in the 1930s following his arrival in London, when the painter recalled also being derailed by political theory. Looking for a way to find the sense of "order" needed in the polarizing, uncertain, political sphere, he briefly "became an abstractionist." The abstract school had seemed a locus for "order and logic," but after attempting to paint that way for nearly a year he realized he could not finish his orderly paintings.

Howard's struggles to balance his early surrealistically inflected paintings with an orderly abstraction encapsulate the unwieldy poles of the British avant-garde during the early 1930s. His arrival in London coincided with the brief life of the aforementioned Unit One, a coalition of British artists and architects linked perhaps only by their varied rejections of the dominant "pedestrian naturalism" of period English art, as architectural historian Sir James Maude Richards has argued.[12] Even the name Unit One attempted to conjoin the sense of a unified movement (Unit) with a focus on individuality (One). Begun by Paul Nash, who issued a manifesto in the form of a thousand-word letter to the editor of *The Times* that was published on June 2, 1933, the group of eleven artists, who all considered themselves moderns, produced work that spanned diverse styles and media, ranging from Nash's surrealist landscapes to Nicholson's geometric abstraction and from Moore's biomorphic sculpture to the reinforced-concrete architecture of Colin Lucas. Informal meetings and the enthusiasm of critic Read, who edited and wrote the introduction for the group's 1934 book, linked the artists together briefly during Howard's early years in London.[13] At their only exhibition, held at the Mayor Gallery in 1934, Read declared, "the aims of the Unit are strategical." Rather than advancing a single stylistic agenda, Unit One aimed to be a starting point for Modernism across the arts.[14] Although the group quickly fell apart, Howard's desire to distance his work from stylistic labels resonates with the aims of Unit One's fiercely independent modern artists.

Although Howard did not officially participate in the Unit One exhibition he quickly entered the orbit of English modernist painters. In 1935 he took over the execution of a mural designed by the group's eldest associate, Edward Wadsworth, a former Vorticist leader, for the De La Warr Pavilion, designed by Erich Mendelsohn and Serge Chermayeff at Bexhill-on-Sea in East Sussex, England. Based on Wadsworth's 1929 painting *Shells and Cones,* the mural design evidenced the artist's post–World War I transition from a Vorticism of chaotic technological forms to marine still lifes (fig. 6). Wadsworth's mural used stylized, recognizable shapes such as shells, starfish, an undulating sea chart, and numerous banners—oceanic motifs linked to Britain's identity as an island nation with imperial power. Art historians Jeremy Lewison and David Peters Corbett have recognized royal regalia in Wadsworth's design, suggesting a conservative turn in his work, but as Bernard Vere suggests the sea also offered a possibility of reconciliation with Europe for modern artists.[15] Although Howard only executed the design, 1935 marks a decisive shift in his own work toward more geometric, abstracted compositions that often float in the center of the page as Wadsworth's floated on the wall.[16]

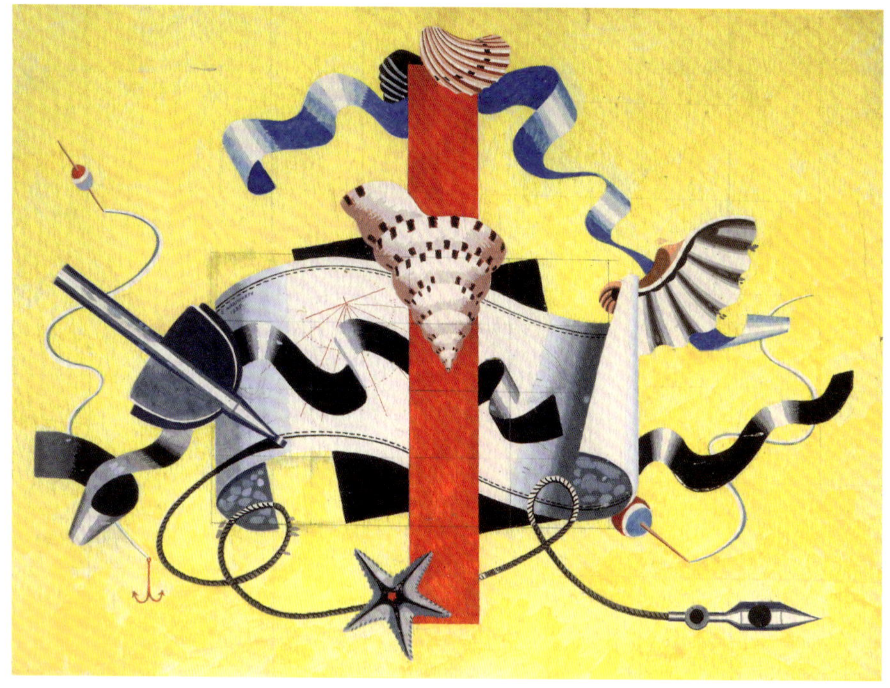

Fig. 6 Edward Wadsworth, mural for the De la Warr Pavilion, Bexhill-on-Sea, East Sussex, England. Replica from 1945 of the original, which was executed by Charles Howard in 1935.

The focus on the ocean at Bexhill may also register the ways English art in this period entered a new dialogue with the wider avant-garde world as tensions mounted in Europe. The Mayor Gallery, where Unit One exhibited, also mounted solo shows devoted to the work of Max Ernst in 1933 and of Paul Klee and George Grosz in 1934. During Howard's years in England the country became a refuge for many avant-gardists associated with particular strains of Modernism. In 1935 the French champion of Purism Amédée Ozenfant opened his Ozenfant Academy of Fine Arts in London (he would move to the United States in 1938). Russian-born Naum Gabo moved in 1936 from Paris, where he had been among the most famous of more than four hundred artists associated with the loosely affiliated Abstract-Creation group. Dutch-born painter Piet Mondrian relocated to London in 1938.

In addition to becoming home to these champions of abstraction's different styles, London also took part in global debates about international Surrealism, which became increasingly political as war broke out. For example, Howard attended a meeting in winter 1939–40 with leading English Surrealists to discuss securing unity with André Breton's *International Federation of Independent Revolutionary Art,* whose program called for a proletarian revolution, a ban on participation in other groups, and a requirement to only exhibit and publish as Surrealists.[17] This unified movement failed to find sufficient signatories in England. Howard continued to exhibit at venues associated with Surrealism and abstraction.[18]

While living in London, Howard continued to exhibit work in San Francisco, likely with the assistance of fellow artists in his family. Contacted by San Francisco critic Junius Cravens to explain the paintings on display at Paul Elder Gallery in 1935, Howard defined both Surrealism and his work's departure from it in a letter. He avowed that Surrealism was an "intellectual formula" distinct from the "art of painting." It focused on realistic depictions of objects to stimulate emotion. In contrast, Howard abstracted objects so that their emotional meaning became secondary to the formal problems of painting—"unity, adjustment, poise, subtlety, style, grace, variety, quality, etc." Howard also pointed to decisive personal splits, explaining, "I suspect the Surrealists, such as Dalí, Ernst, and Miró, would scorn me as still being a painter."[19] A voice directly connecting the West Coast of the United States with Europe, Howard charted his differences from the Surrealists specifically and didactically for an American audience, focusing on the formal qualities of his painting and individual reactions.

In London, however, Howard's painting was celebrated by Surrealists. In 1939 Russian poet George Reavey wrote an admiring review of his exhibition at the Guggenheim Jeune Gallery in the *London Bulletin,* a magazine published by the Surrealist Group in England. According to Reavey period viewers might have found it tempting to call Howard an abstract painter, however, upon closer examination his work diverged from the varied types of late-1930s abstraction, styles so specific that he tied them to the names of individual artists;

Howard was "certainly not a pure abstractionist like Mondrian or a constructivist like Ben Nicholson," nor did he have any affinity with Purists Ozenfant or Fernand Léger. Instead Reavey suggested Howard's links to Surrealism, while allowing he also departed from its characteristic "pictorial realism." He evocatively described the ambiguous elements that filled Howard's canvases, as in *Presage* (1938, plate 22), which illustrated his account.[20] Reavey likened the painting's forms to "restless *mobile* architecture, a world in dissolution and remaking, a sort of animated jigsaw puzzle the liberated parts of which are struggling to form a new organic unity of their own." Here, in contrast to the static qualities that had defined Howard's earlier work, compositional elements seem to flex and assemble. In *Presage* neutral colors replace the earlier blue sky and brown landscape to create an increasingly ambiguous emptiness. Tall vertical forms nearly span the right side of Howard's paper, orange and blue masses rest on and under attenuated black and gray legs, which seem to lean on or stand in a rectilinear brown formation that creates a kind of architectural corner. On the right thin washes of yellow overlap beige and black shapes, passing behind and over, interrupted by strained, hair-like lines that conjoin forms across the paper. Reavey mused that the painter's vision momentarily arrested these shapes in order to show "the stress and [strain] of some sort of revolution going on." Even without human figures Howard's

crowded composition evokes a dramatic puzzle inflected by contemporary global politics.[21]

The Howards left England for San Francisco in early July 1940. Many other modern artists similarly fled to the United States, but for Howard this exile brought him back to his family. Charles and Madge avidly participated in the San Francisco Bay Area art world of the 1940s. Both exhibited in the San Francisco Art Association's annual exhibitions and mounted solo shows at the San Francisco Museum of Art (SFMA, now the San Francisco Museum of Modern Art). Examining Madge Knight's gouache *Bone* suggests the two painters shared a parallel biomorphic abstract style (fig. 7). In addition to painting, Charles Howard worked as a shipfitter, as well as for the Works Progress Administration, Office of War Information, and CSFA.[22] *First War Winter* (plate 27), which Howard completed in San Francisco, marks a shift toward the dark backgrounds that would characterize much of his wartime work.[23] The foreboding black forms on the edges of the canvas create an ominous atmosphere and also suggest blackouts in wartime London, which Howard would have experienced, having left the city just months before the aerial bombings began. Howard's central forms appear lit internally, casting no shadow, as if light emanates from an intense spot or searchlight in the bottom center of the composition. A thin, vertical form resembling a mast or a flag, along with a bright red oval, bisects the

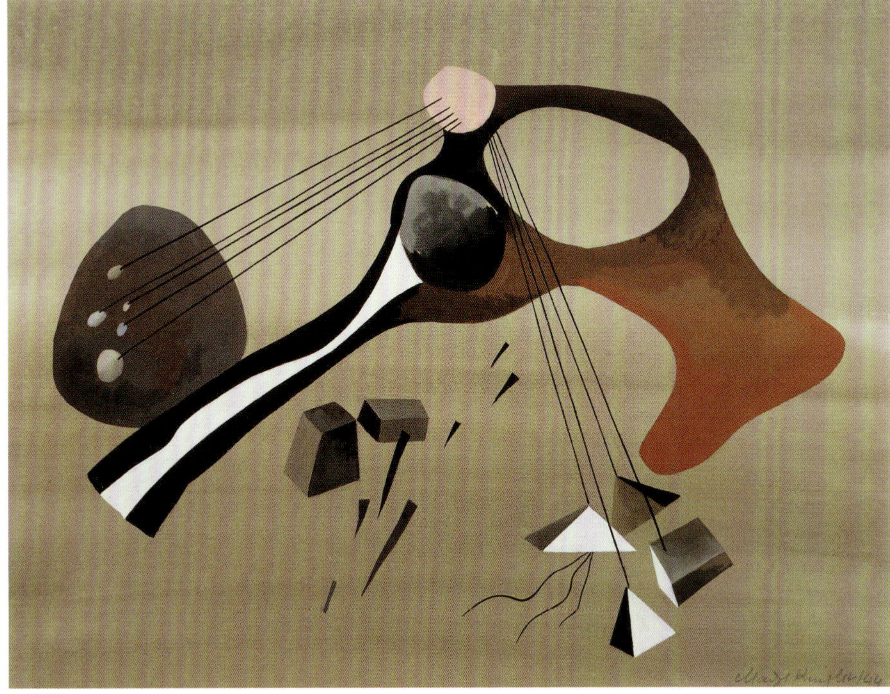

Fig. 7 Madge Knight, *Bone*, 1944. Gouache on paper, 8⅞ in. × 12 in. (22.6 × 30.5 cm). San Francisco Museum of Modern Art, gift of Jermayne MacAgy, acquired 1955

center, and just to the left is a blue blob in an "R"-like shape with a yellow accent and a bright white semicircular gleam. Although difficult to describe in words, these central elements retain an ambiguous individuality against the darkness. Are they endangered by it or holding out a kind of hope?

In addition to supporting the war effort by working at a shipyard in Sausalito, California, Howard participated in projects for the federal government's Works Progress Administration (WPA), which was intended to produce public art. A design for an unrealized tapestry intended for the lounge of Officers' Recreational Building at the Alameda Naval Air Station evidences his ongoing interest in textile design. Although Howard's plans for Alameda never came to fruition, two other textile works, *The Spot* and *The Virgin,* were created in collaboration with the V'Soske workshop in Manhattan and included in the exhibition *New Rugs by American Artists* at MoMA in 1942.[24] That same year Howard also finished a large oil painting titled *Abstraction in Flight* (see page 27) that is based on the tapestry design he had proposed for the Naval Air Station. Banded by dark stripes of muted blue at top and bottom, the rectangular painting frames five stacked, undulating waves in varying shades of muted blue. Resembling both the sea and the sky, the design's field points ambiguously to the dual domains of the naval air base. The silhouette of a propeller airplane with straight, tapered wings fills the center of the composition, a schematic symbol over an ambiguous landscape. Howard laid another shape and linear system over top—a cross section of a plane's wing with rainbow circles decorating the lightening holes, an engineering innovation that enabled buoyancy and strength. Thin brown lines arch across the wing, tracing the basic diagram of the air movement that creates lift. In this Howard's abstraction resembles the iterations of a technical diagram as much as a puzzle in motion.

Howard also designed popular posters for the Office of War Information in the 1940s. Period artists ranging from Norman Rockwell to Ben Shahn participated in the war effort by offering representations of aspects of American life that must be defended, examples of American strength, or depictions of the dangers posed by the enemy. Advertising specialists encouraged designs that would "appeal to the emotions of viewers" and offer "a literal picture in photographic detail."[25] In contrast to the realist illustrations that dominated war poster production, Howard's posters attempted to use geometric abstraction and Surrealism to direct American audiences. In *Panic Defeats Defense!* he layers gray, amorphous biomorphic forms, which rhyme with those from his abstract paintings, over a scrap of architecture, a window with ornate molding (recalling his 1927 watercolor), and blackout curtains (fig. 8). Here Howard's ambiguous forms gain clear symbolism from the caption, which warns viewers to prepare for a gas attack. In rendering the invisible threat of gas in tangible form, Howard arrived at a strategy of visualization that escaped other posters of the period, which turned to gas masks in order to communicate the threat. Howard's striking anti-Japanese poster *Serve in Silence* also belongs to period campaigns that figured racist caricatures of the Japanese emperor Hirohito (fig. 9). Such posters attempted to envision the danger posed by domestic spies and often featured exaggerated representations of Japanese figures listening on phones and with ear horns, or through keyholes, windows, and open doors. In these images artists depicted the Japanese enemy as easy to identify visually through ethnic caricature but also potentially everywhere unseen. Instead Howard deploys an experimental aesthetic that duplicates the biological, layering biomorphic forms that spring from the caricature to become excessive ears. With features dangerously out of control like monstrous mushrooms, Howard's design suggests the counterintuitive ways that organic Surrealism might be used in the service of the war effort.

Howard's painting became recognized for its contribution to American democracy when his *Prescience* (1942, plate 33) won a purchase prize at the Metropolitan Museum of Art's *Artists for Victory* exhibition. The painting links formally with *First War Winter* (1934–40, plate 27), offering another red form in the center, this one larger, undulating, and bisected by thick black lines. A small spot of bright blue in the upper center of the image appears held in place by similar curling lines, which do not obey a geometric logic but meander or dangle like hairs, ligaments, or irregular wires. Again, complex shapes in browns, blacks, and grays flank the composition with small areas of primary colors, yellow, red, and blue surrounded here by bright white shapes. *Prescience* is a brighter painting than *First War Winter*, but one with a more ambiguous space. Howard layers planes in which, as in the off-white area on right, floating forms oscillate like apertures cut through the surface to provide a look at a distant horizon. Although the meaning of the painting remained ambiguous to contemporary viewers, it suggested wartime victory over Adolf Hitler's regime, which had attacked abstraction and Surrealism in *Degenerate Art,* an exhibition staged in Munich in 1937. The very ambiguity of the painting also forced viewers to think for themselves, encouraging the development of a discerning vision and skepticism that would allow individuals to resist propaganda and despotism. In 1942 Howard's notion of painting as a means beyond language for common communication between individuals—a

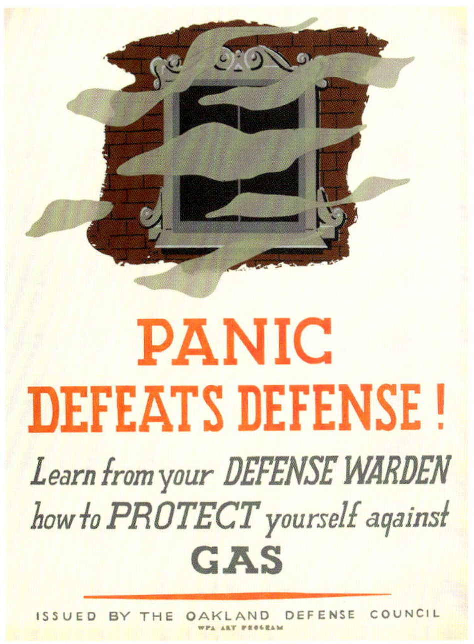

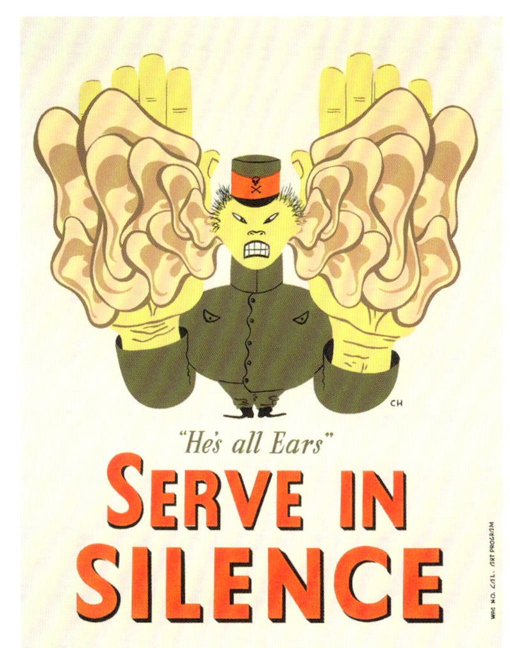

Fig. 8 Poster for the Oakland Defense Council, Works Progress Administration Art Program, 1940s.

Fig. 9 Poster for the San Francisco Junior Chamber of Commerce, Works Progress Administration Art Program, 1940s.

psychologized abstraction that roamed between organic and geometric—had democratic and anti-fascist potential.

Created in the middle of World War II, Howard's painting and design projects underscore the complex, productive space between abstraction and Surrealism. Examining Howard's compositions broadens our view of the art world, envisioning connections between stylistic wings, as well as between media—oil painting, illustration, and decorative arts. The broader history of art during the 1930s and 1940s suggests that Howard's movement between period styles should be regarded not as an equivocation but as the deliberate aesthetic position of an intermediate genius.

Notes

1. Herbert Read, *Art Now: An Introduction to the Theory of Modern Painting and Sculpture,* 2nd ed. (New York: Pitman Publishing Corporation, 1948), 100.

2. David Goodway, "Introduction," in *Herbert Read Reassessed* (Liverpool, UK: Liverpool University Press, 1998), 2.

3. Read, *Art Now,* 131.

4. Douglas MacAgy, "A Margin of Chaos," *Circle* 10 (Summer 1948): 39–42.

5. These and other quotations by Charles Howard in this essay come from his text "What Concerns Me," reprinted on pages 57–59 of this volume, unless otherwise noted. This reprinting is based on an unpublished typescript in the Howard family archives. A slightly revised version of the text was published as "What Concerns Me," *Magazine of Art* 39, no. 2 (February 1946): 63–65.

6. Douglas MacAgy, "Charles Howard," *Magazine of Art* 47 (April 1953): 158. Here MacAgy made reference to the theories of William James. In a review of Howard's retrospective at the California Palace of the Legion of Honor, critic Alfred Frankenstein argued that Dalí represented "psychological literature" by painting things for which there were words, while Howard managed instead to grapple with objects for which no name exists. See Frankenstein, "Art Galleries," *San Francisco Chronicle,* May 12, 1946.

7. Andrew Carnduff Ritchie, *Abstract Painting and Sculpture in America* (New York: The Museum of Modern Art, 1951).

8. Lawrence Alloway, "Art News from London" *Art News* 55, no. 3 (May 1956): 14.

9. "Charles Houghton Howard," in *California Art Research: John Galen Howard, Robert Boardman Howard, Charles Houghton Howard, Adaline Kent, Jane Berlandina,* ed. Gene Hailey (San Francisco: Works Progress Administration California Art Research Project, vol. 17, 1936–37), 41.

10. "Variety Included in Howard Exhibition," *San Francisco Chronicle,* March 18, 1928, quoted in Ibid., 43.

11. For more on Madge Knight see Ilene Susan Fort, Terri Geis, and Tere Arcq, eds., *In Wonderland: The Surrealist Adventures of Women Artists in Mexico and the United States* (Los Angeles: Los Angeles County Museum of Art, 2012), 227.

12. Sir James Richards, "Foreword," in *Unit One: Spirit of the '30s* (London: Mayor Gallery, 1984), 5.

13. Mark Glazebrook, "Unit One: Spirit of the 'Thirties'," in *Unit One: Spirit of the '30s,* 13.

14. Herbert Read, "Unit One," in *Unit One: Spirit of the '30s,* 47.

15. See Jeremy Lewison, *A Genius of Industrial England: Edward Wadsworth, 1889–1949* (London: Arkwright Arts Trust and Bradford Art Galleries and Museums, 1990); David Peters Corbett, *The Modernity of English Art, 1914–1930* (Manchester, UK: Manchester University Press, 1997); Bernard Vere, "Enigma Variation: Edward Wadsworth's 'Marine Still-Lifes' and Giorgio de Chirico," *Visual Culture in Britain* 7, no. 1 (June 2006): 39–58.

16. In contrast, Howard's mural work in and around New York frequently responded to the existing decorative elements in the room. See for example the wall paintings he created for Hobart G. Erwin, illustrated on page 16 of this volume.

17. Among those at the meeting were Read, Penrose, Mesens, Jennings, Jacques Brunius, Ithell Colquhoun, Eileen Agar, Edith Rimmington, Hayter, A. C. Sewter, Dr. Grace Pailthorpe, Rueben Mednikoff, John Banting, and Gordon Onslow Ford. Charles Harrison, *English Art and Modernism, 1900–1939* (Bloomington, IN: Indiana University Press, 1981), 20.

18. Howard participated in the *International Surrealist Exhibition* at New Burlington Galleries, London, in 1936, and had a solo exhibition at Peggy Guggenheim's first gallery, Guggenheim Jeune, Paris, in 1939.

19. Junius Cravens, *San Francisco News,* May 4, 1935, quoted in "Charles Houghton Howard," 48.

20. Reavey incorrectly reproduced *Presage* with the caption *The Cage,* another painting from 1938 now in the collection of the Solomon R. Guggenheim Museum, New York.

21. George Reavey, "Charles Howard" [review of Guggenheim Jeune Gallery exhibition], *London Bulletin,* no. 13 (April 1939): 14.

22. For an in-depth discussion of Howard's time in San Francisco see pages 24–29 of Apsara DiQuinzio's essay in this volume.

23. For more on this shift in Howard's work see Susan M. Anderson, "Journey Into the Sun: California Artists and Surrealism," in *On the Edge of America: California Modernist Art, 1900–1950,* ed. Paul Karlstom (Berkeley: University of California Press, 1996), 194.

24. Press release and checklist for *New Rugs by American Artists,* the Museum of Modern Art, New York, June 30 to August 9, 1942, Archives of the Museum of Modern Art, https://www.moma.org/calendar/exhibitions/3044.

25. Young & Rubicam [Advertising Firm], "How to Make Posters that Will Help Win the War," ca. 1942, quoted in *Design for Victory: World War II Posters on The American Home Front,* by William L. Bird, Jr. and Harry R. Rubenstein (New York: Princeton Architectural Press, 1998), 28.

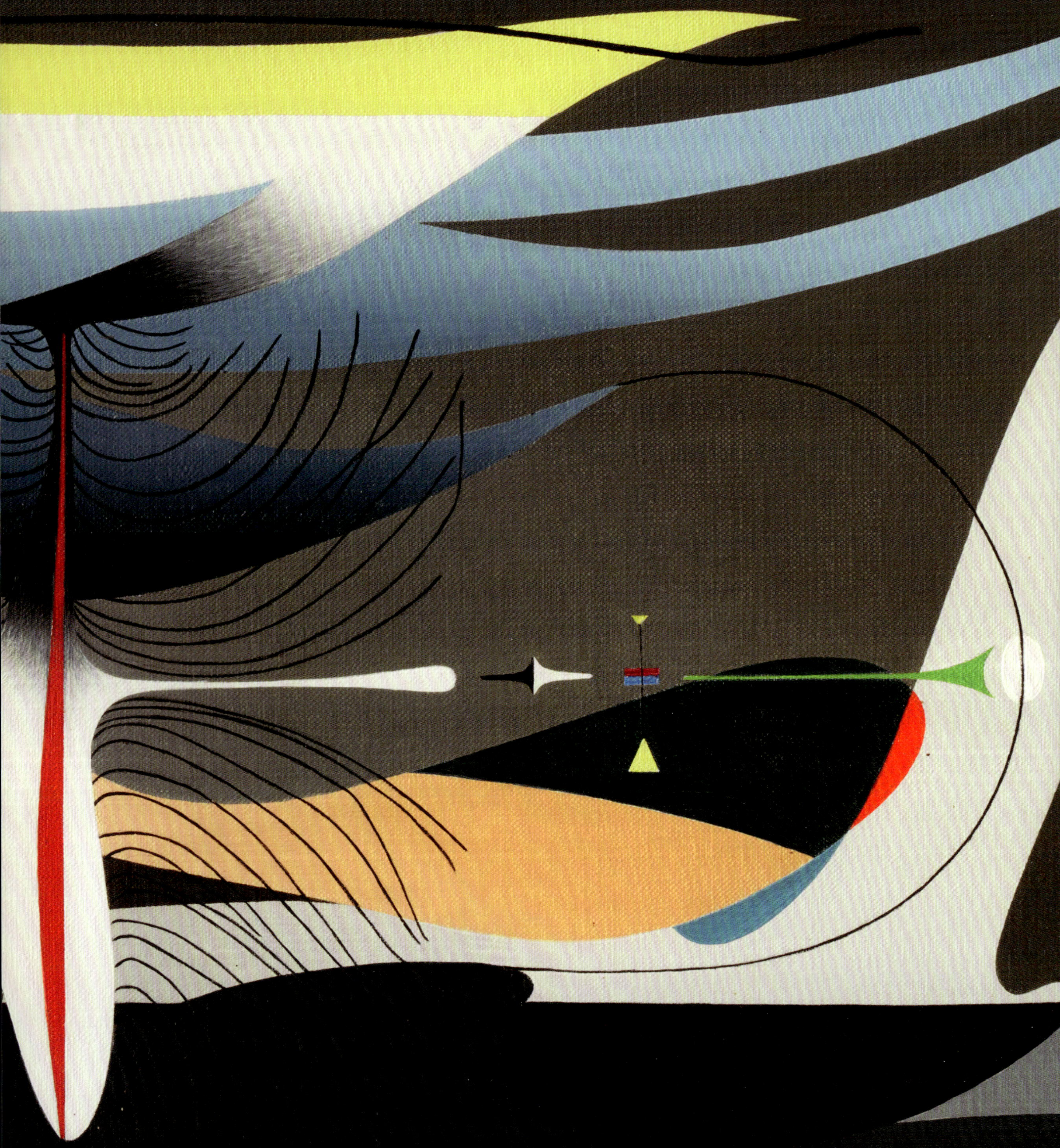

What Concerns Me

Charles Howard

The language of a modern artist is the tongue of people who are living. It refers to the whole world, everything in it, the little and the big and the medium-sized, what's over the earth and underneath, the insects, the birds, the trees, the minerals, fish, mountains, the motes in the eye — all these things and the million million more; accidents, hazards, and the unconsidered. It is expressive of what these things have done to mankind and what man makes of them: their totemic significance, their poetry and their everyday use. It is where we start, and it is our experience. We understand, if we want to, and all that is necessary is an open mind.

———————————

The railroad that runs from Venice to Milan passes near the small hinterland town of Castelfranco. It is a wayside station. There was a picture there that I had seen mentioned in the guidebook. I thought, if time could be managed, perhaps I ought to make the effort to see it—another item covered in the general tour I was making, a point in an itinerary, between trains, so to speak. I was in a hurry. I was young. There was a lot else planned.

From the station a straight, tree-lined road leads directly through the lovely country to the town. It was a charming day, about eleven o'clock in the morning, I think. I remember a gateway through a medieval wall, and a cobbled street to the church. When I entered, there was no one within except the sacristan. He was down near the altar but spotted me at once and waved me grandly to him. Fixing a chair against one side of the apse, he bowed. I sat down. I was charmed: it was like being in a set piece. With a flourish, he swept aside a large curtain hanging opposite.

I looked at the picture for a quarter of an hour. I looked at nothing else. It may be that I thought of all the other pictures I had been looking at in Italy, when I had been spending time in galleries that should by rights have been spent on something else, writing a novel, say. It may be that I ruminated on the somber, analytical, philosophical approach of the Florentine painters, and then [on] the free, warm, romantic fervor of Venice. I think it is fairly certain that I realized even in those few minutes that here, in this picture before me, was a combination of both these approaches, that here for once was a synthesis.

Well, really I don't remember what I thought. I don't know what my state of mind was. I only know for sure that I was not a painter then, nor had I any idea of becoming one.

After a while I simply got up and left. I went out of the church and down the street to the walled gate. When I was outside the town, on the road in the calm, sunlit air, with the trees and the fields, I had a quick and sudden reaction, and was violently ill.

I cut the tour at once and hurried immediately back to Paris, to begin painting. I have been painting whenever I could ever since.

———————————

I paint as much as I can. It is a wearing occupation. Paint itself is an unimaginative substance, and the affair of putting it on a support is enervating. But it is an obsession for me to paint, and I am exceedingly restless when I don't.

And there is always the obsessive subject.

I make many small drawings, automatic and otherwise. I make a lot of these drawings in my head. It isn't a question of copying, but of remembering. I am astonished at the amount of material that is lying around. You see it on any walk through the streets and fields, on the shores and in the woods. A lot comes from waste things, the amiable objects that people throw away, the shapes left over after the fine, neat, arbitrary palaces of our civilization have been made. They are very revealing shapes.

These sorts of notes go on like a soliloquy without end, awake or asleep. Then, sooner or later, as if from nowhere, some association will suddenly seem to come alive, a tiny spark, a flash, a momentary passion. That will be the beginning of a picture, and from there on the wheels grind. I will go through literally hundreds of drawings and trials, pulling and pushing, simplifying and elaborating, erasing, redrawing, setting traps, springing them, discarding, planning, memorizing. In my mind's eye I'll know absolutely what should be there, and with patience and deep looking I set myself to draw it out.

All this goes on before any paint actually gets on the canvas. Every line, shape, color, gradation is screened and caressed until it is there but for the painting. A laborious method of working, I'll agree, and the so-called fun of painting is not apparent. Actually it is not there. I do not get what you might call fun out of painting. It is not a frisky business. It is drudgery. It is a tedious, circuitous battle with an intractable medium. It is disappointing at every turn, painstaking as one may be, and using every bit of experience and adroitness that one may. I suppose that's why I am what is known as a slow painter. I look more than I paint, and I struggle with the paint and with myself. No, it is not an easeful pursuit.

When you paint this way you have a strong sense that the endless spiral of completion slowly swings around, the tension mounts, the passion closes in, the painting starts to make itself. It takes a long time to get to that point; it is near the end, and when it does come it doesn't last long. And you only get back a fraction of what you originally saw. The drama is only partially revealed; only a facet of the subject is divulged. But even with that small bit, it is utterly and completely rewarding. Or so it seems for a few minutes. Then you start again.

I've always found it difficult to keep track of my pictures once I can no longer work on them. I have tried occasionally, but my mind is not on it. The cord once broken, my interest goes; or rather the interest is of a different kind, and to a degree worldly. Yet I am aware that the pictures "look" better if there are a dozen or so together, as if they complete, or tend to complete, one another. In a sense they do. They are links in a chain. They are not isolated or disconnected, far from it. Nor are they individual pieces turned out on a factory belt, all complete and nicely packaged for exhibition here and there. They are closely related, regardless and quite apart from style and presentation. They are in fact all portraits of the same general subject, of the same idea, carried as far as I am able at the time.

We hear of pictures being spoken of as communicating, or of being a communication. I have no sense of that, so far as my own pictures are concerned. They are not messages. I am not telling anybody anything he doesn't already know, nor drawing attention to something special and reserved. I do not belong to an *élite*. I don't uncover secrets. I am dealing with material that is the possession of all people, presenting it with the fundamental anonymity of a human being on the face of the earth. I make pictures with shapes common to man anywhere, of any race, of any generation, regardless of time. I leave myself open for these shapes, and when I find them I use them exclusively.

———————————————

When I first went to London, in 1933, I suddenly found it impossible to make *pictures*. I could paint all right, but the picture eluded me. I sweated and rationalized, but the paintings remained blind, and only with considerable embarrassment would I force myself to finish them. When I found the trouble, its resolution was also implied. I had for some time been living in a city where everything had seemed easy to paint, where you could go out into the street and in a couple of blocks get a dozen ideas. It was a stimulating place, like a cocktail. If you ran dry you simply went outdoors and there it was. You turned it on like a faucet. It was wonderful, and easy as pie. Nothing to it, and who was I to recognize the lightness? I was used to it, and dependent on it, the fair enchantment.

That could have gone on for the rest of my life, I fancy, and probably I would have liked it a lot. I count myself fortunate that it didn't. For my time of life, I had been there long enough, though when I left I didn't know it. I'd got into trivial habits. It took a simple accident of displacement to indicate the existence of far richer ore, lying there free for the taking. The several years of close work that followed to find a way to mine it were worth it. Now I can return blithely enough to New York, but the fun and games are far behind.

Another thing happened in the thirties. Like a good many other people I was overwhelmed by political theory. The pattern was perhaps not unusual—arguments, refusal, cause, consequence, inevitable conviction, and the following urgency to reconcile one's own activity—but the shock was telling. I saw its effects on other artists as bewildered and desperate as myself. Some were abandoning themselves to extraneous subject matter; others dutifully followed the various hand-picked dicta of interested individuals; still others gave up production altogether. An anxious and vociferous period in our time. But however others solved the problem to their own satisfaction, painting as such had to remain the central point for me. I became an abstractionist. The way I understood it, what we needed, fundamentally and ideally, was order. And I thought also that these things, to be of good will, should start at home. I set out to find them for myself, as a painter. Abstraction was order and logic, so I became, just like that, full of logic, an abstractionist.

That interlude lasted just about a year, or until I realized I was losing picture after picture. Regardless of the worthiness of the intention, and aside from whether I was trying to work under an original pictorial misconception or not, it was clear that overt, effortful, and conscious admonition on the one hand, or extrovert and purposeful abstraction on the other, were not my pigeon. I gave up both overnight, and have never returned.

This text is based on an unpublished typescript in the Howard family archives. A slightly revised version was published as "What Concerns Me," *Magazine of Art* 39, no. 2 (February 1946): 63–65.

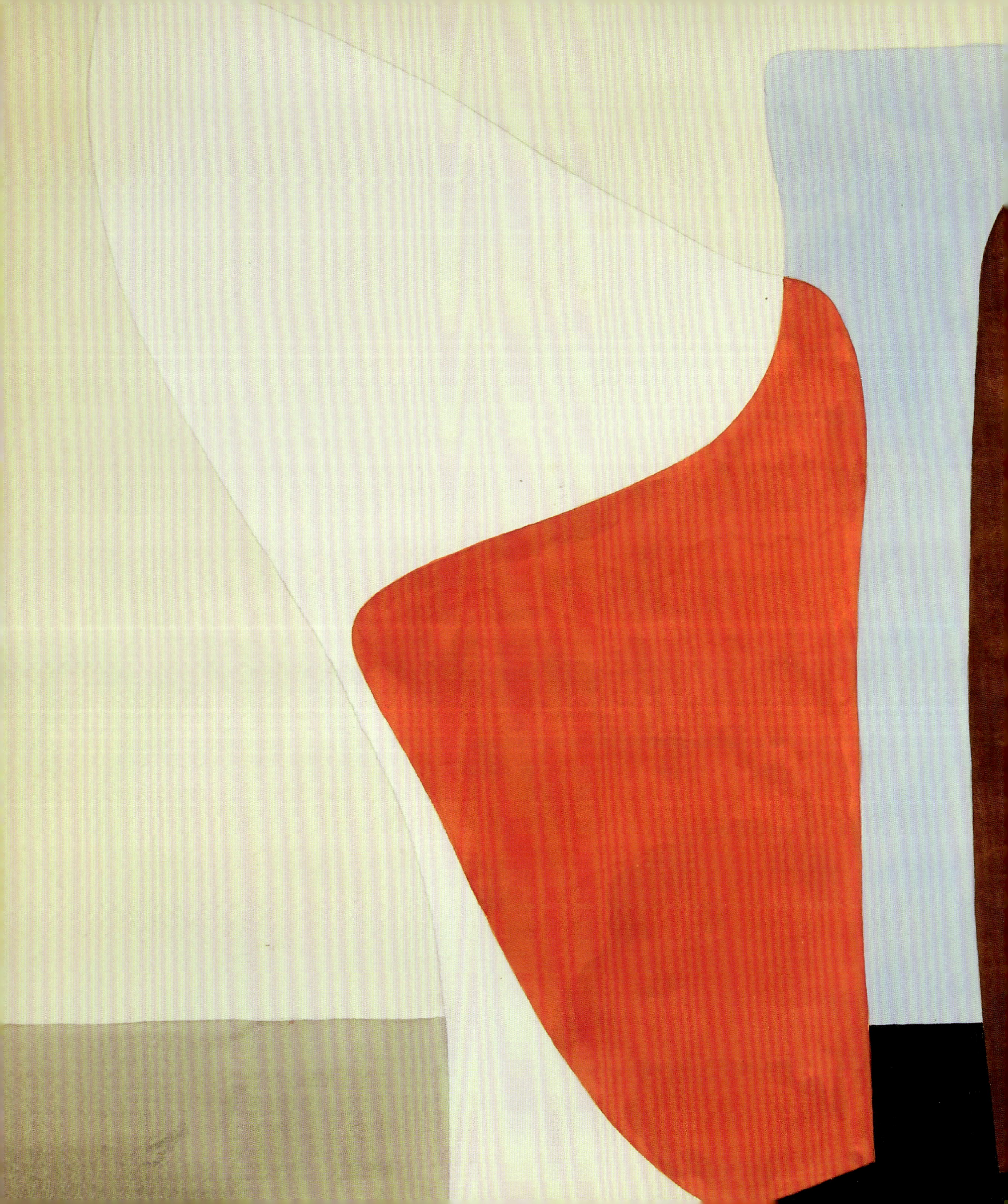

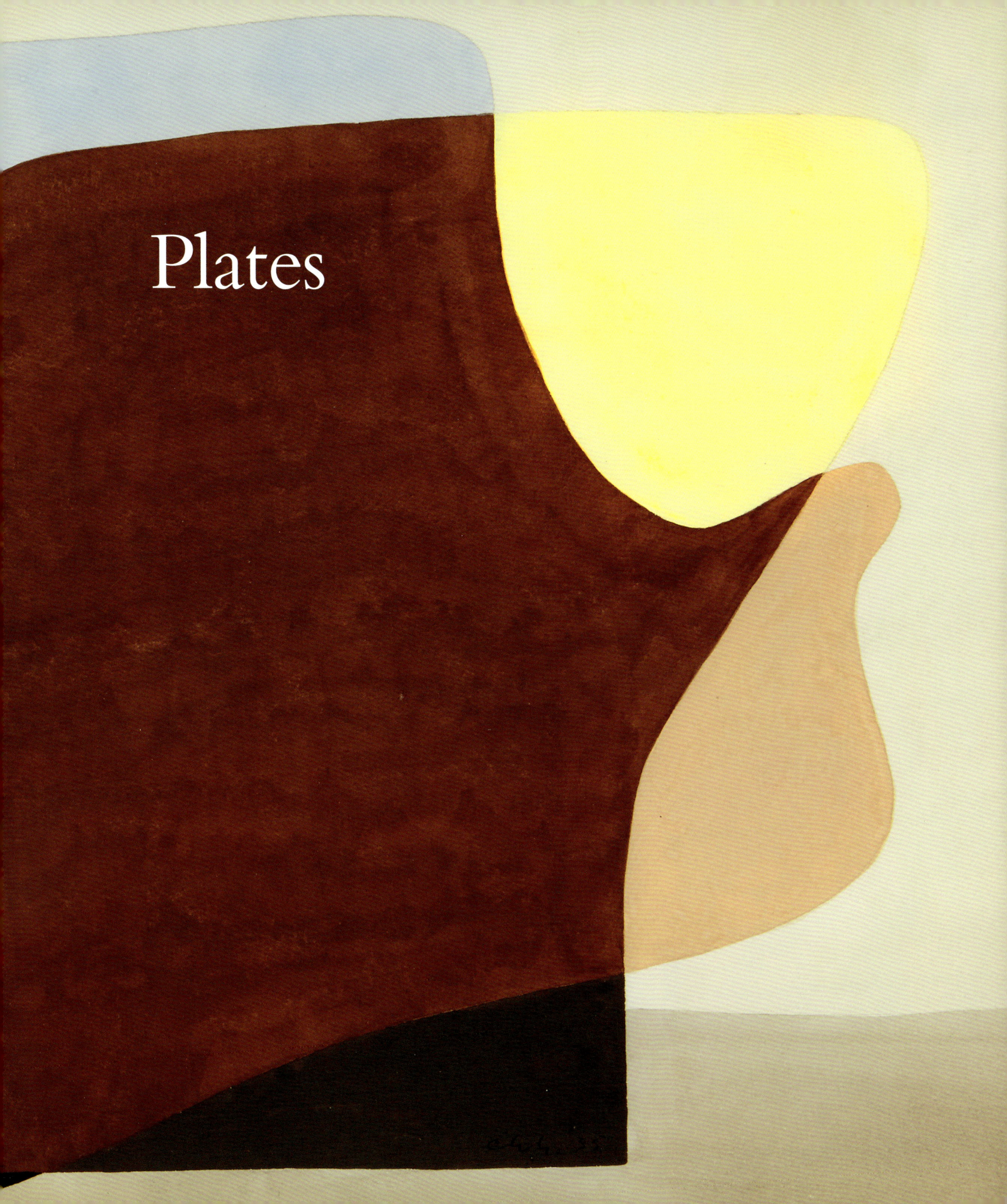
Plates

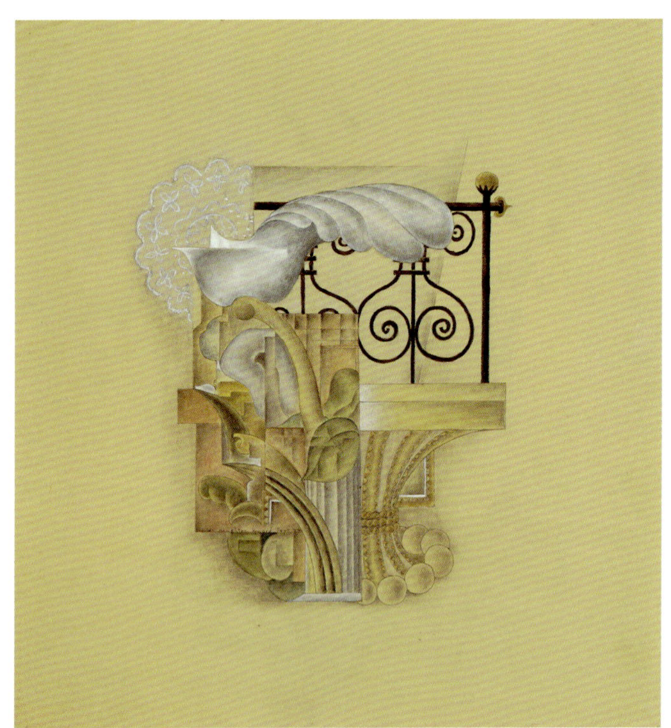

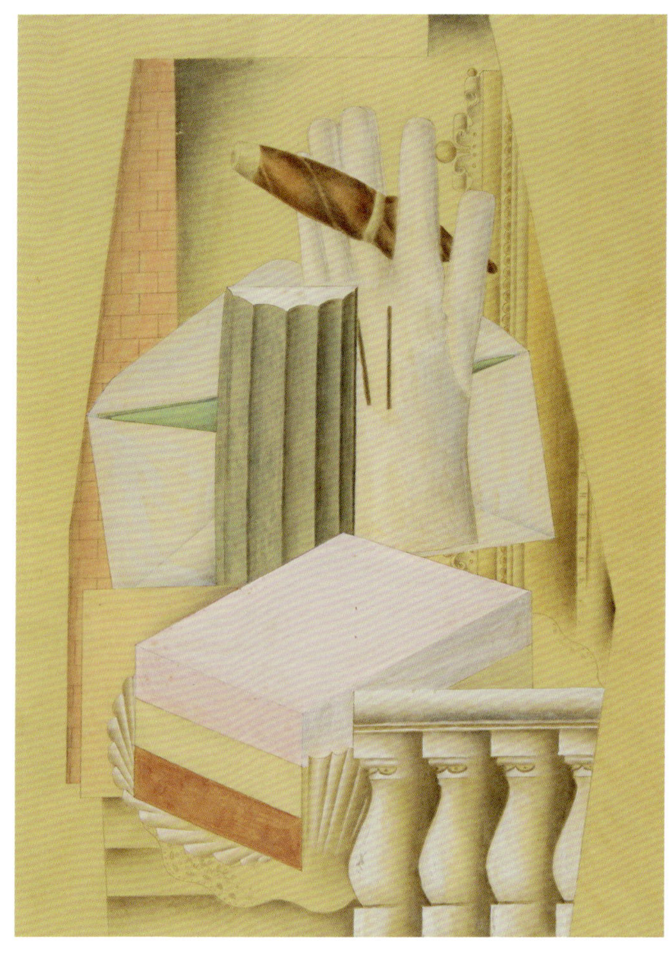

1 *1826 into 1926*, 1927.
Watercolor and graphite on paper,
13½ × 13¼ in. (34.3 × 33.7 cm).

2 *Untitled*, ca. 1927–29.
Gouache and graphite on drafting
paper, 19 × 14³⁄₁₆ in. (48.3 × 35.6 cm).

3 *Untitled*, 1931.
Ink on paper, 22 × 15 in. (55.9 × 38.1 cm).

4 *Untitled*, 1931.
Ink on paper, 15 × 21½ in. (38.1 × 54.6 cm).

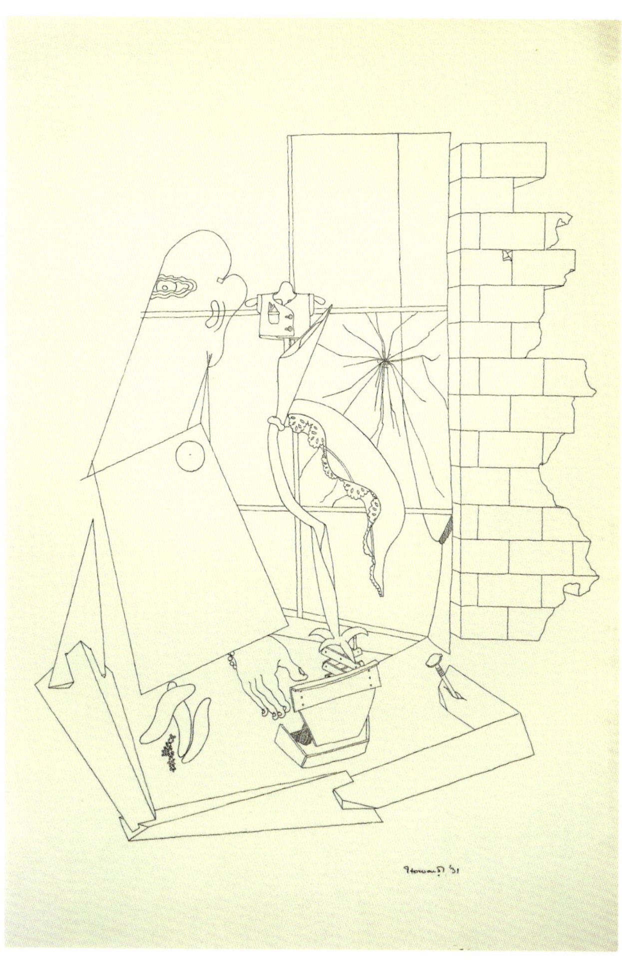

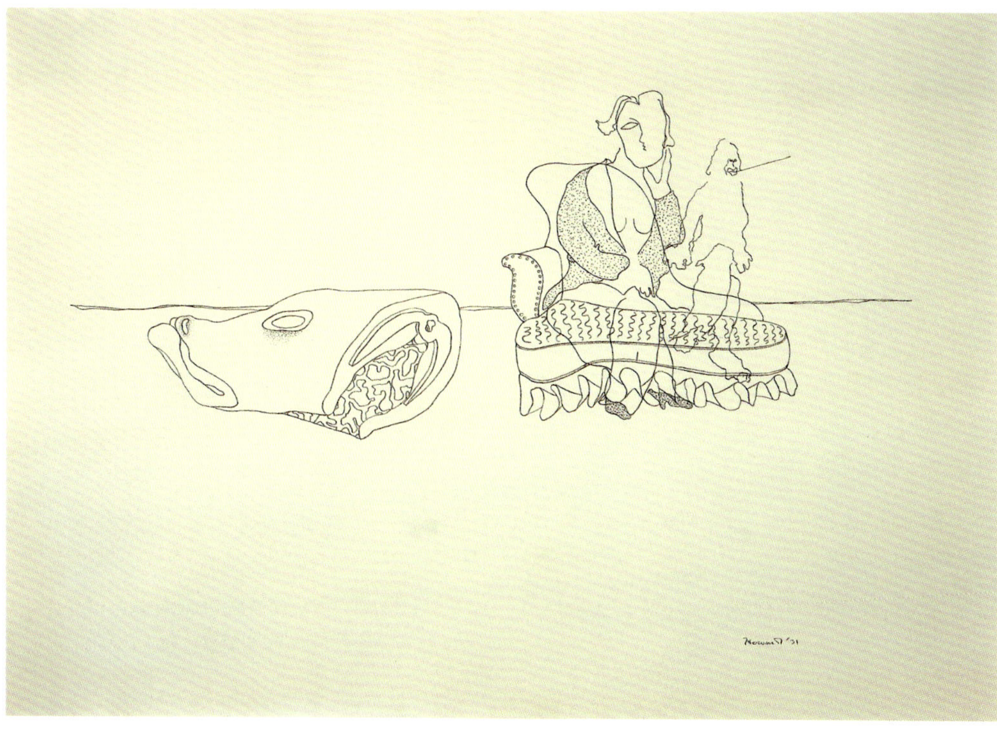

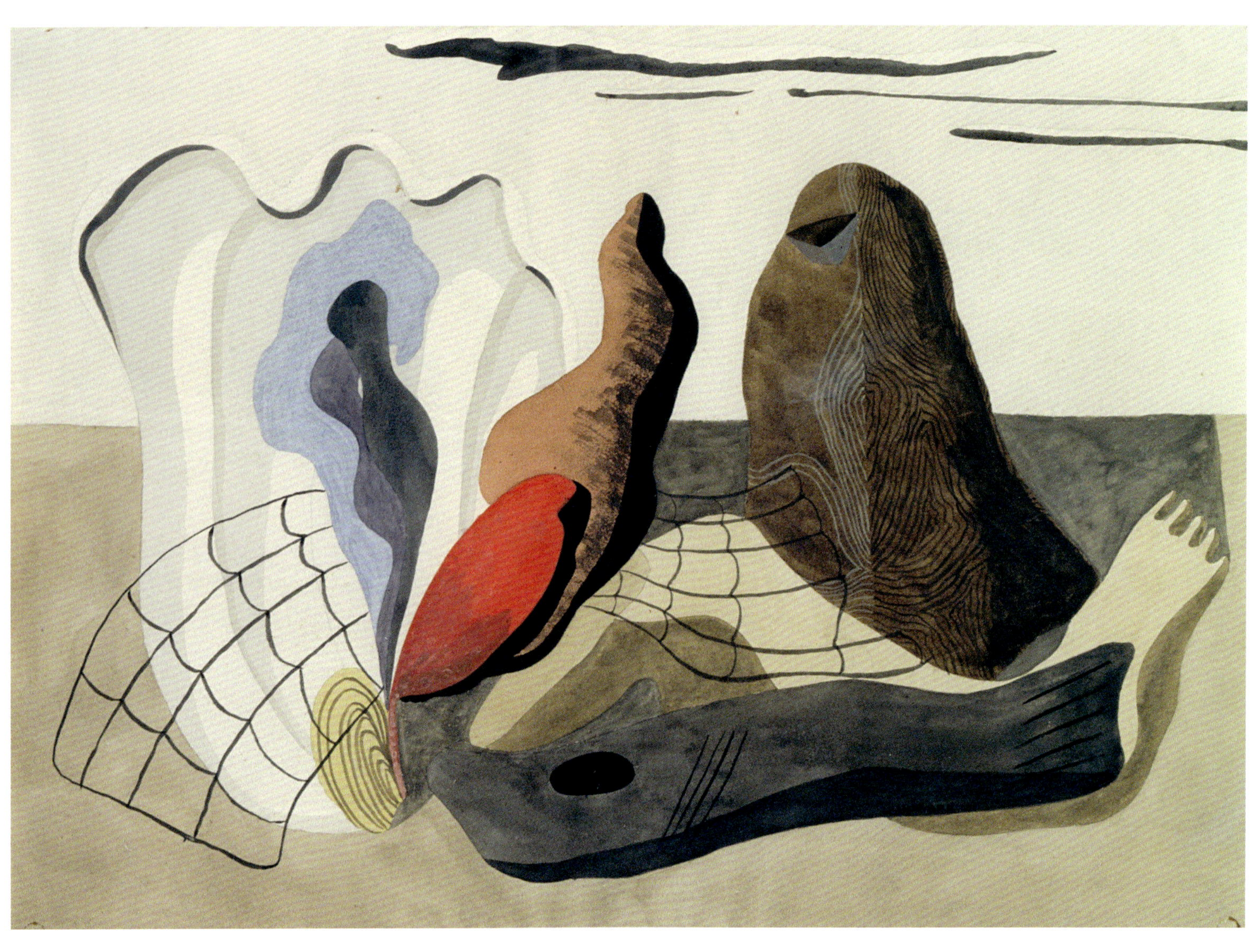

5 *Untitled*, 1931.
Gouache and watercolor on paper,
14 × 20 in. (35.6 × 50.8 cm).

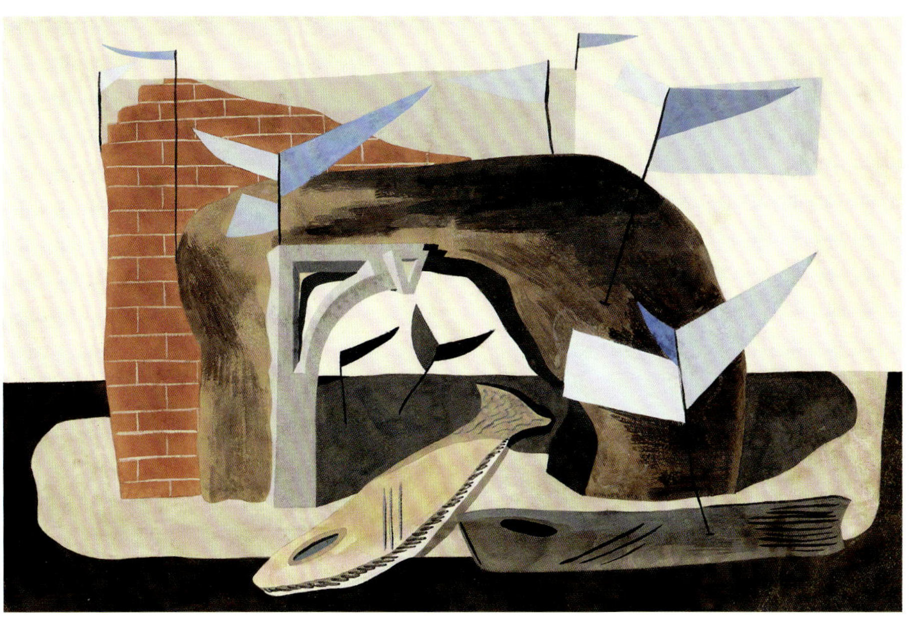

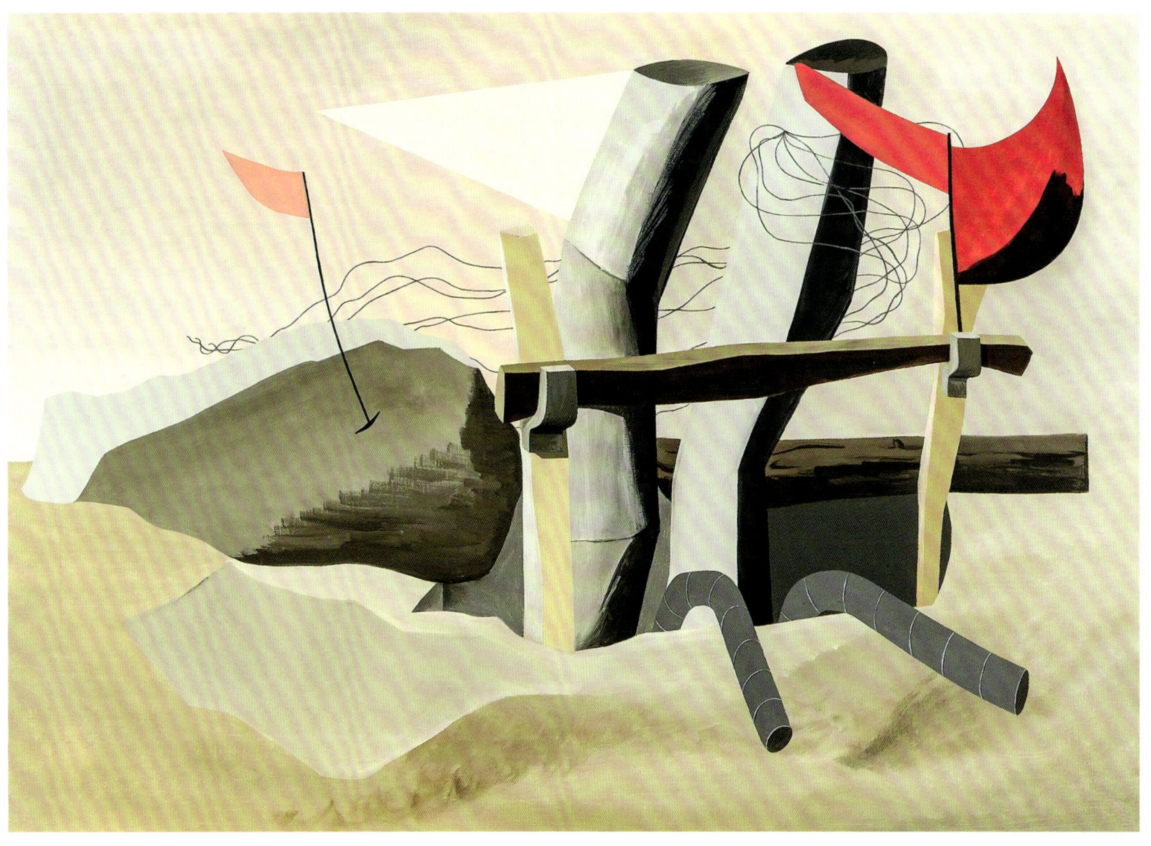

6 *Untitled Abstract Landscape,*
ca. 1931–32.
Watercolor on paper, 13¾ × 21⅛ in.
(34.9 × 53.3 cm).

7 *Excavation,* 1932.
Oil on canvas, 24 × 34 in.
(61 × 86.4 cm).

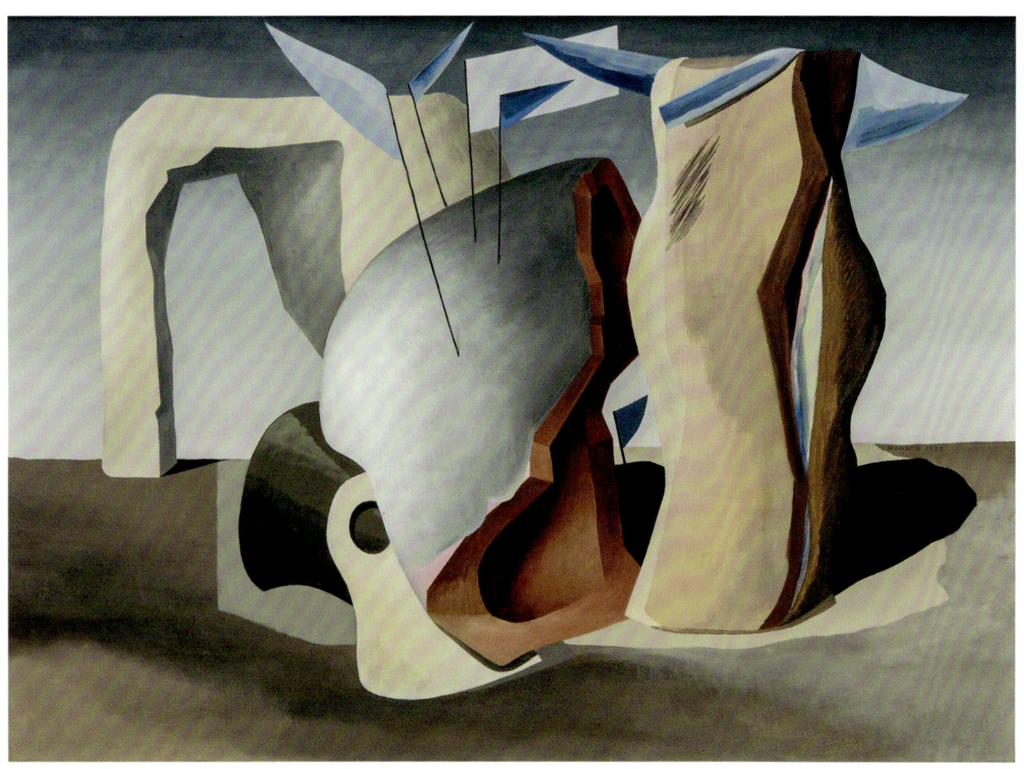

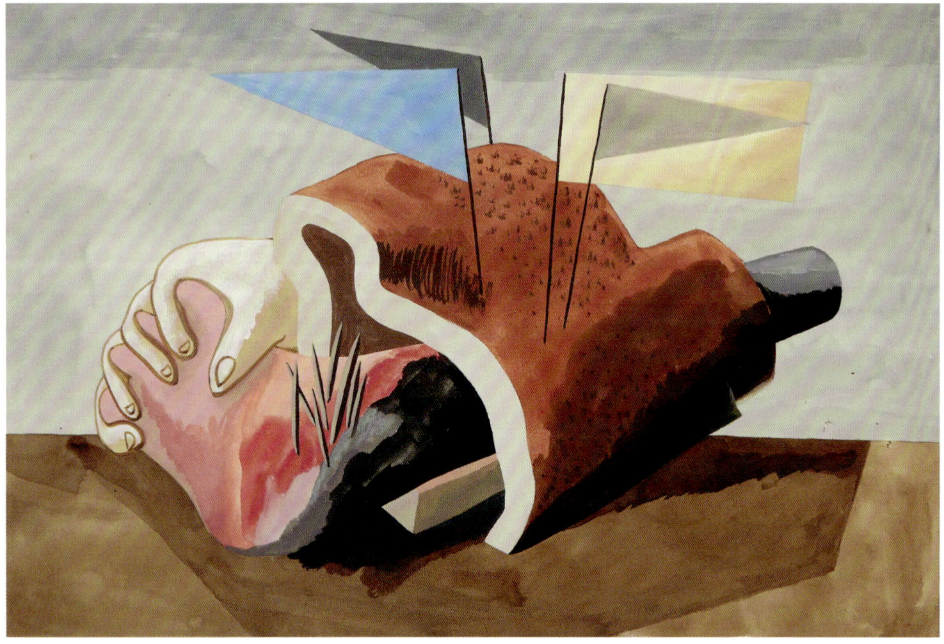

8 *Grotto*, 1932.
Oil on canvas, 24 × 34 in.
(61 × 86.4 cm).

9 *Untitled*, 1932.
Gouache and graphite on paper,
14½ × 21¾ in. (36.8 × 55.3 cm).

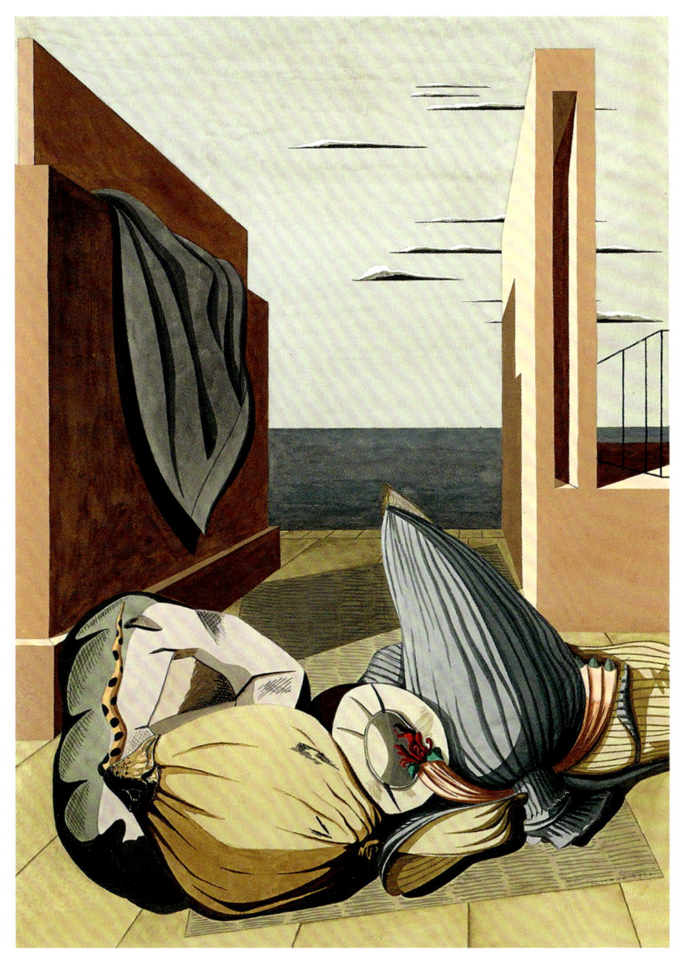

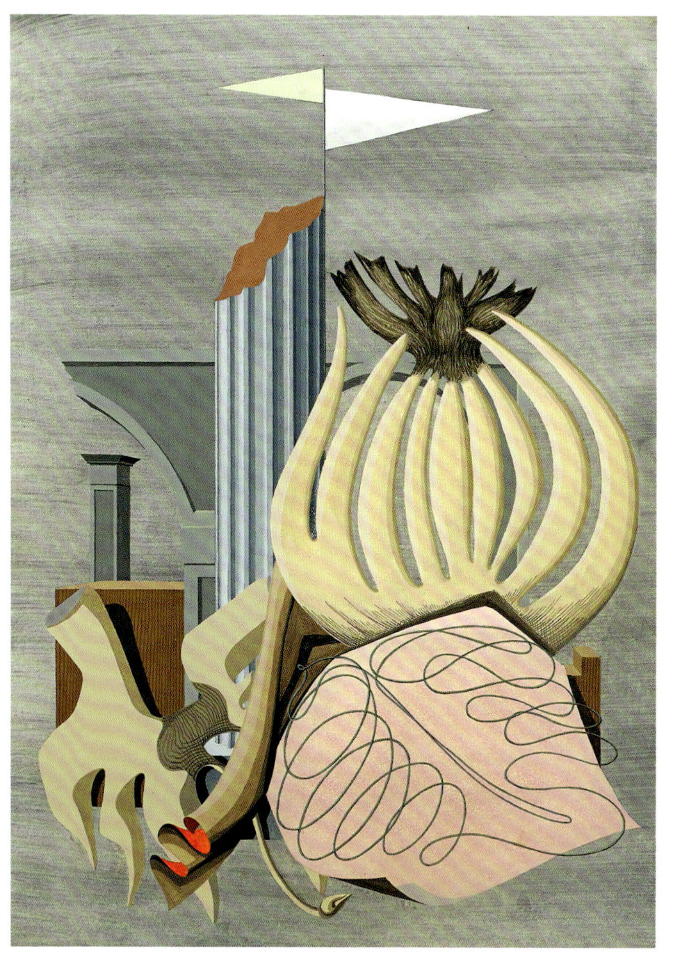

10 *Untitled (#1)*, 1932.
Gouache and graphite on paper,
18½ × 13½ in. (47 × 34.3 cm).

11 *Untitled (#2)*, 1932.
Gouache and graphite on paper,
18⅜ × 13⅜ in. (46.7 × 34 cm).

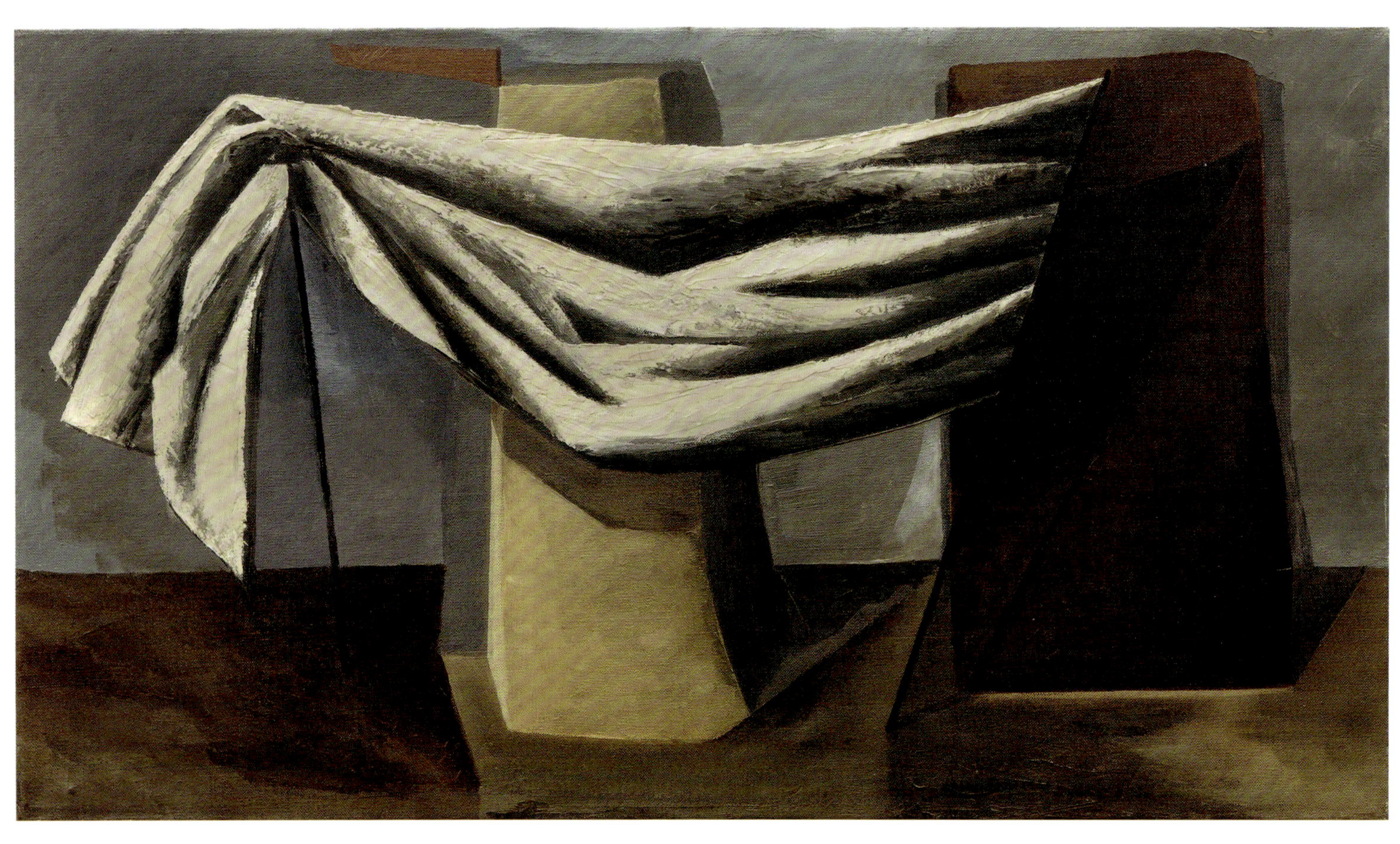

12 *Banner*, 1934.
Oil on canvas, 15 × 26¾ in.
(38.1 × 68 cm).

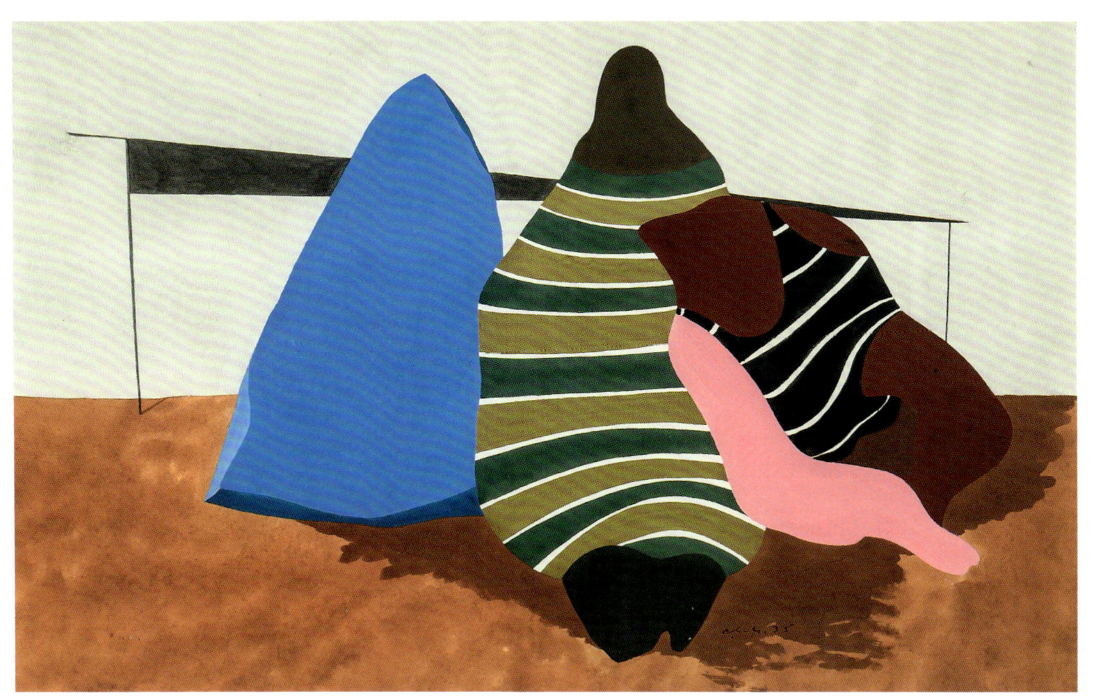

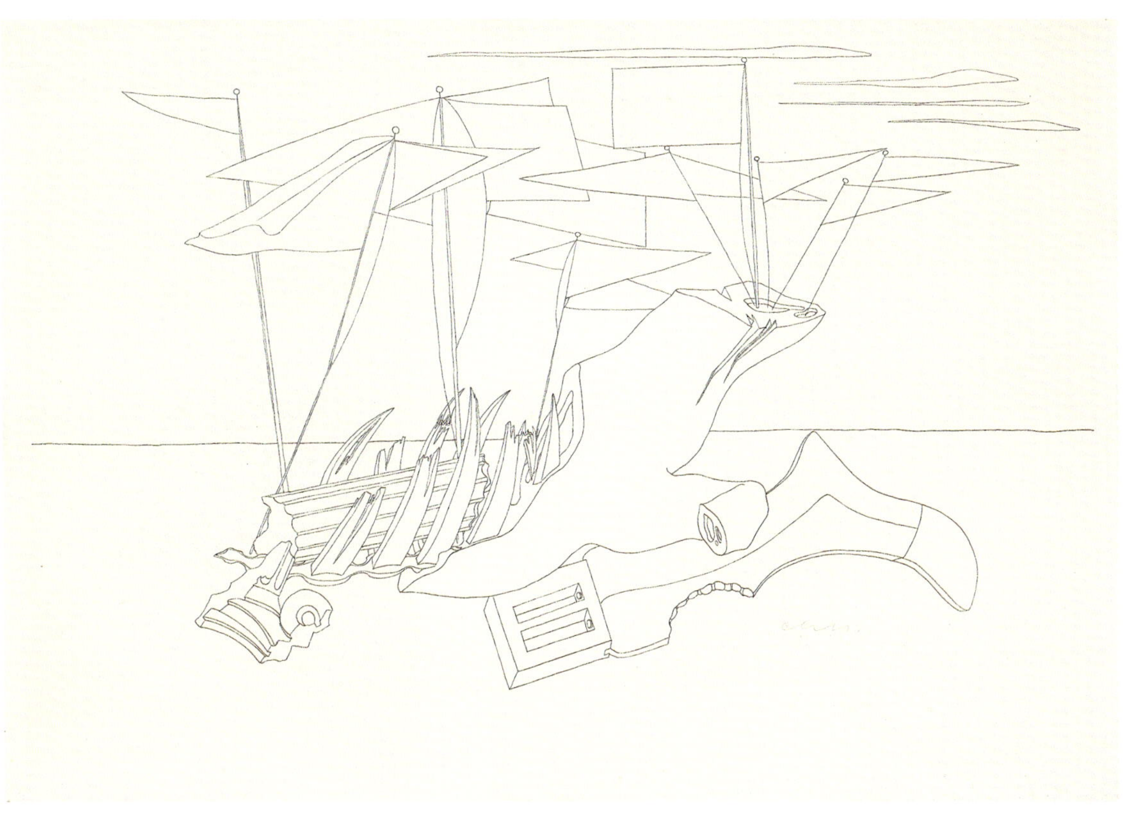

13 *Untitled*, 1935.
Gouache and graphite on paper,
13 × 21 in. (33 × 53.3 cm).

14 *Untitled*, ca. 1935.
Ink on paper, 15¼ × 22¼ in.
(38.7 × 56.5 cm).

15 *Untitled*, 1935.
Gouache and graphite on paper,
13³⁄₁₆ × 20¼ in. (33.5 × 51.4 cm).

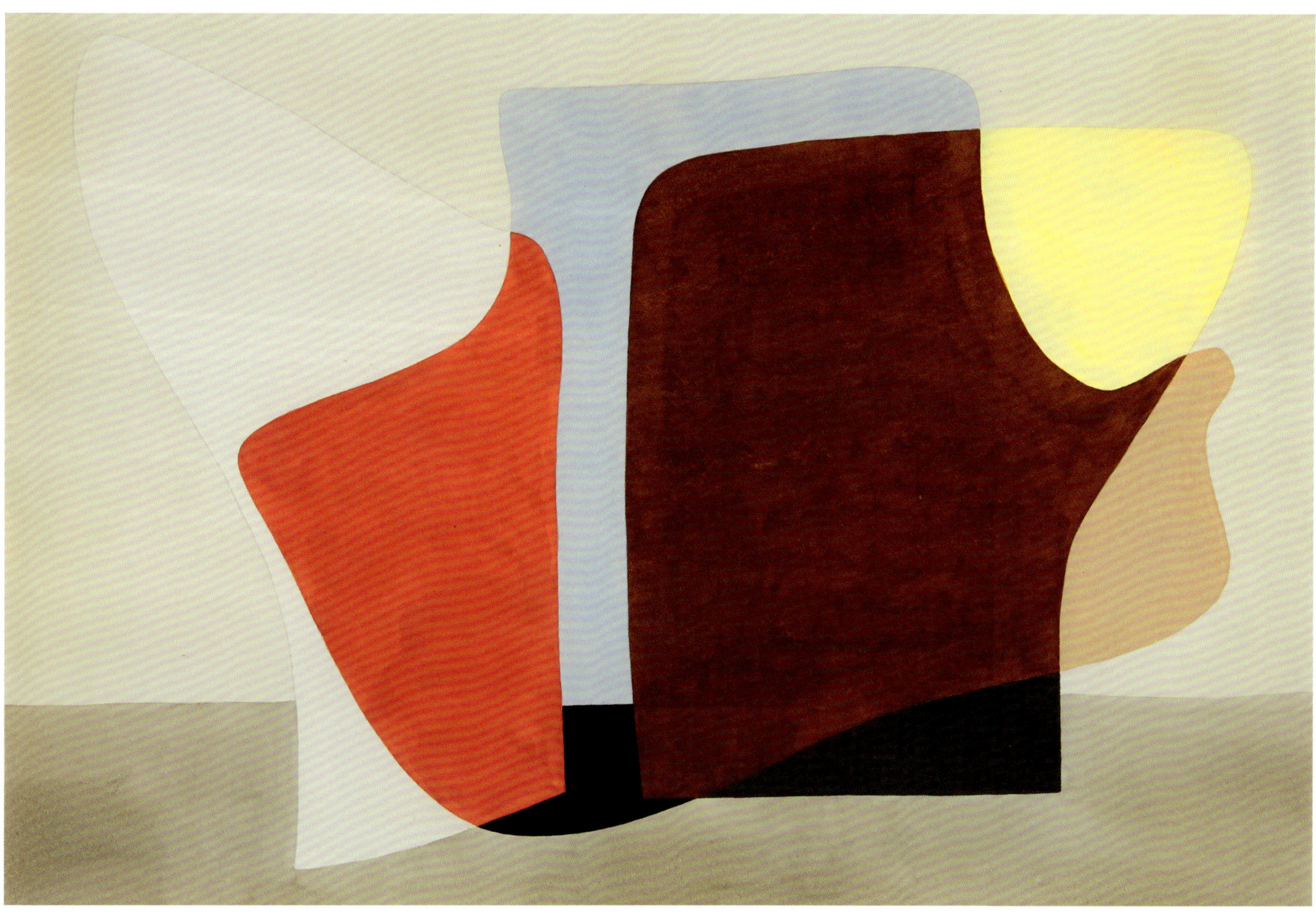

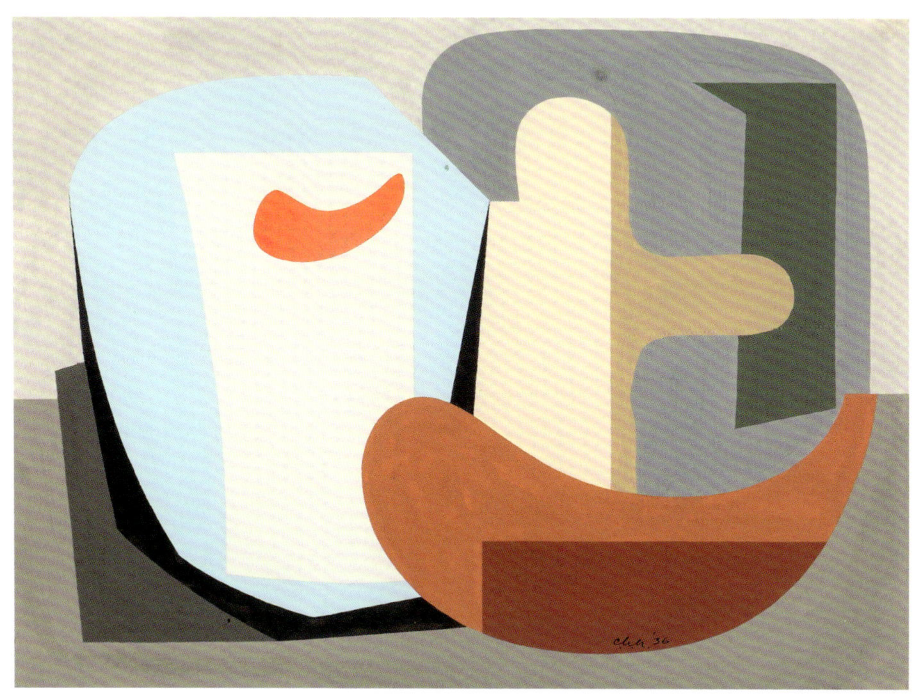

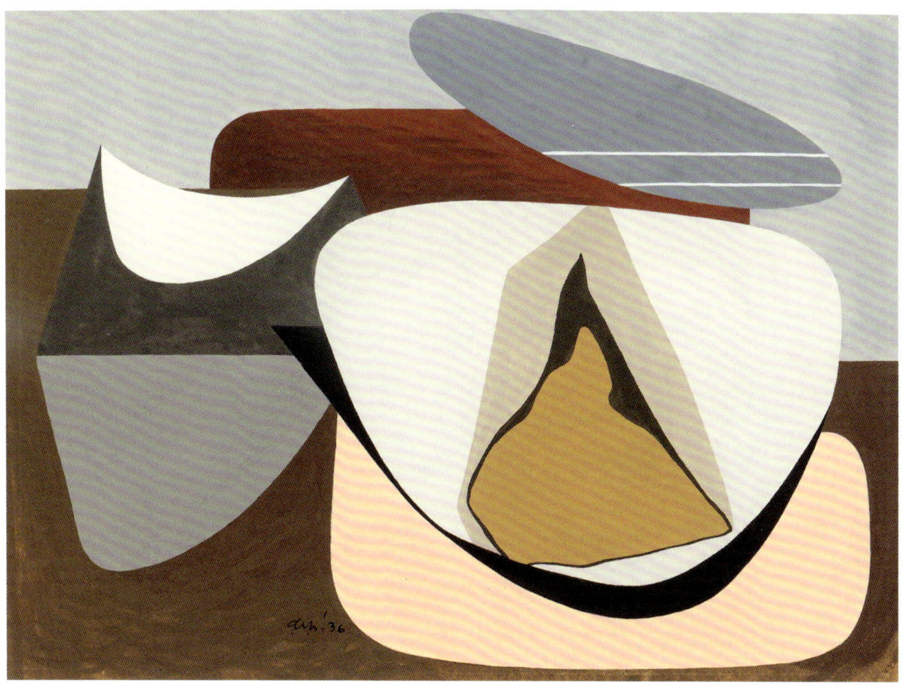

16 *Concretion*, 1936.
Gouache and graphite on paper,
10 × 14 in. (25.4 × 35.6 cm).

17 *Sketch for an Abstract Painting*, 1936.
Gouache and graphite on paper,
9¼ × 13 in. (23.5 × 33 cm).

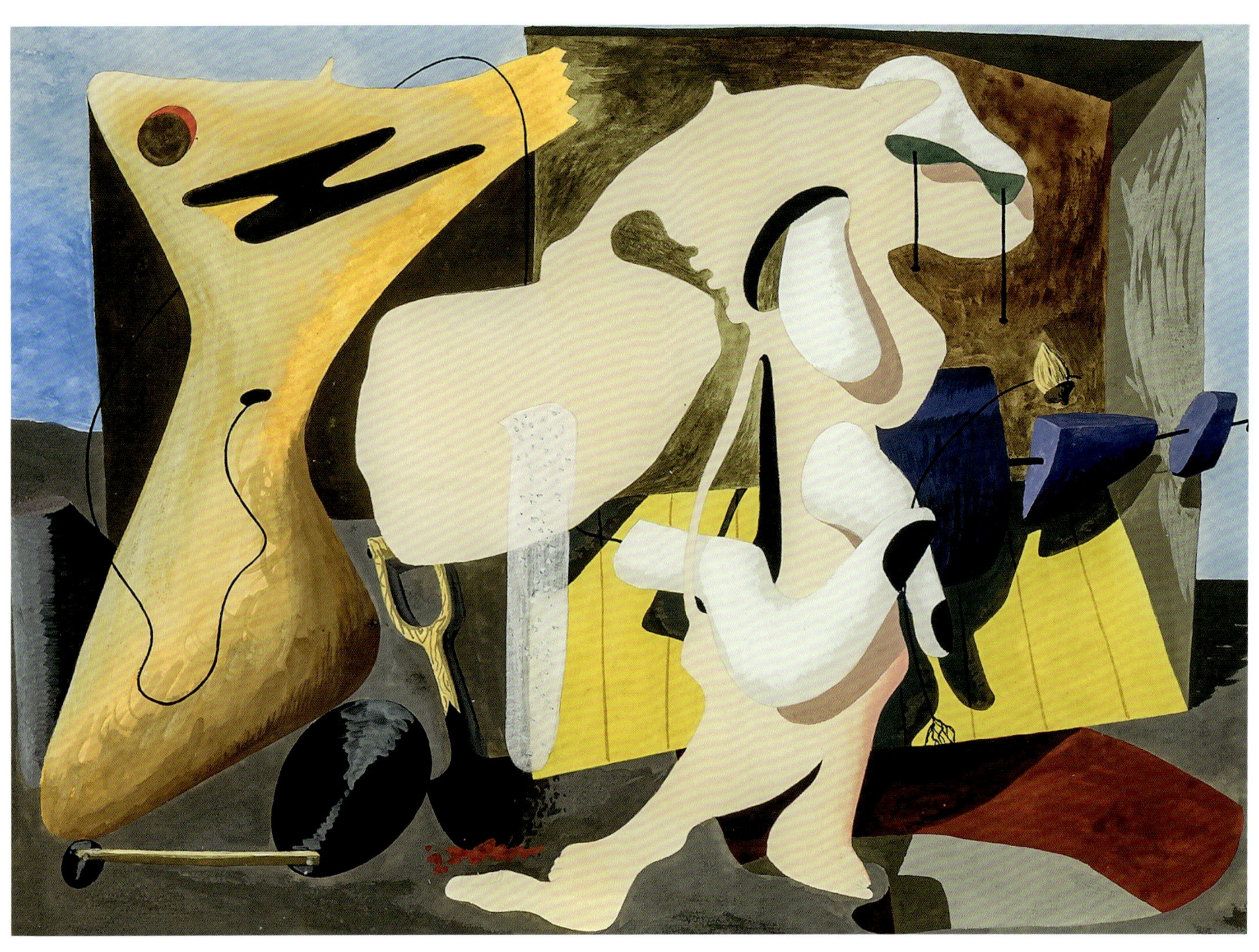

18 *The Mother (Makes the Son)*
Plants the Seed, 1937.
Gouache and graphite on paper,
$10\frac{3}{8} \times 14\frac{5}{8}$ in. (26.4 × 37.2 cm).

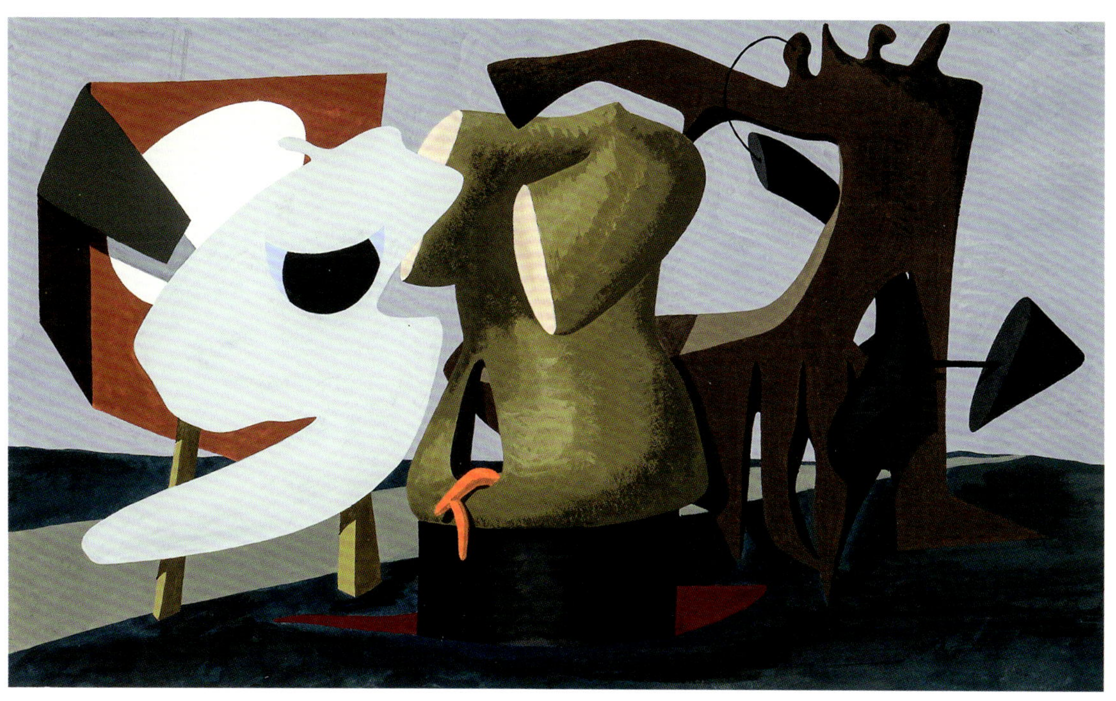

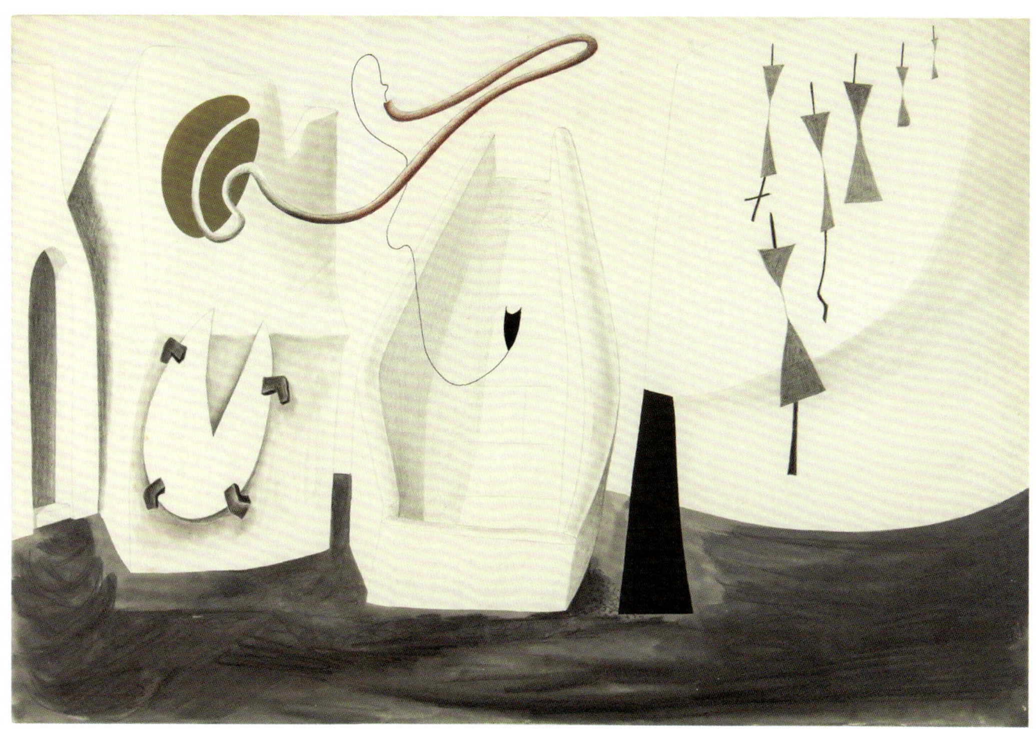

19 *The Sons Await Tradition*, 1937.
Gouache on paper, 9¼ × 16 in.
(23.5 × 40.6 cm).

20 *Untitled*, ca. 1937.
Graphite, ink, and watercolor
on paper, 12⁷⁄₁₆ × 18½ in.
(31.8 × 47 cm).

21 *Precinct*, 1938.
Gouache and watercolor on paper,
18½ × 27 in. (47 × 68.6 cm).

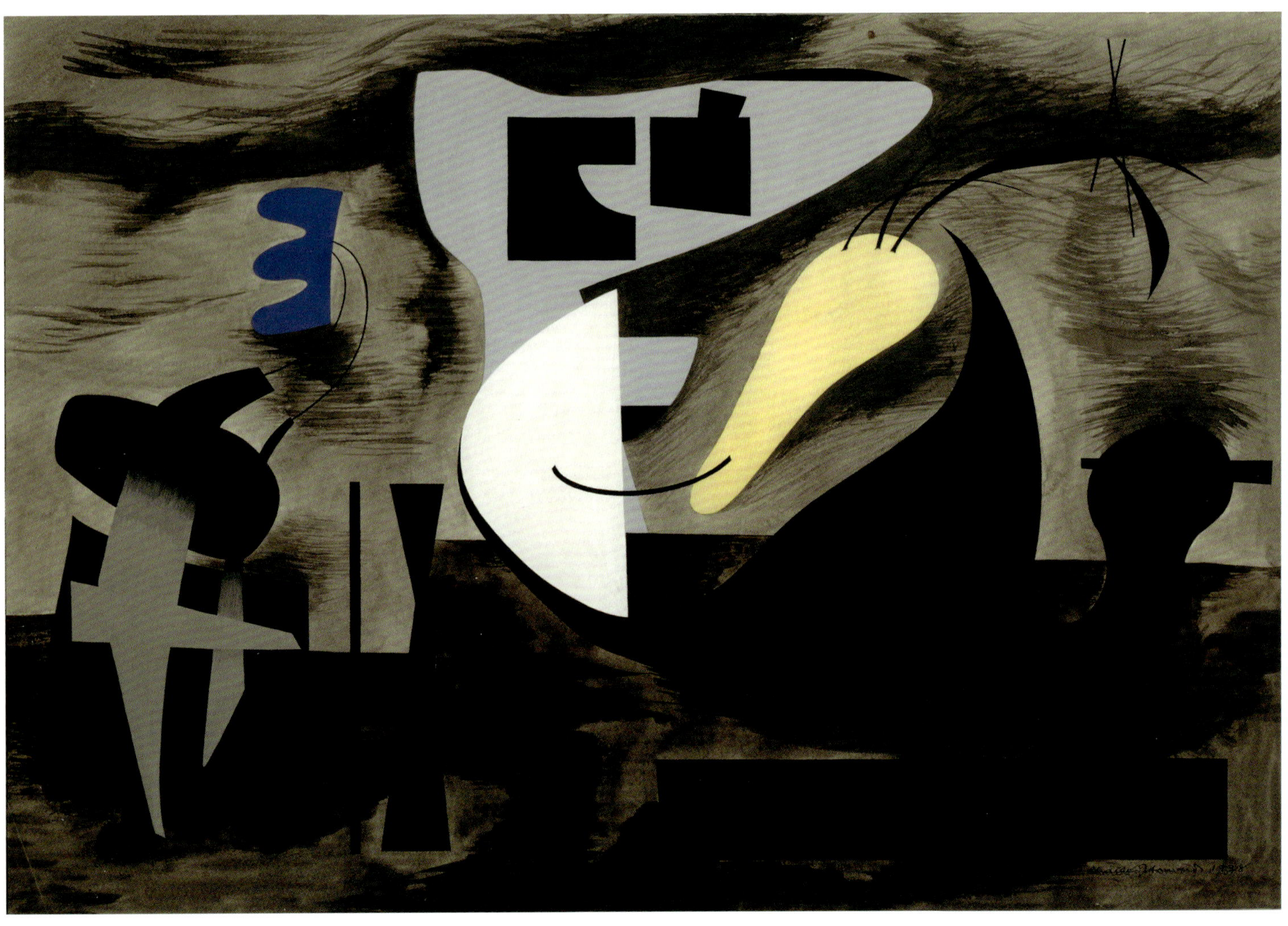

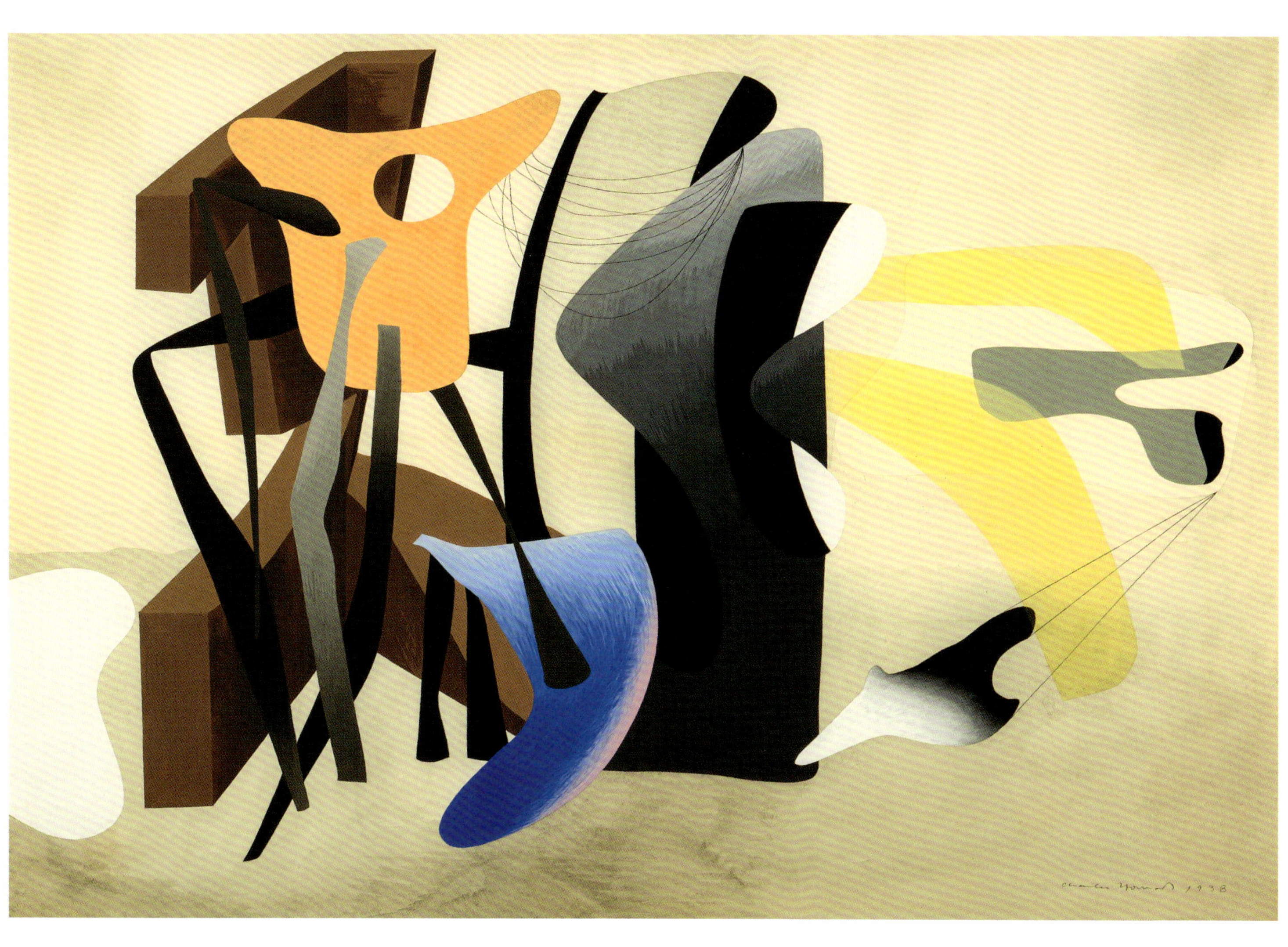

22 *Presage*, 1938.
Gouache, watercolor, ink, and
graphite on paper, 14⅞ × 22 in.
(37.8 × 55.9 cm).

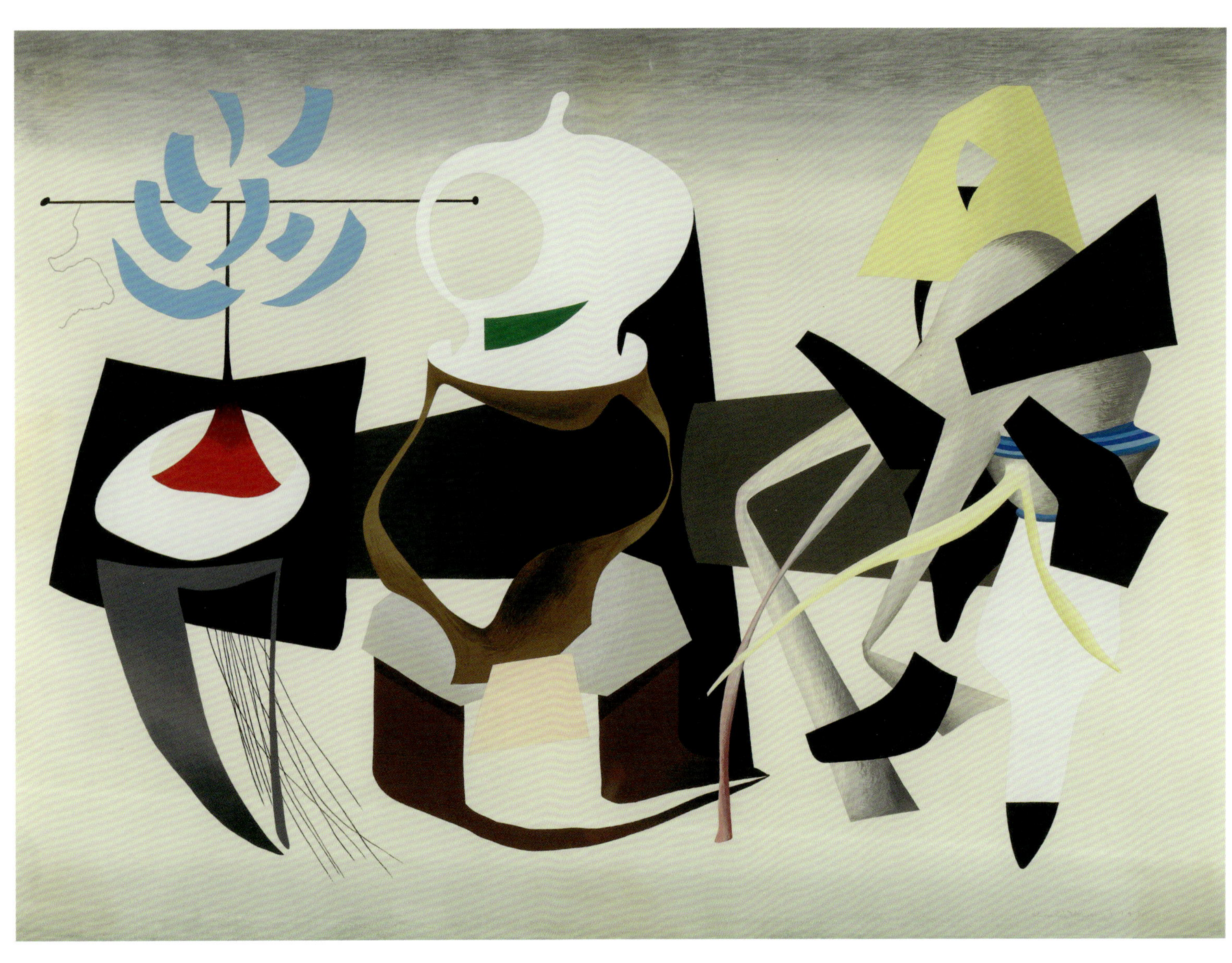

23 *The Cage*, 1938.
Tempera and watercolor on paper,
21⅝ × 29⅝ in. (54.9 × 75.3 cm).

24 *Elevation*, 1939.
Gouache and graphite on paper,
21⅜ × 29½ in. (54.3 × 74.9 cm).

25 *Hare Corner*, 1939.
Gouache and graphite on paper,
26⅝ × 35⅞ in. (67.6 × 90.9 cm).

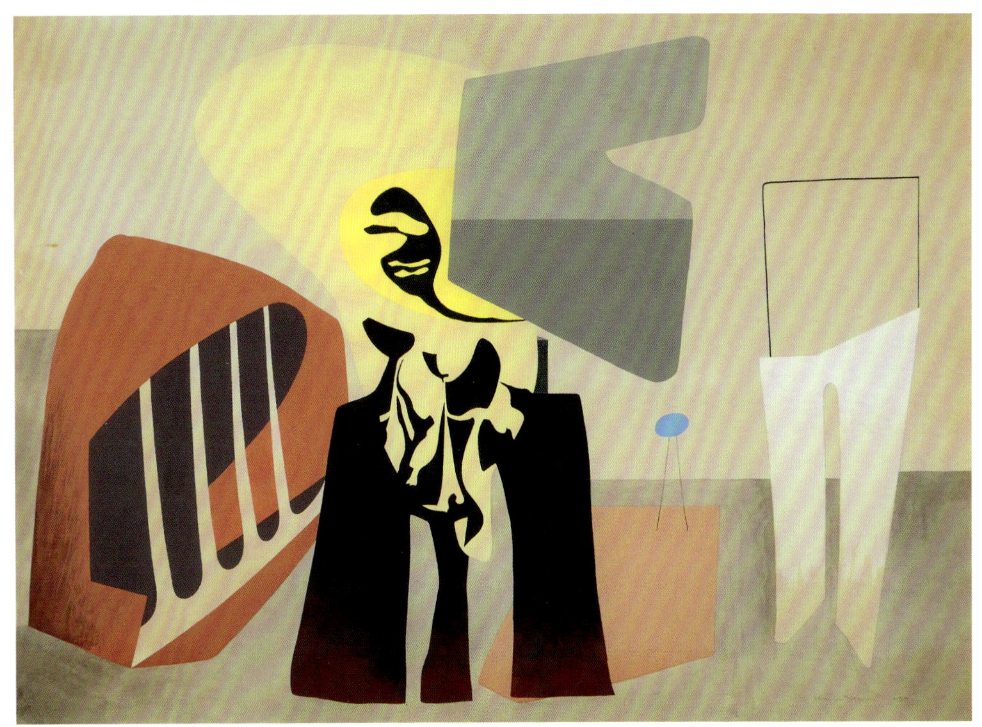

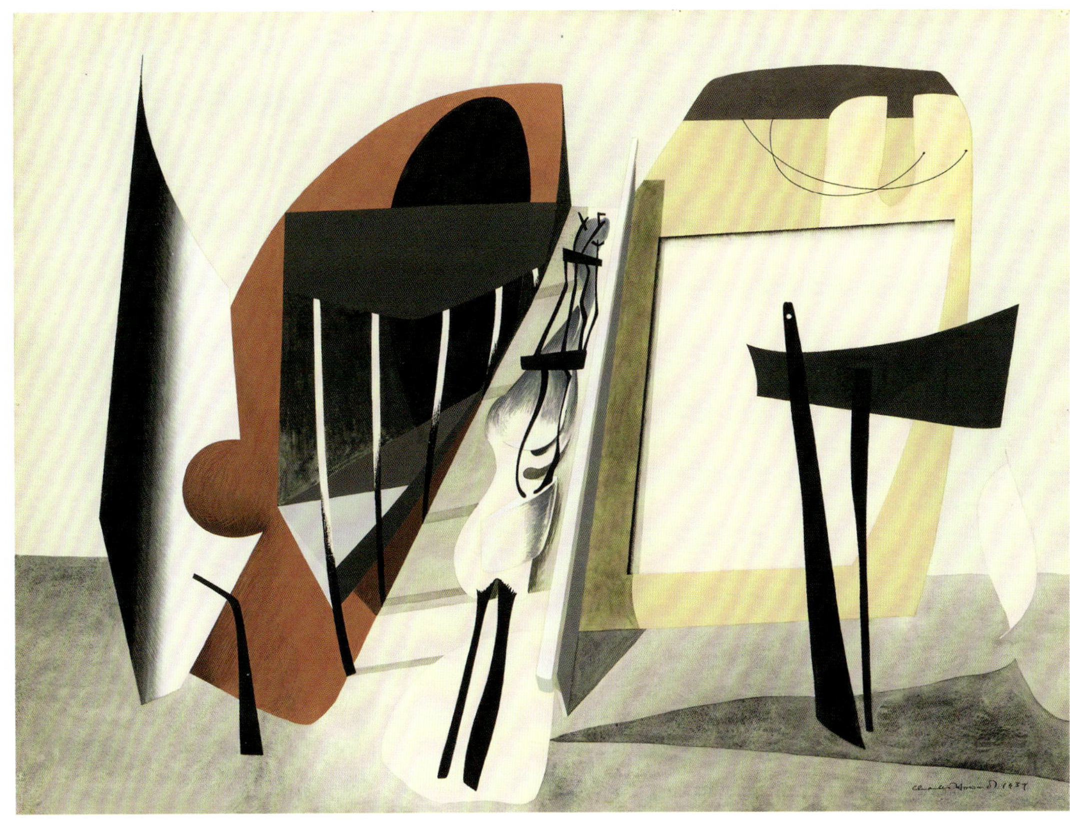

26 *The Dove*, 1939.
Oil on canvas, 11¹⁵⁄₁₆ × 13¹⁵⁄₁₆ in.
(32.4 × 51.8 cm).

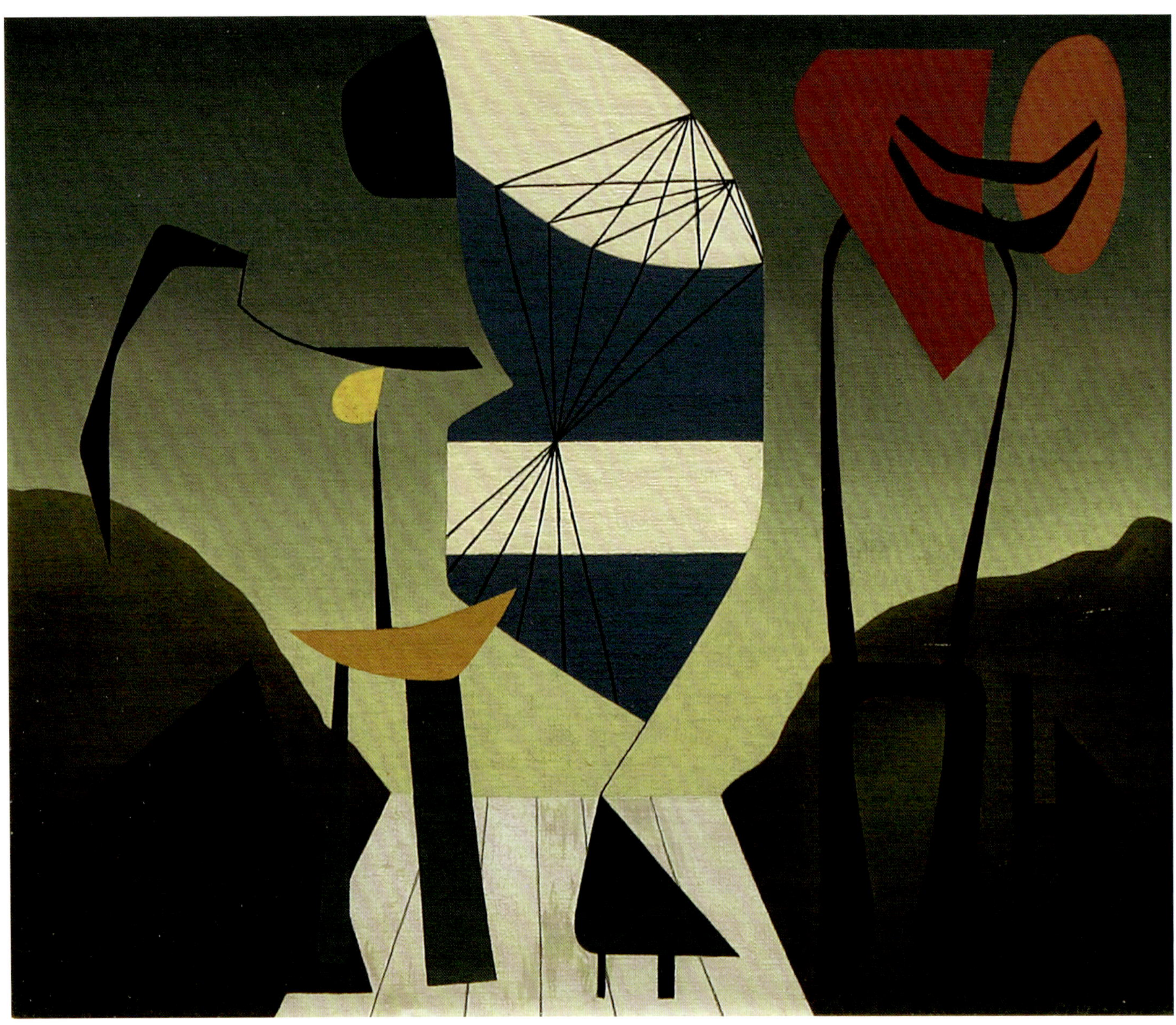

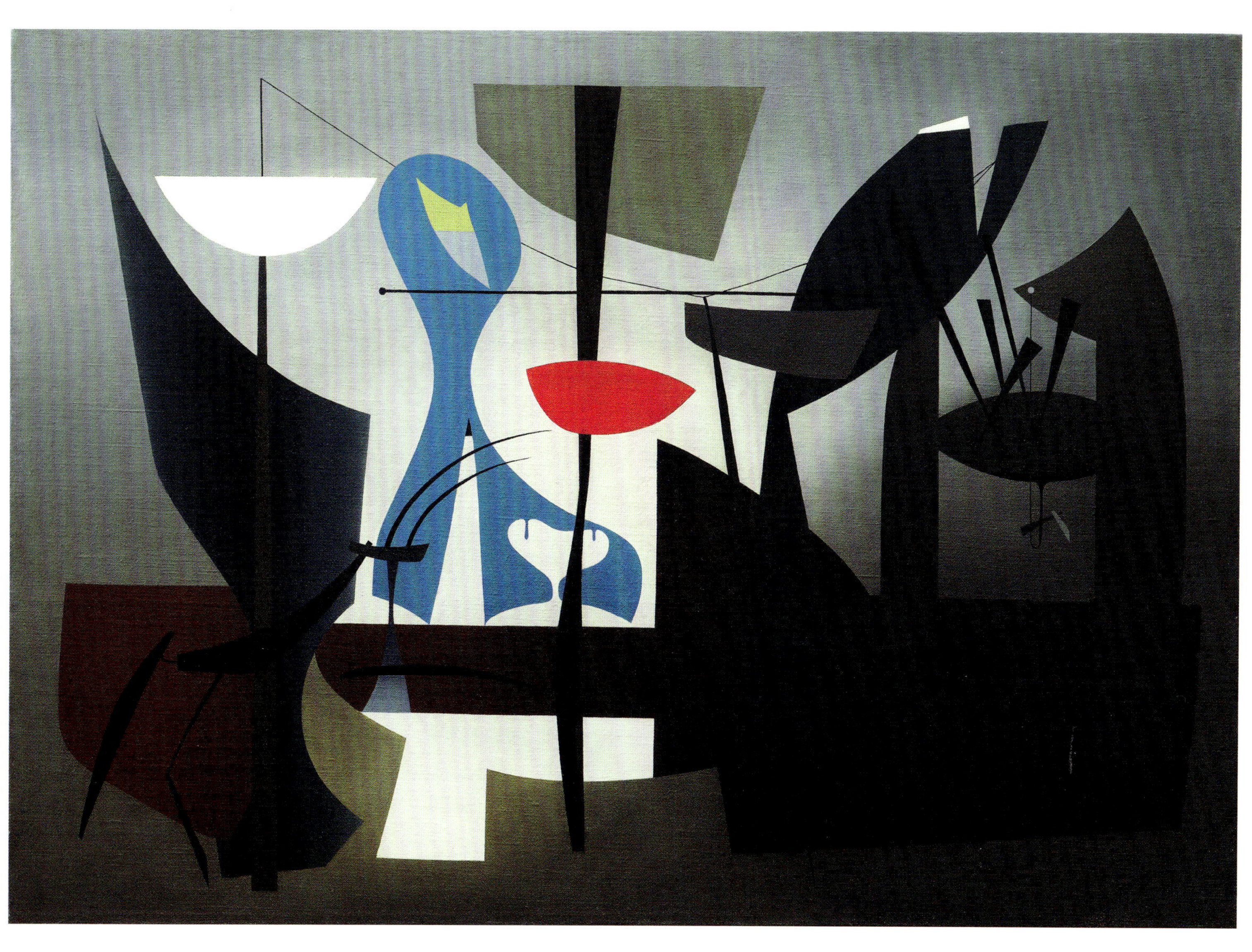

27 *First War Winter*, 1939–40.
Oil on canvas, 24¼ × 34 in.
(61.6 × 86.4 cm).

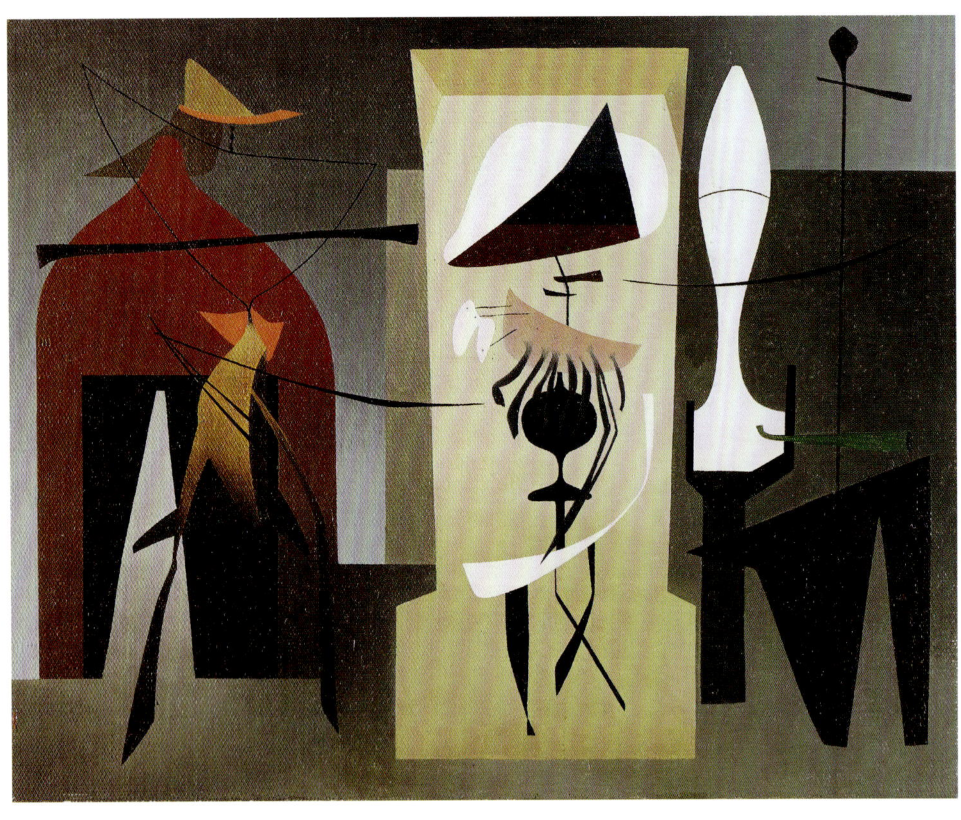

28 *Bivouac*, 1940.
Oil on board, 16 × 20 in.
(40.6 × 50.8 cm).

29 *Generation*, 1940.
Oil on canvas, 22¾ × 25¾ in.
(57.8 × 65.4 cm).

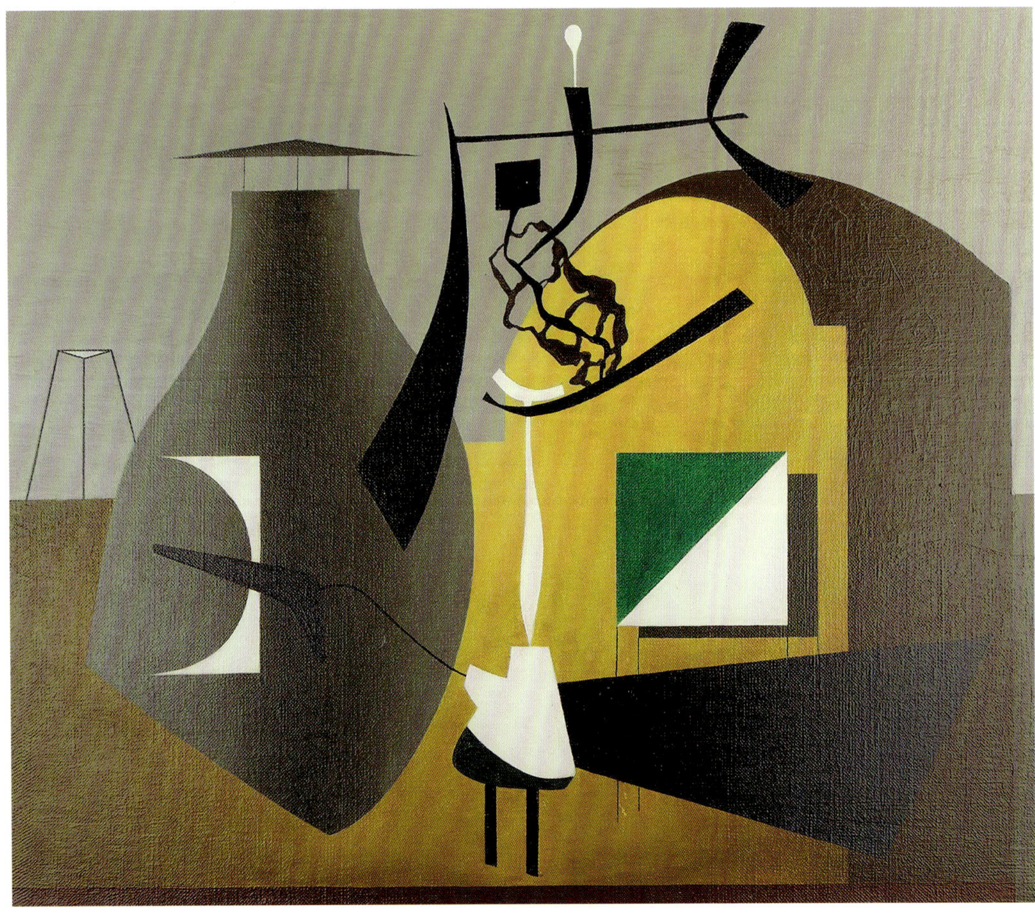

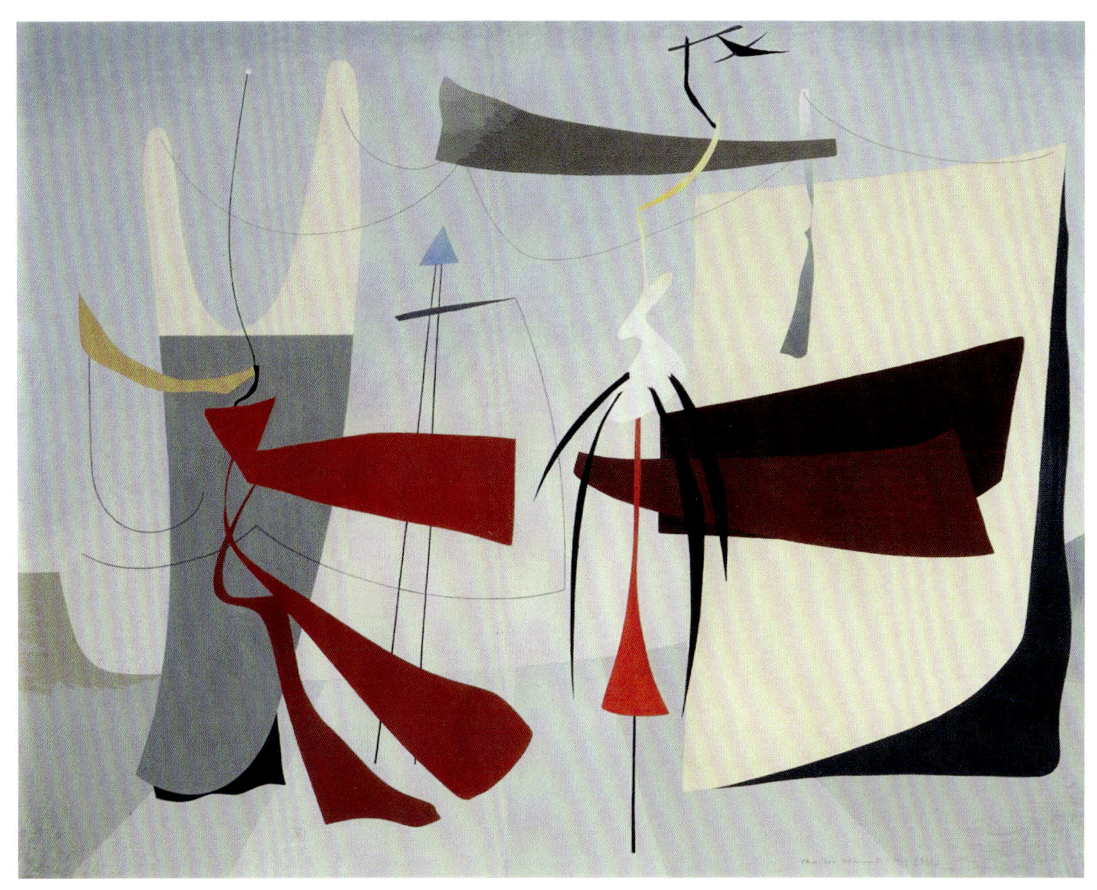

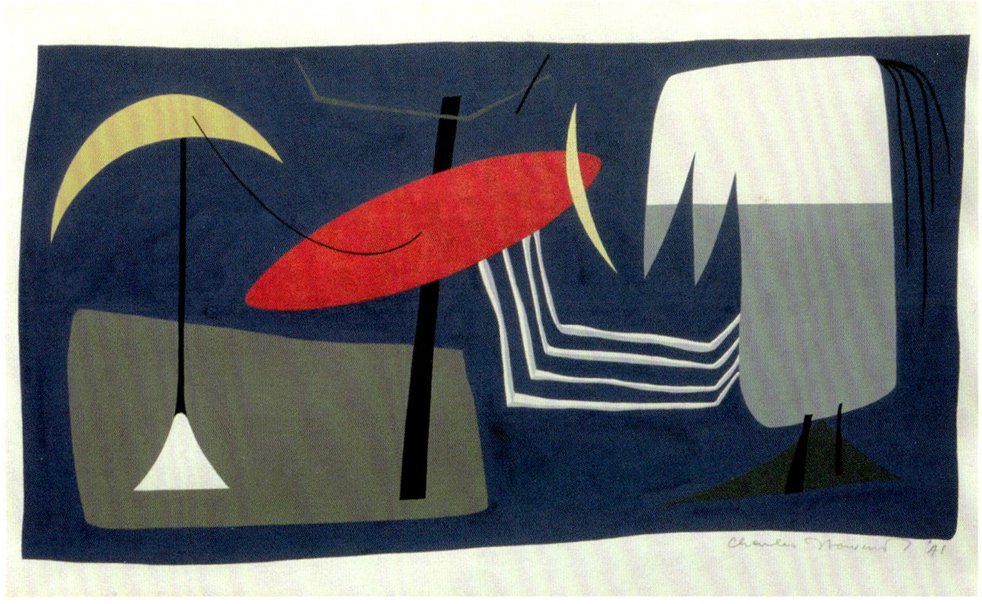

30 *Esplanade*, 1941.
Gouache on paper, 20⅝ × 27 in.
(52.4 × 68.6 cm).

31 *Hieroglyph*, 1941.
Gouache on paper, 15½ × 22⅝ in.
(39.4 × 57.5 cm).

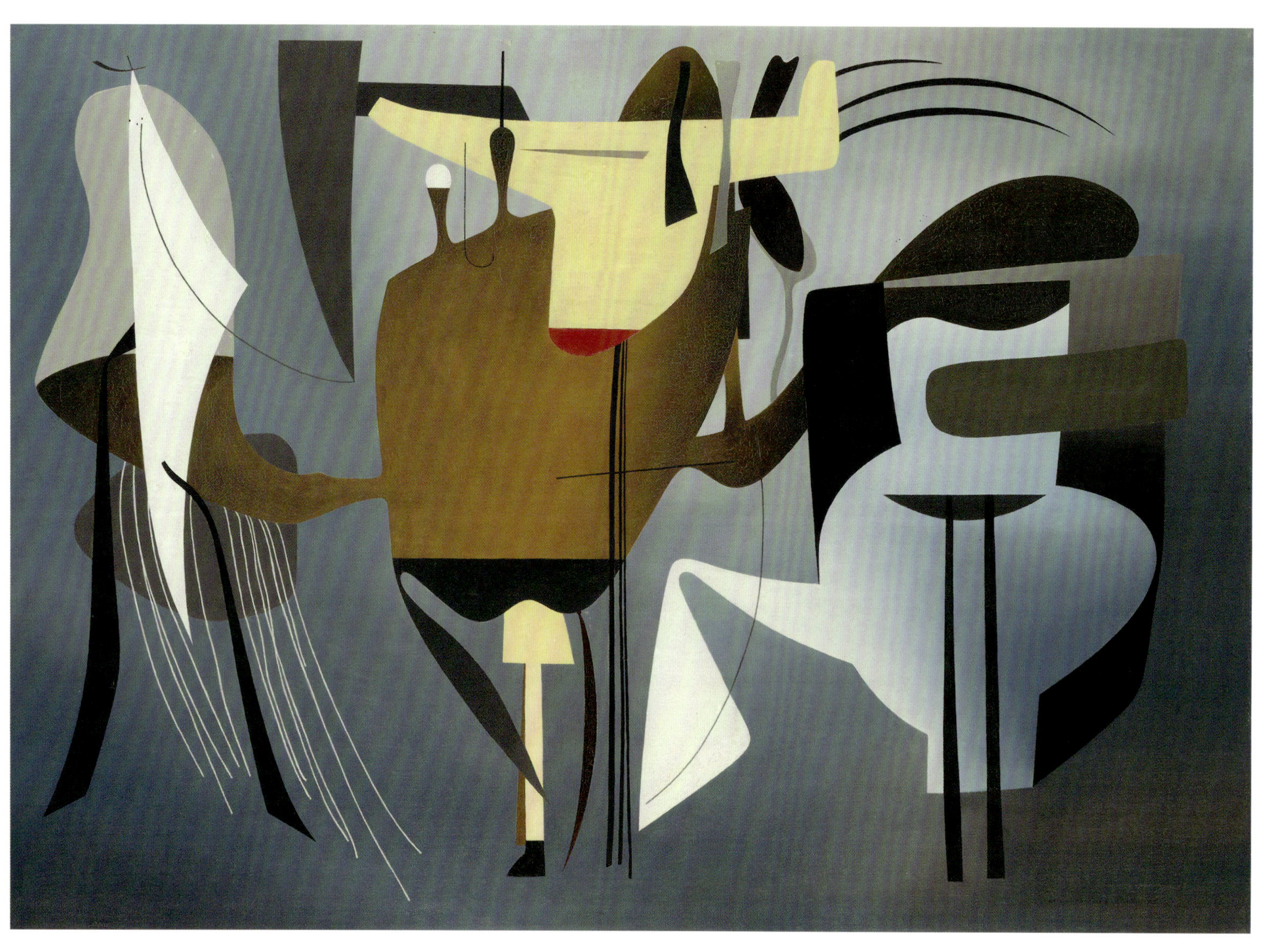

32 *Trinity*, 1941.
Oil on canvas, 24 × 34 in.
(61 × 86.4 cm).

33 *Prescience*, 1942.
Oil on canvas, 28¼ × 40½ in.
(52.4 × 102.9 cm).

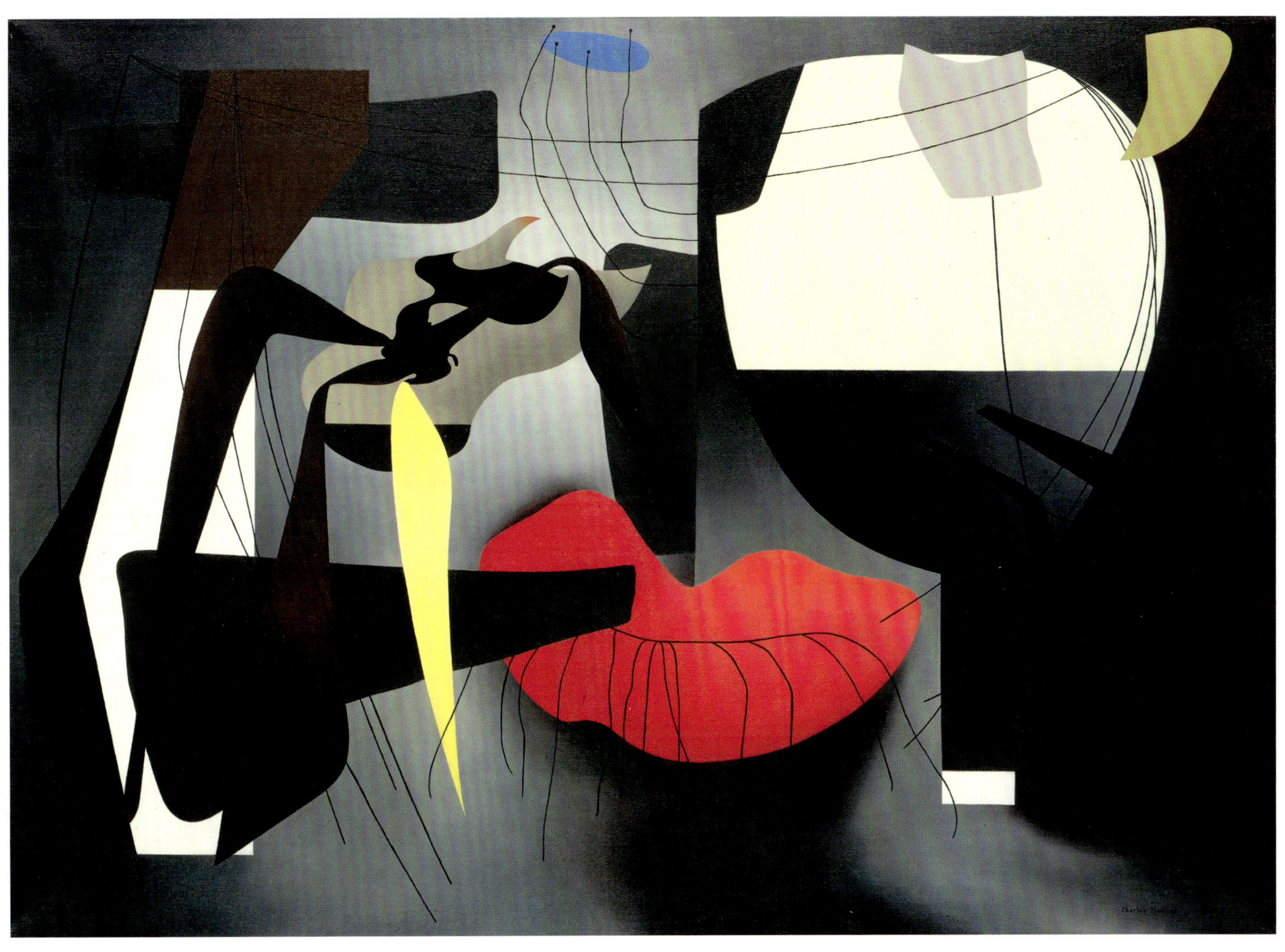

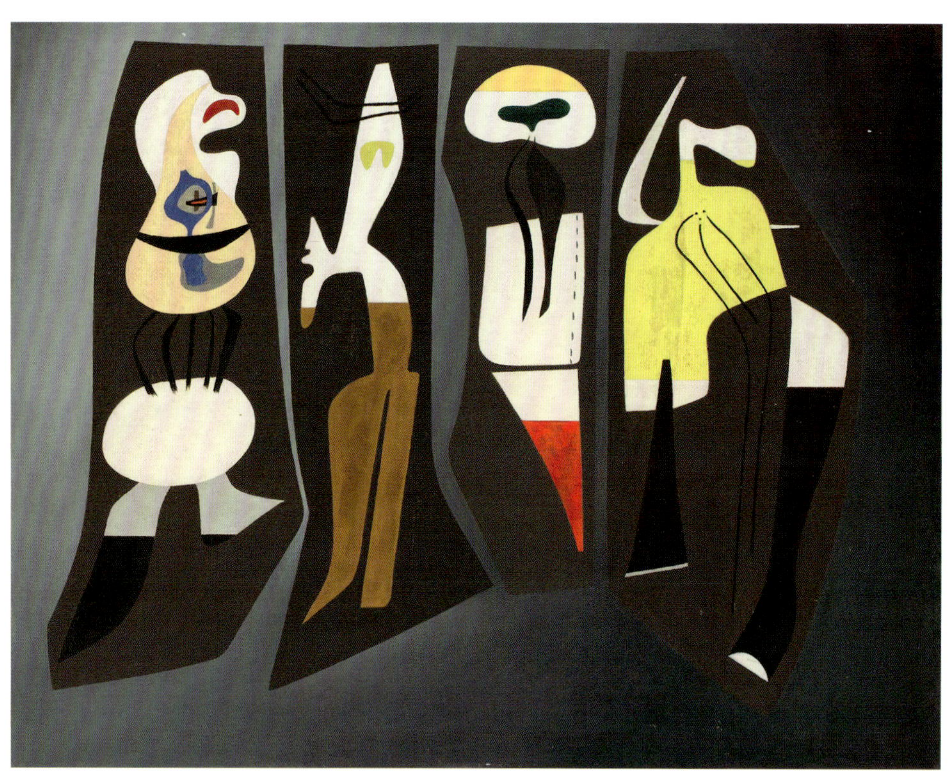

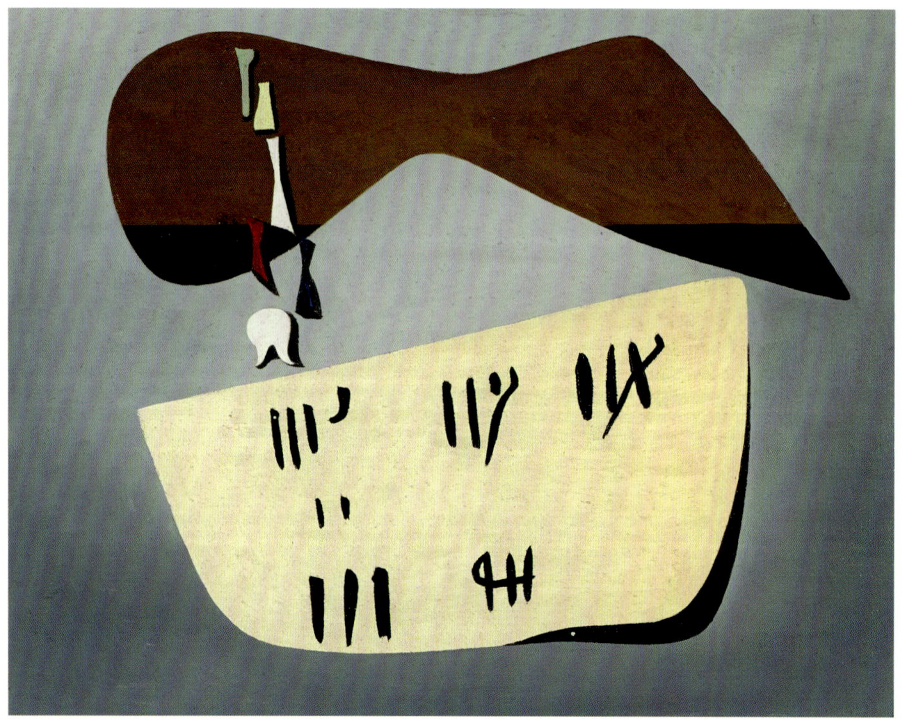

34 *Departure*, ca. 1943.
Oil on canvas, 13¹⁵⁄₁₆ × 17¹⁵⁄₁₆ in.
(35.4 × 45.6 cm).

35 *Glyptic*, 1943.
Oil on canvas board, 9 × 12 in.
(22.9 × 30.5 cm).

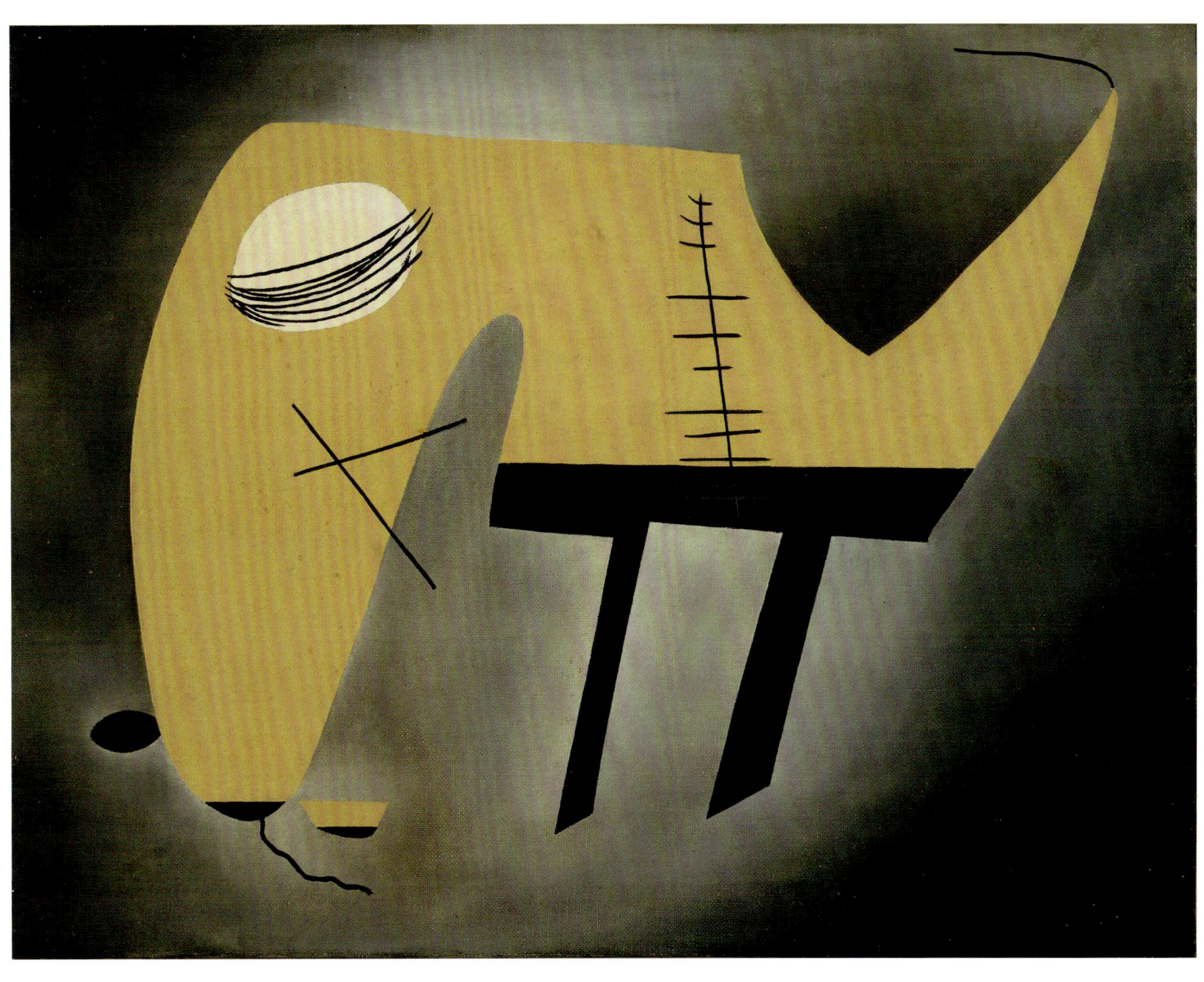

36 *Untitled*, 1944.
Oil on canvas, 12 × 15⅞ in.
(30.5 × 40.3 cm).

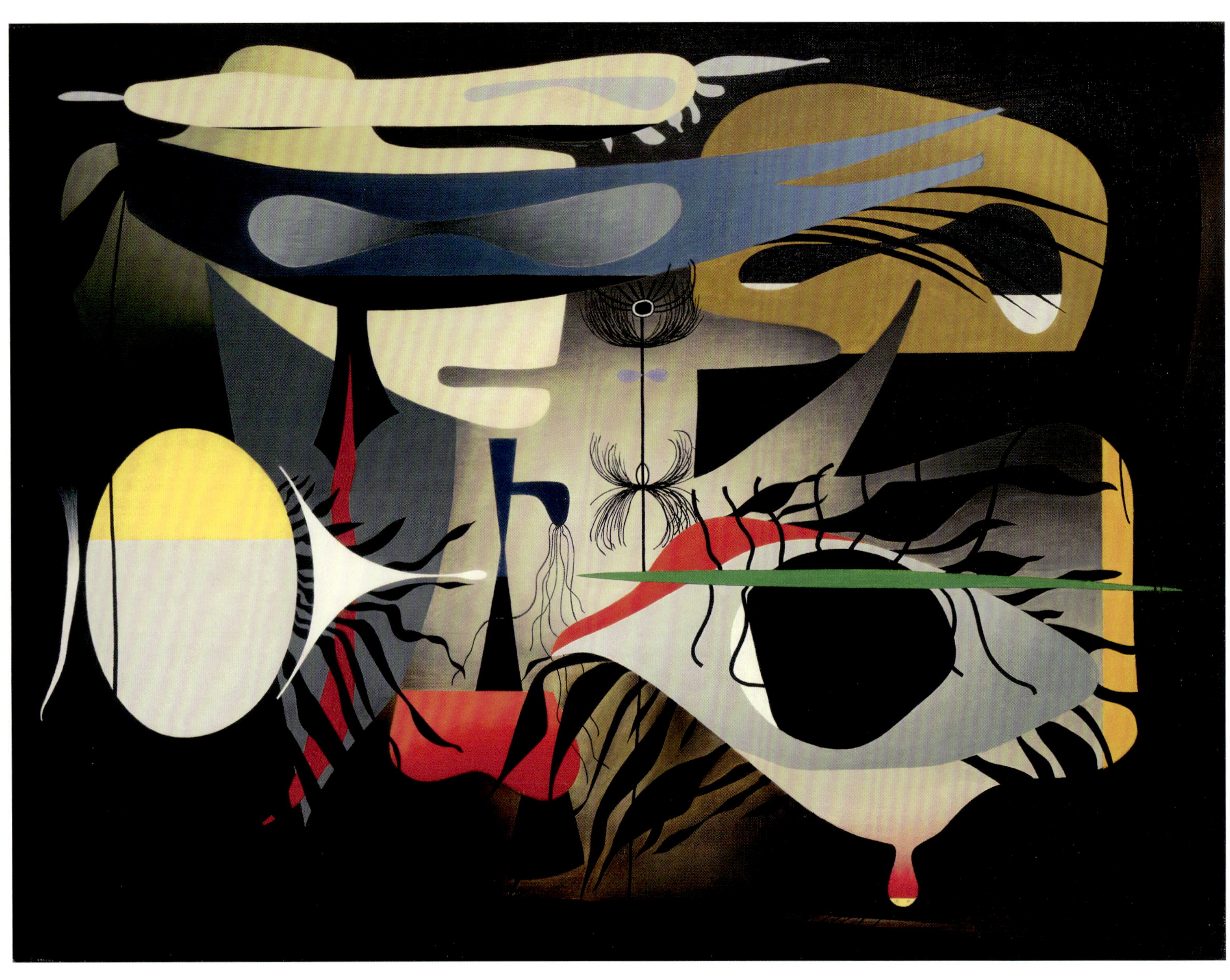

37 *Dove Love*, 1945.
Oil on canvas, 18 × 24⅛ in.
(45.7 × 61.3 cm).

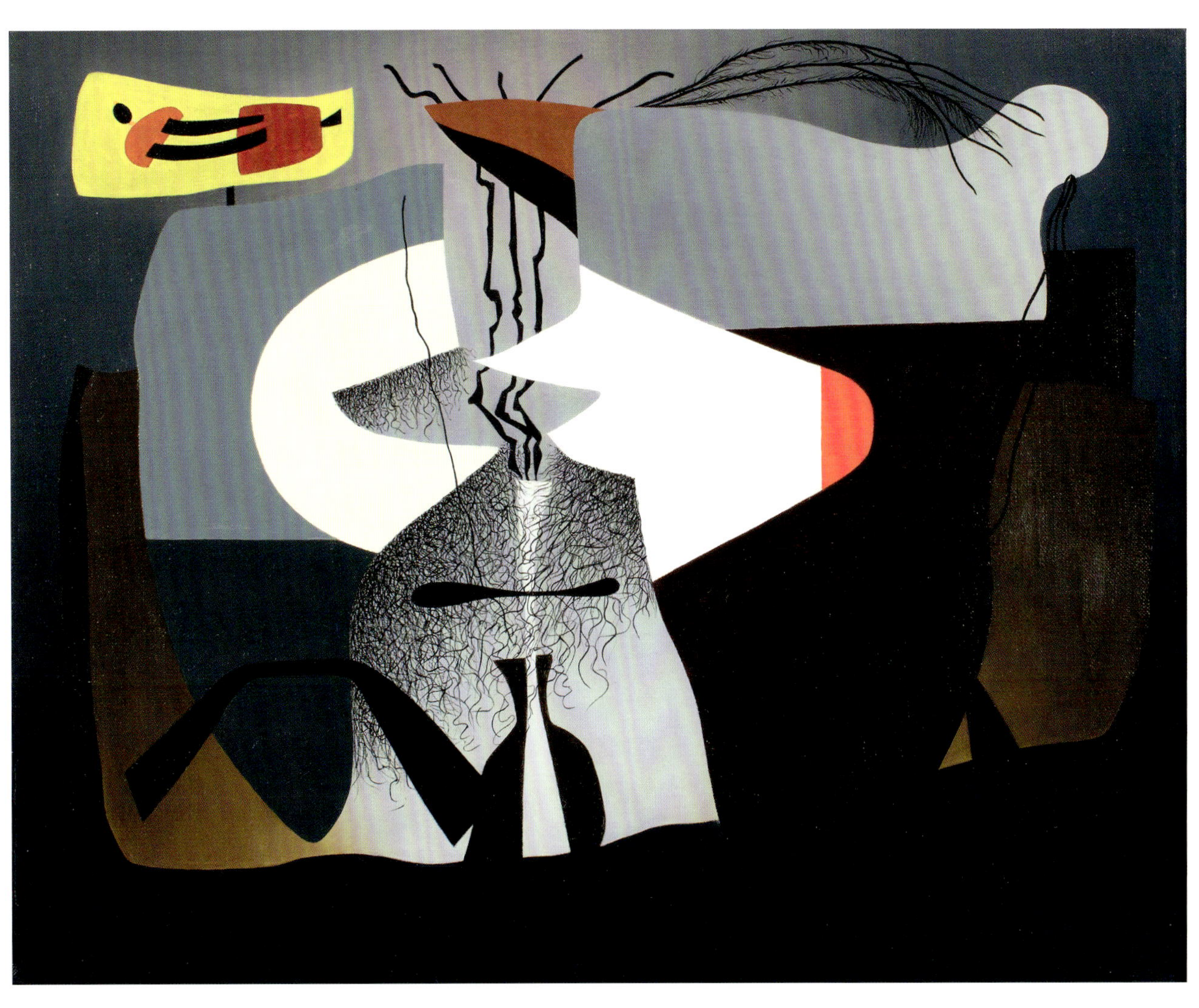

38 *The Medusa*, 1945.
Oil on canvas, 14$\frac{1}{8}$ × 18$\frac{3}{16}$ in.
(35.9 × 48.3 cm).

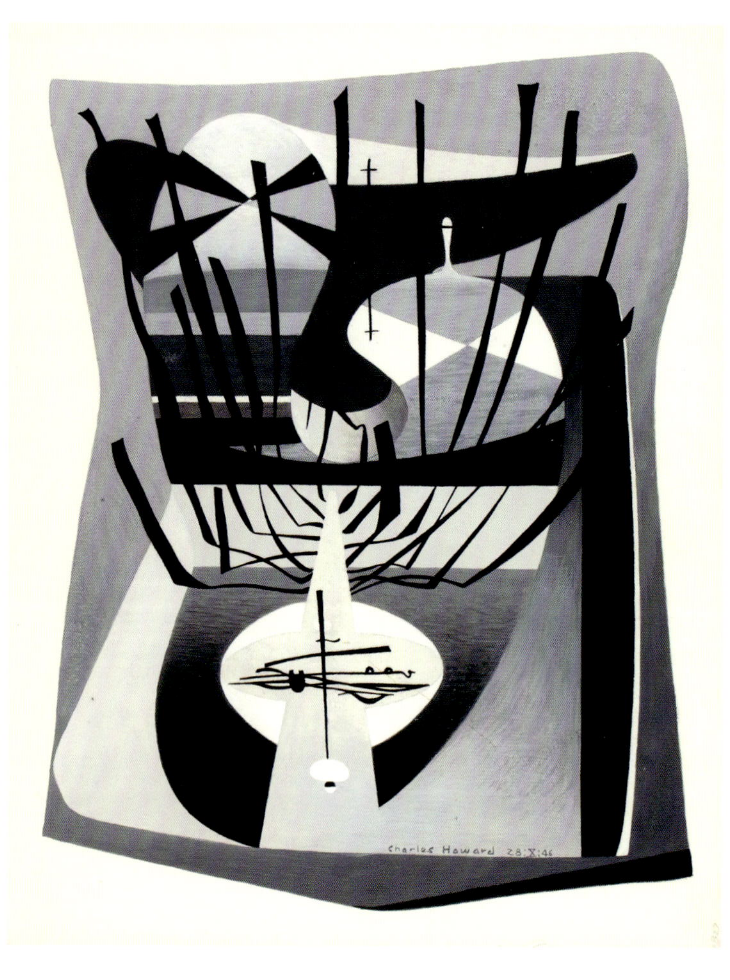

39 *California*, from the *United States Series*, 1946.
Gouache on paperboard,
13 × 10⅜ in. (33 × 26.4 cm).

40 *The Chain of Circumstance*, 1946.
Oil on canvas, 12⅛ × 24⅛ in.
(30.8 × 61.3 cm).

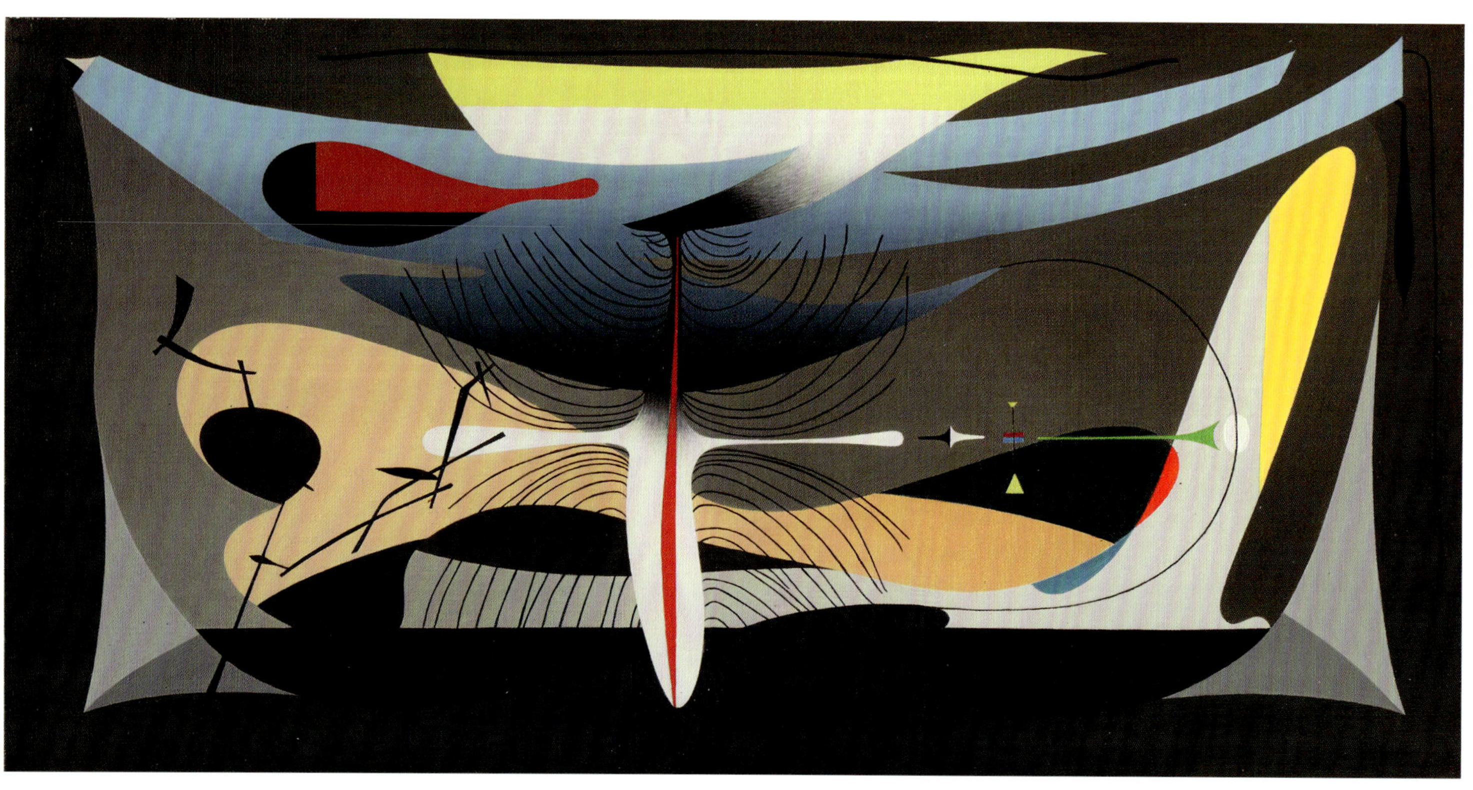

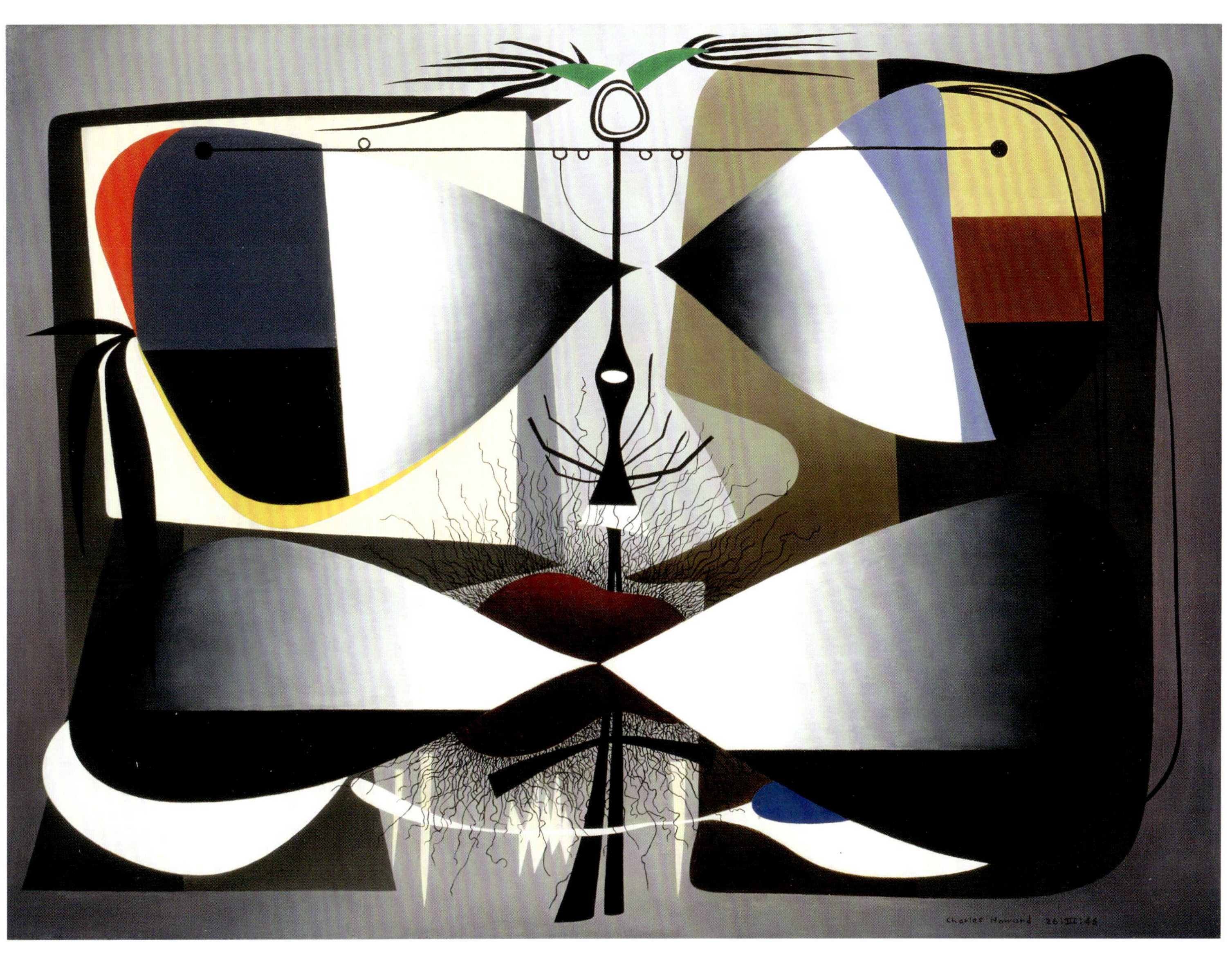

41 *The First Hypothesis*, 1946.
Oil on canvas, 16¼ × 22⅛ in.
(41.3 × 56.2 cm).

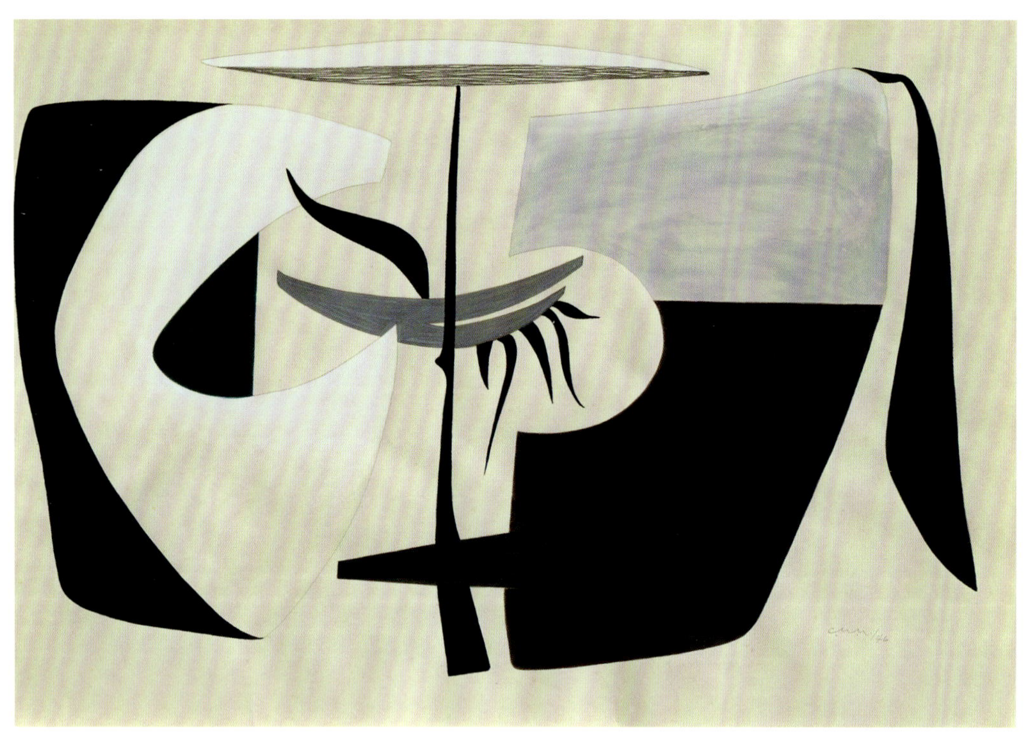

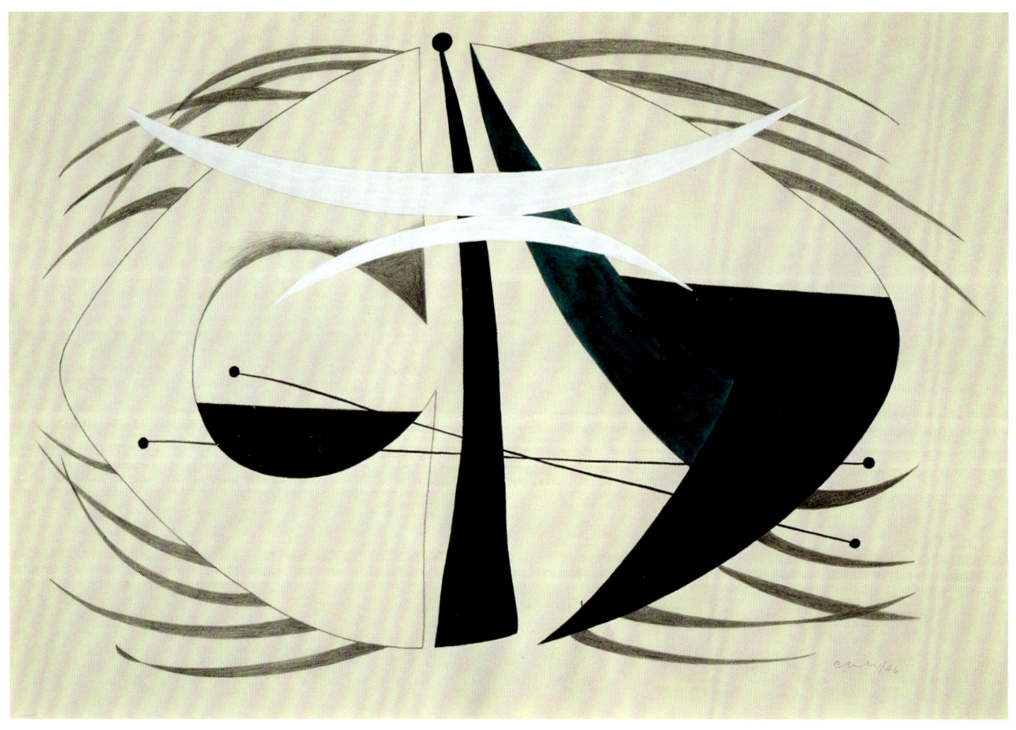

42 *Nasty 7: VII: 46*, 1946.
Gouache, pen and ink, and graphite on
paper, 15 × 21¹⁵⁄₁₆ in. (38.1 × 55.9 cm).

43 *Nasty 8: VIII: 46*, 1946.
Gouache and graphite on paper,
15 × 22 in. (38.1 × 55.9 cm).

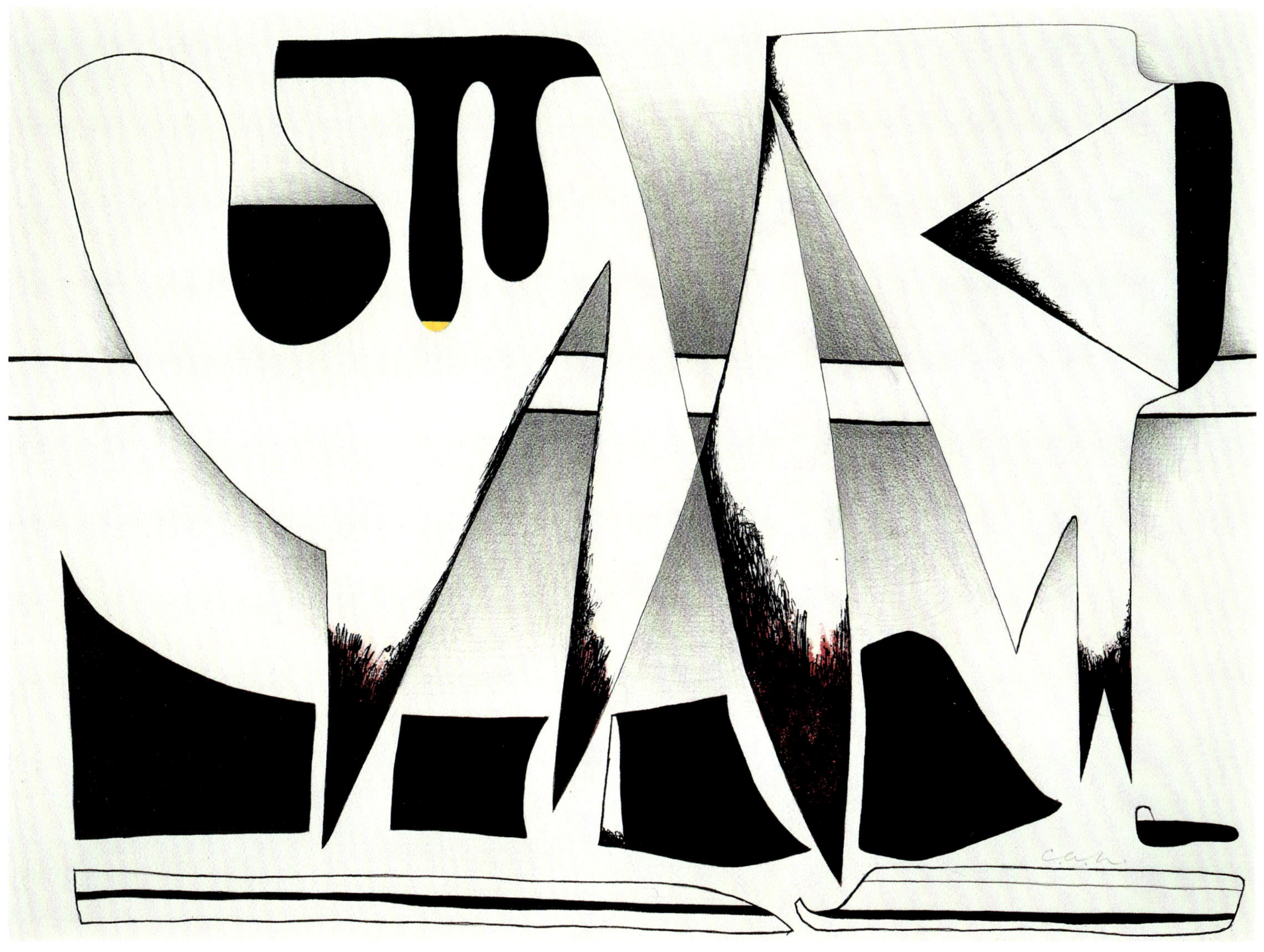

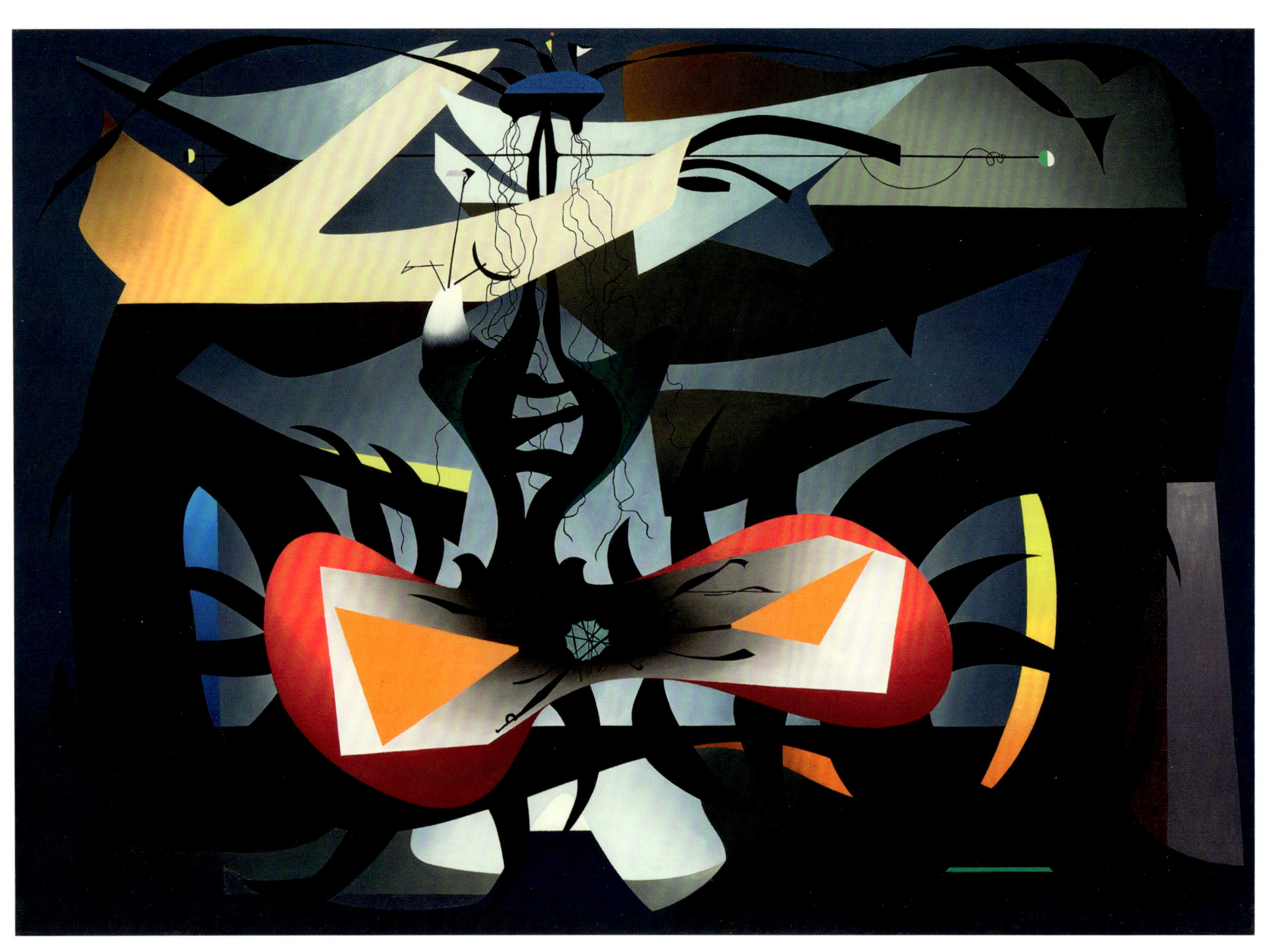

45 *The Progenitors*, 1947.
Oil on canvas, 24⅜ × 34½ in.
(61.9 × 87.6 cm).

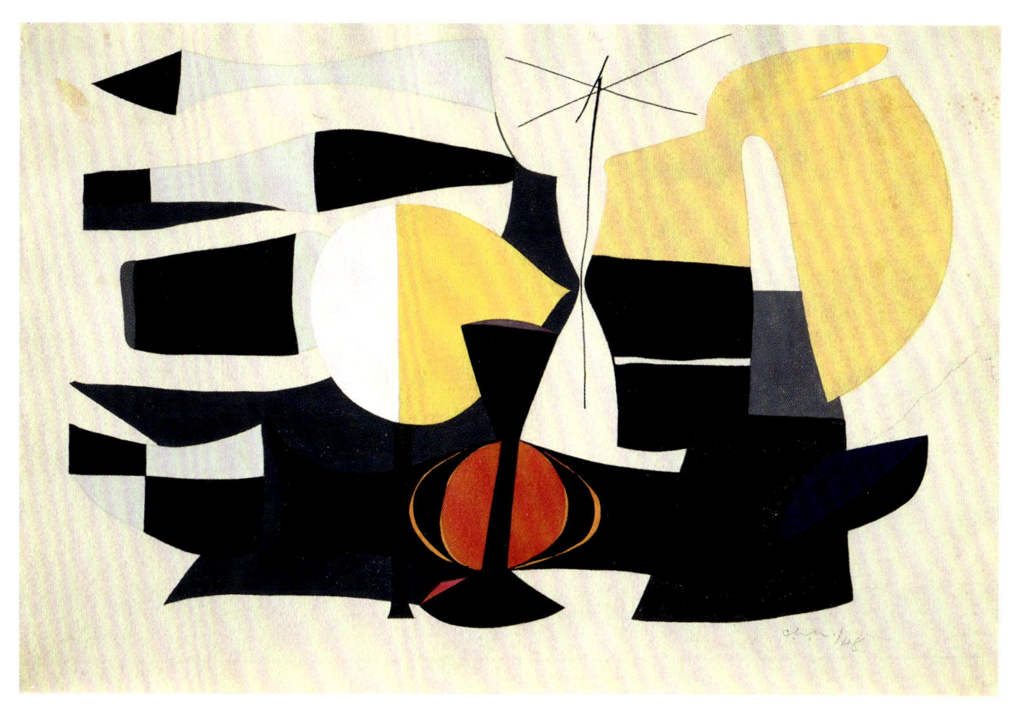

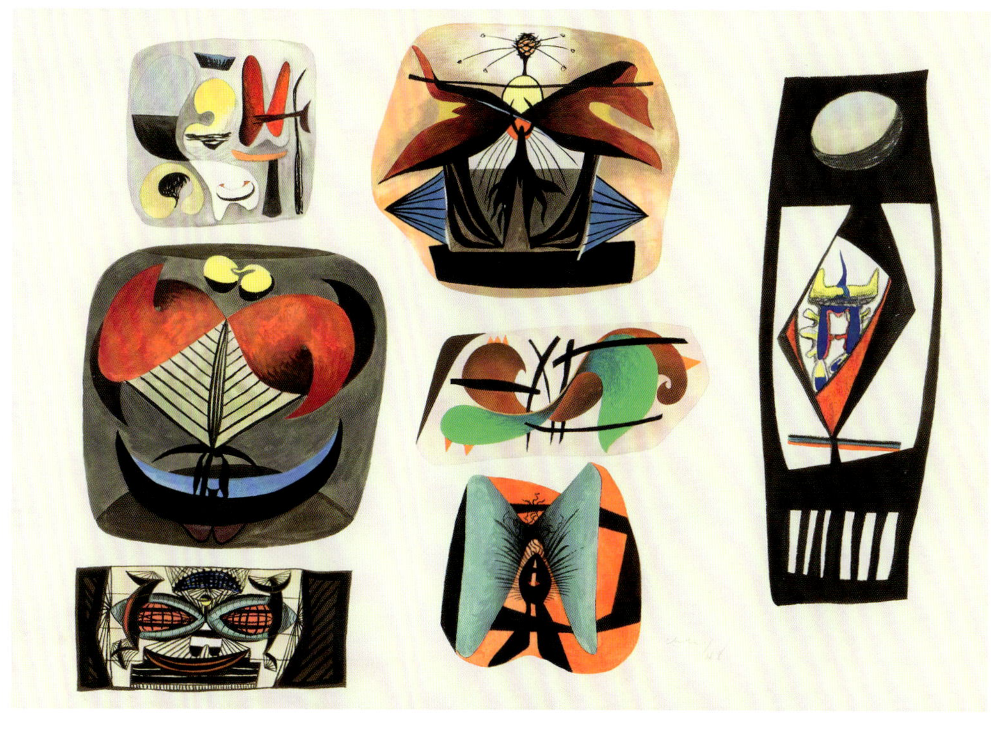

46 *The Gift*, 1948.
Gouache on paper, 13¾ × 20³⁄₁₆ in.
(34.9 × 51.3 cm).

47 *Untitled*, 1948.
Watercolor and ink on paper,
15⅜ × 21⅞ in. (39 × 55.6 cm).

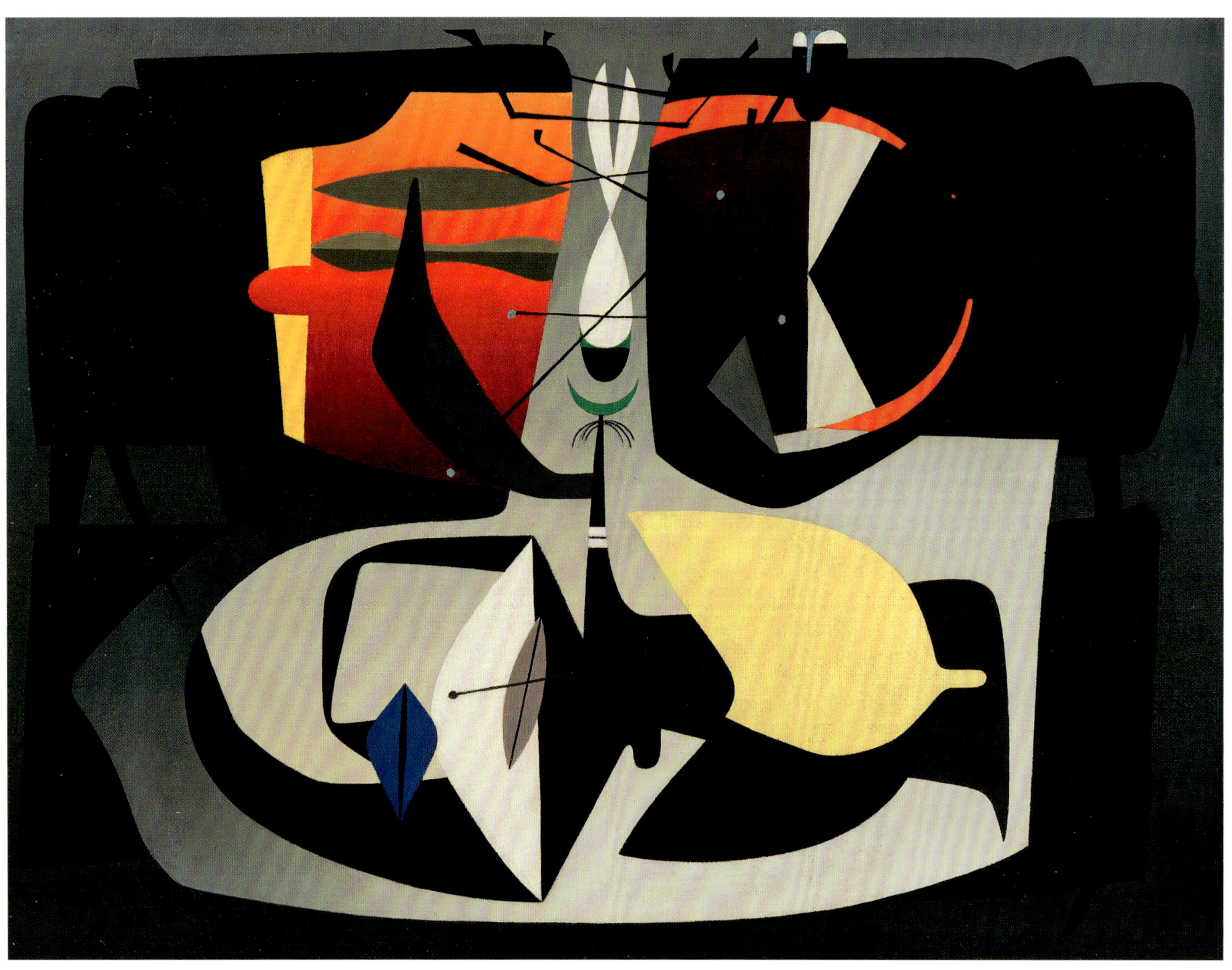

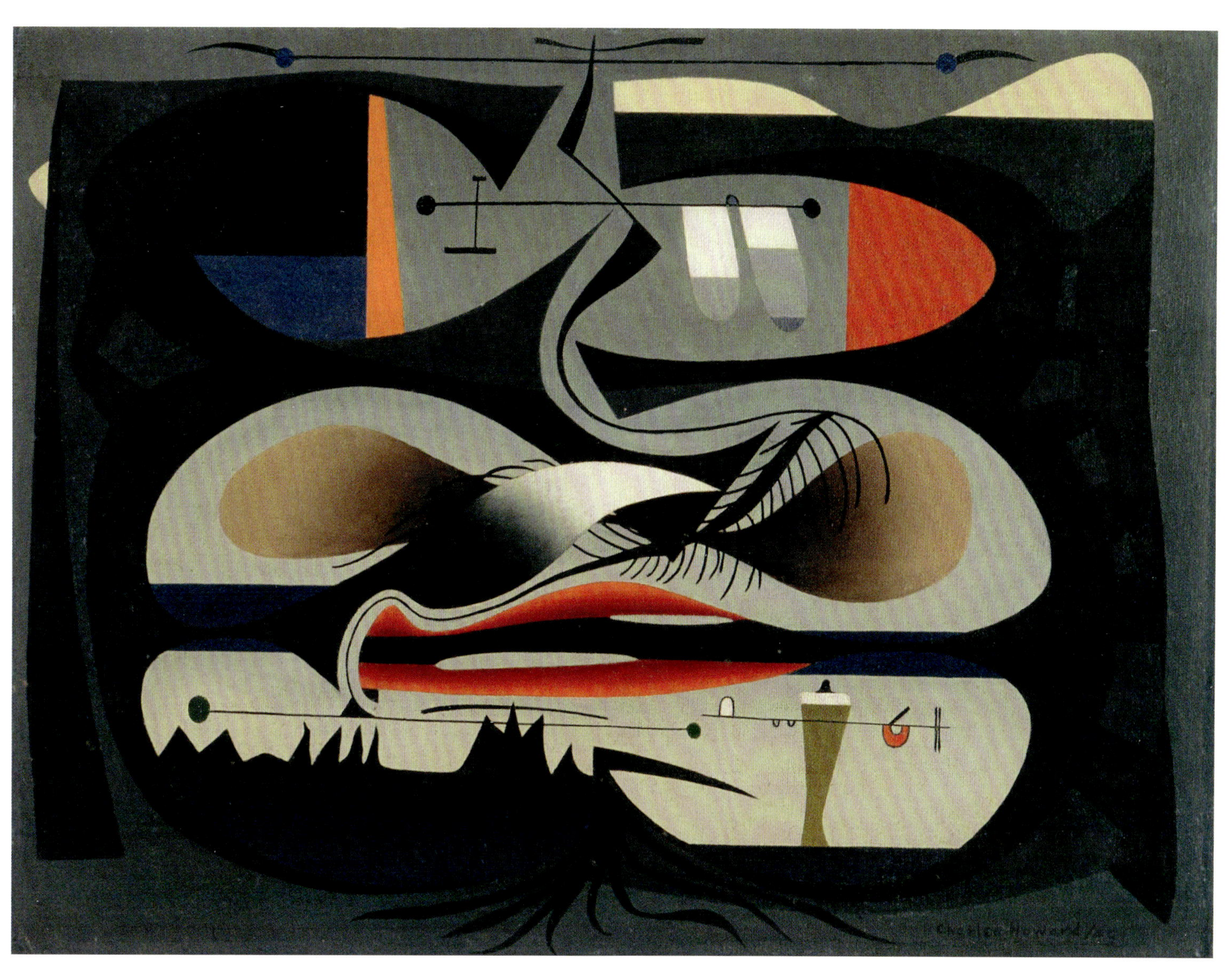

49 *The Ascending Aperture*, 1949.
Oil on canvas mounted on board,
12 × 16 in. (30.5 × 40.6 cm).

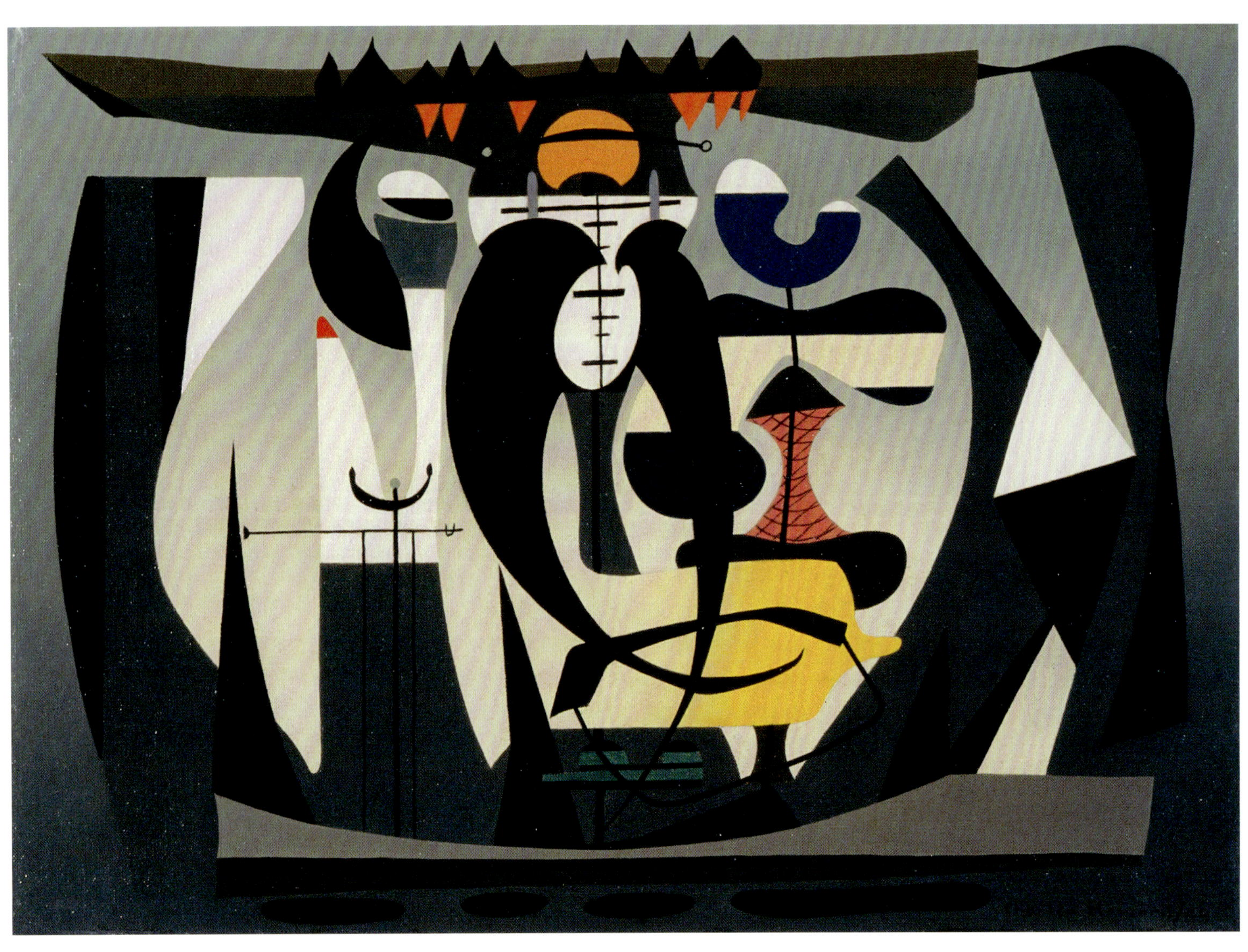

50 *The Cumulative Emblem*, 1949.
Oil on canvas, 10 × 13¹⁵⁄₁₆ in.
(25.4 × 35.6 cm).

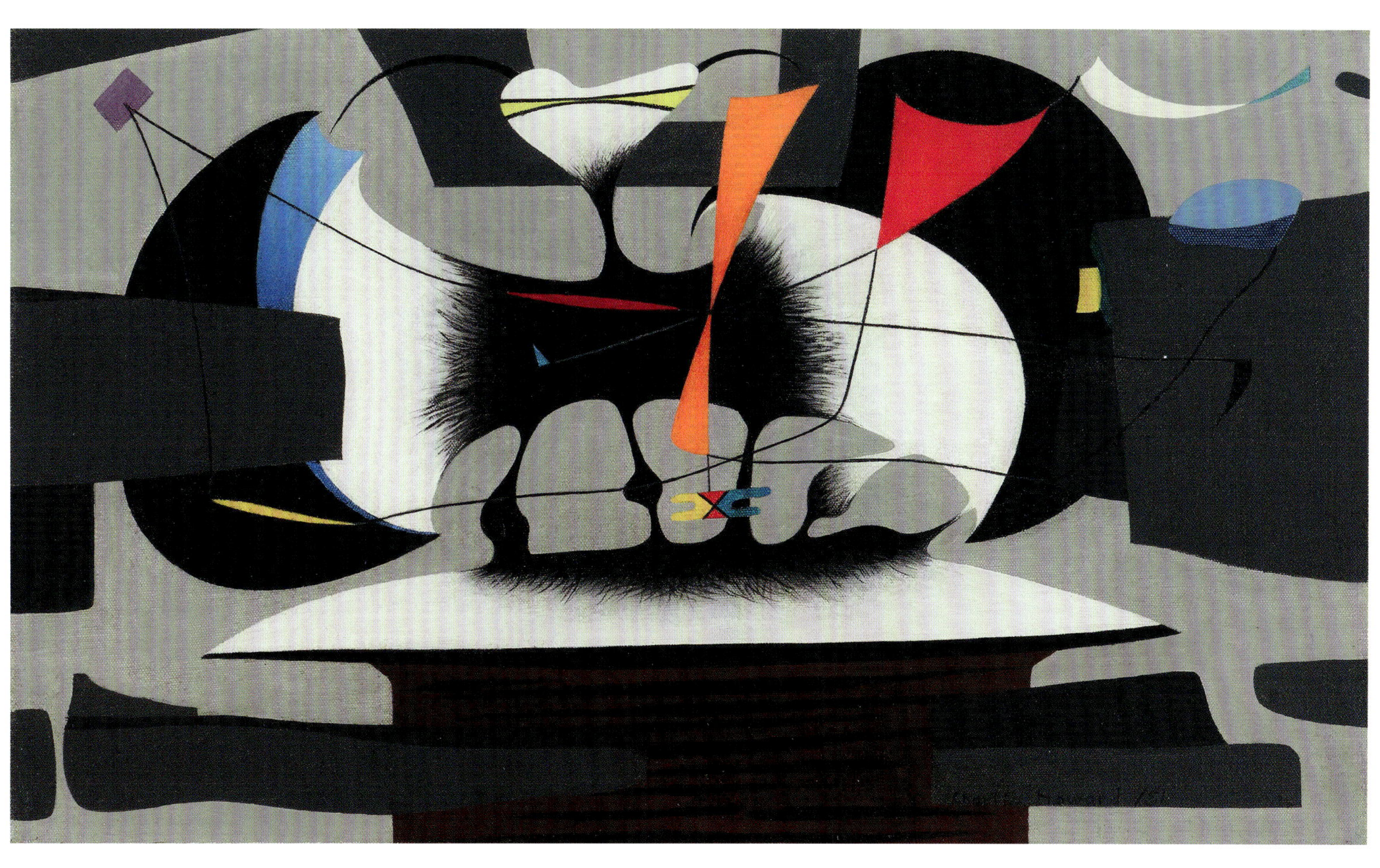

51 *Binary Armature*, 1951.
Oil on canvas, 10 × 17 in.
(25.4 × 43.2 cm).

52 *Night Painting*, 1955.
Oil on canvas, 40¼ × 57¼ in.
(102.2 × 145.4 cm).

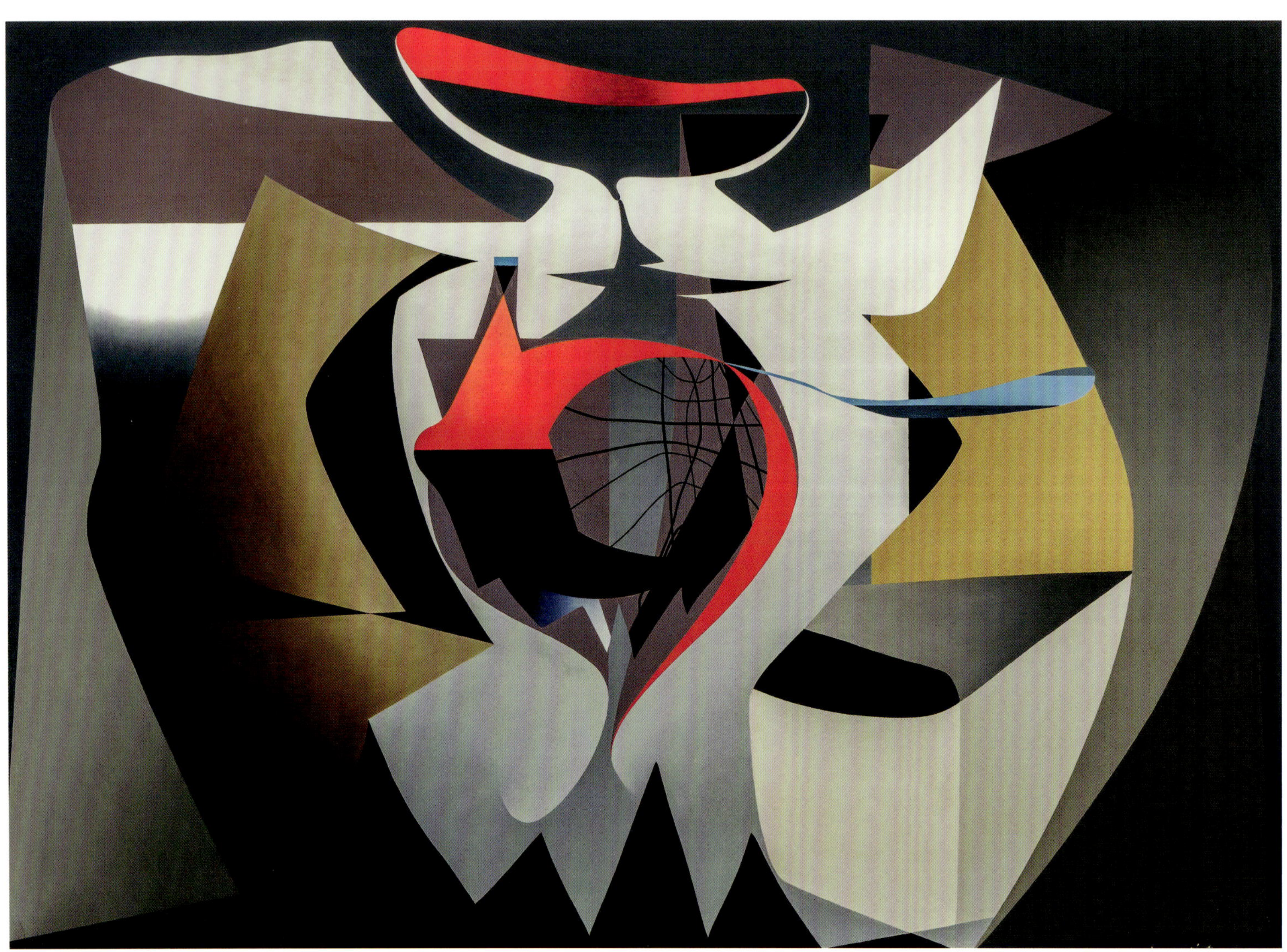

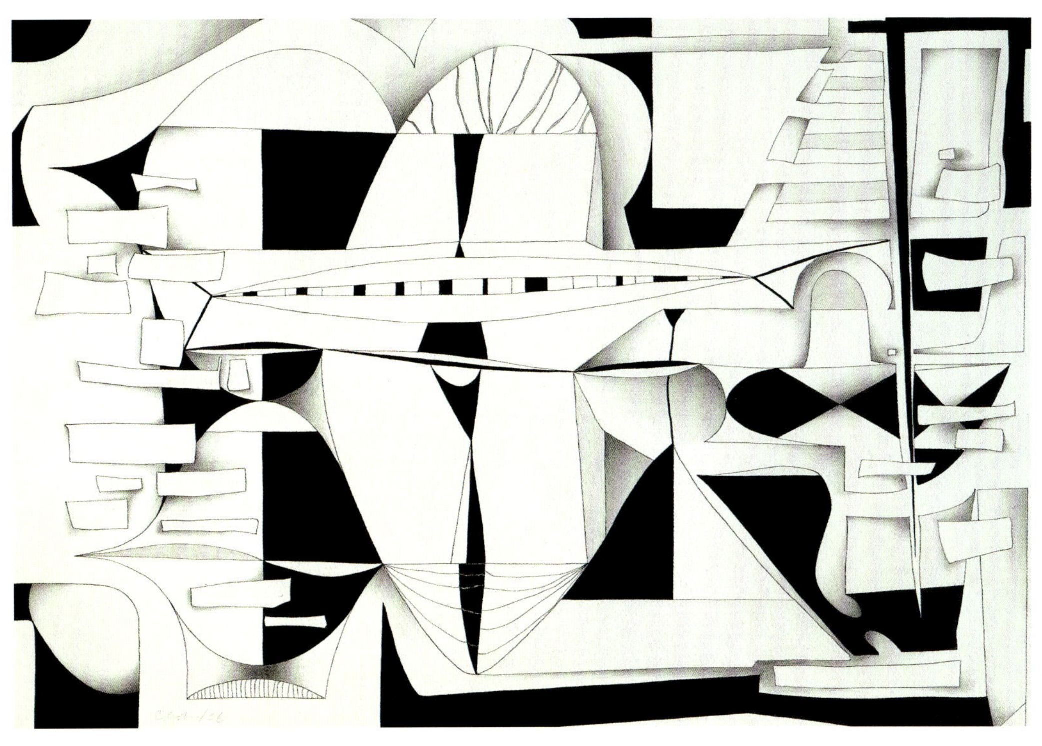

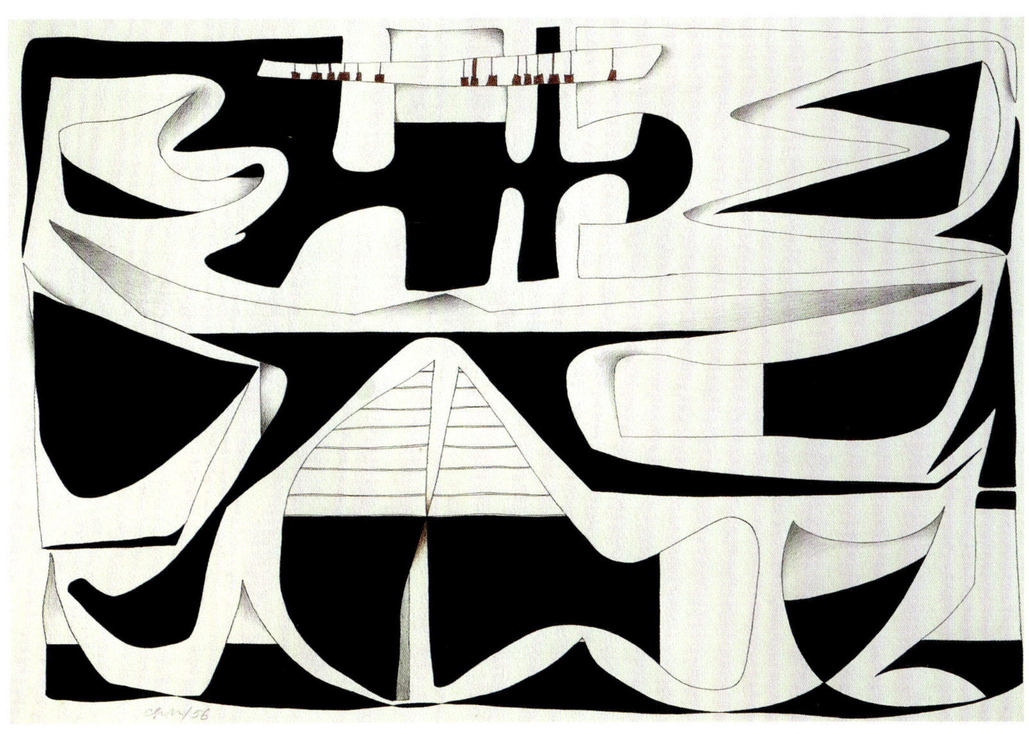

53 *Untitled*, 1956.
Pen, ink, and graphite on paper,
17¾ × 25¹⁵⁄₁₆ in. (45 × 65.9 cm).

54 *Untitled*, 1956.
Pen and ink on paper, 17¾ × 25⅞ in.
(45 × 65.7 cm).

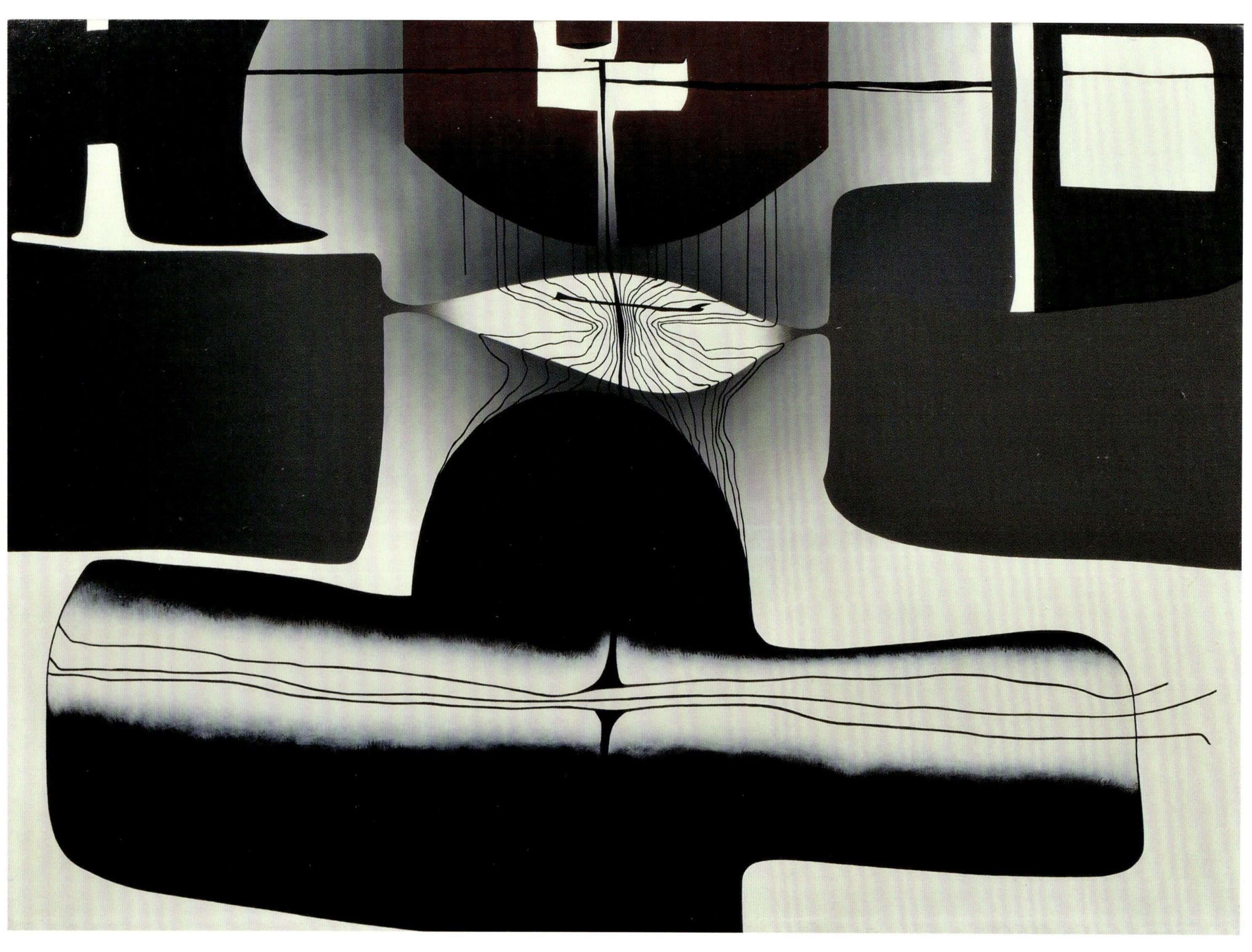

55 *Painting (I)*, 1962.
Oil on canvas, 24⅛ × 34¾ in.
(61.3 × 88.3 cm).

56 *Painting (VI)*, 1962.
Oil on canvas, 33¹/₁₆ × 46¹/₁₆ in.
(83.8 × 116.8 cm).

57 *Painting (VI)*, 1964.
Oil on canvas, 33¼ × 46¼ in.
(84.5 × 117.5 cm).

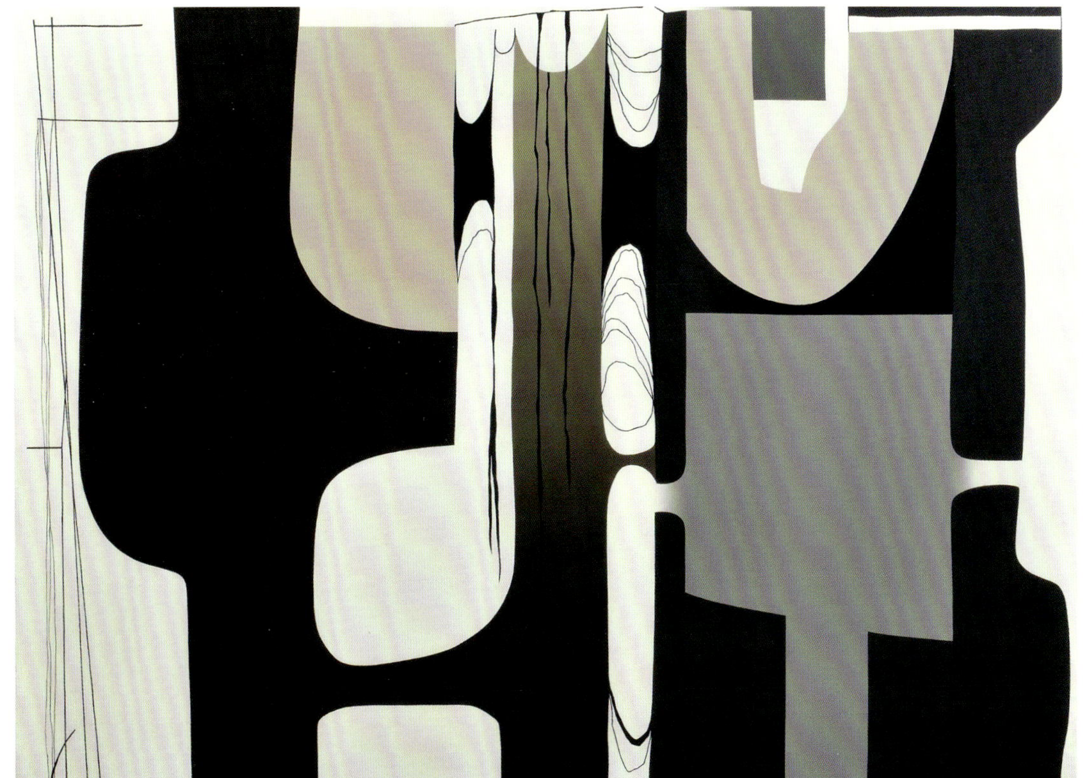

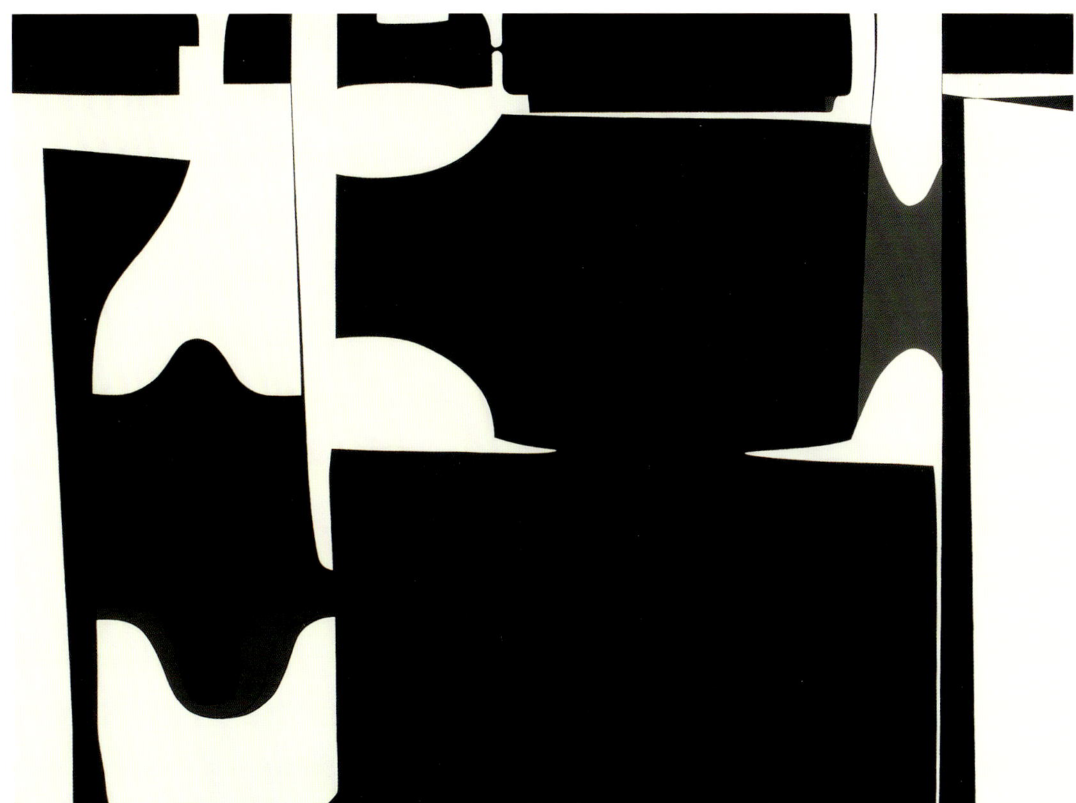

Chronology

Valerie Moon

1899

• Charles Houghton Howard is born on January 2 in Montclair, New Jersey, to John Galen Howard and Mary Robertson Bradbury Howard. Charles is the middle child of five; he and his siblings, Henry, Robert, John, and Janette, will all become artists and architects like their parents.

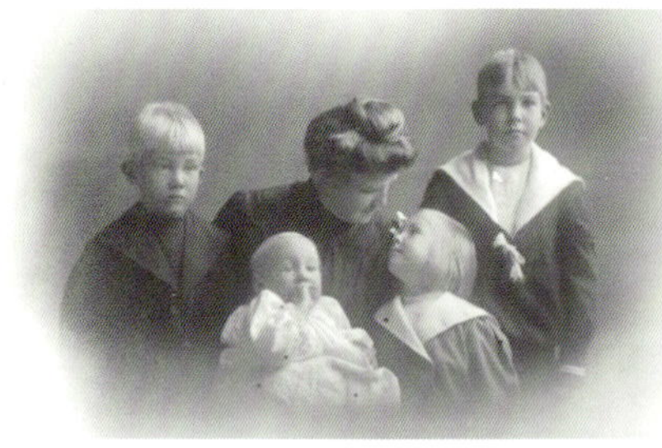

Mary Robertson Bradbury Howard and her children—Charles looking up, n.d.

• Psychologist Sigmund Freud's *The Interpretation of Dreams* is published. Freud lays out theories of the unconscious, dreams, and the Oedipus complex that will provide the intellectual basis for Surrealism in the 1920s.

1902

• The Howard family moves to Berkeley from New York when John Galen Howard becomes supervising architect and founder and professor of the architecture program at the University of California, Berkeley.

• The Art Department is founded at UC Berkeley.

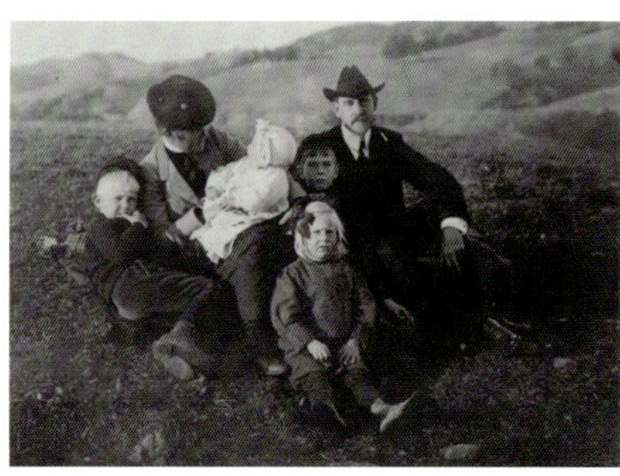

The Howard family in the Berkeley Hills on Thanksgiving Day, 1902. Clockwise from top left: Mary Robertson Bradbury Howard, John Langley Howard, John Galen Howard, Henry Howard, Charles Howard, and Robert Howard.

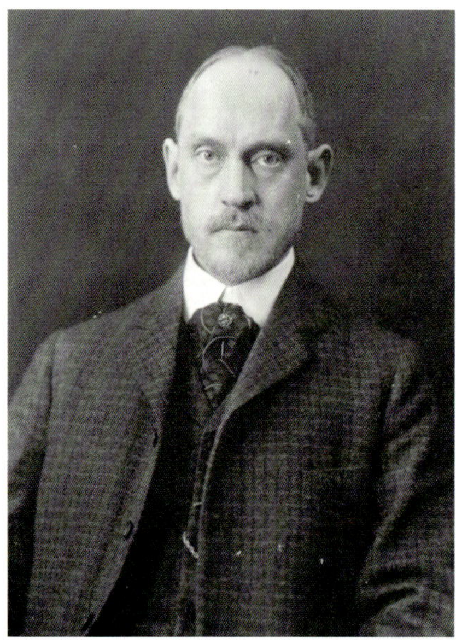

John Galen Howard, n.d.

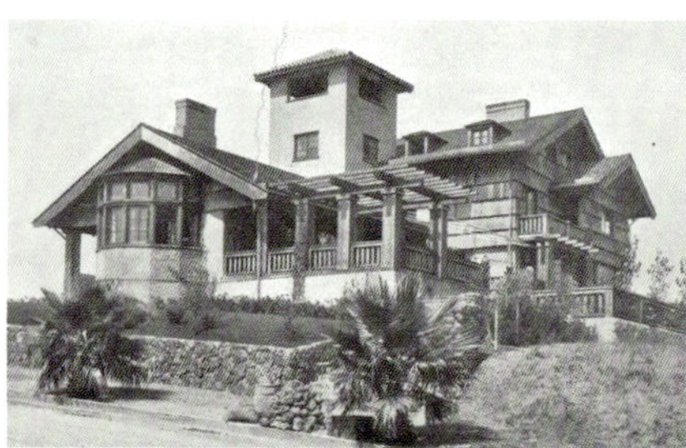

Howard family home on Ridge Road, Berkeley, ca. 1902.

1903

• The coastal Northern California town Carmel-by-the-Sea begins a slow transformation at the hands of real estate developers eager to position it as a cultural center and artists' colony. The Howards begin to spend summers in Carmel, a tradition they will continue until around 1918.

• John Galen Howard's first building at UC Berkeley, the William Randolph Hearst Greek Theatre, opens.

1906

• A deadly earthquake devastates San Francisco, killing thousands and destroying more than half the city.

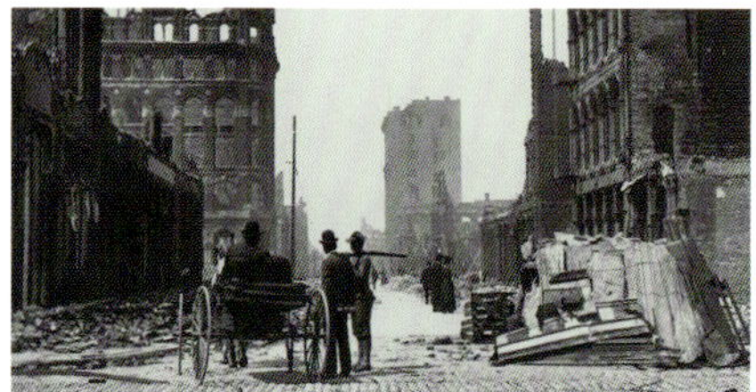

Aftermath of the San Francisco earthquake, 1906.

• Frederick H. Meyer founds the California School of Arts and Crafts (now known as California College of the Arts, CCA) in Berkeley.

• RMS *Titanic* sinks in the Atlantic Ocean, killing more than 1,500 passengers, including Peggy Guggenheim's father Benjamin Guggenheim, German American millionaire John Jacob Astor IV, and Isidor Straus, co-owner of Macy's department store.

• A group of New York artists called The Association of American Painters and Sculptors organizes the *International Exhibition of Modern Art,* also known as the Armory Show. The exhibition, staged at New York's 69th Regiment Armory before traveling to the Art Institute of Chicago and the Copley Society of Art in Boston, is the first major survey of modern American and European art in the US. Featured works address themes of rapid technological change and pictorial fragmentation; Marcel Duchamp's *Nude Descending Staircase (No. 2)* (1912) particularly scandalizes audiences.

• Sather Tower, the campanile on the UC Berkeley campus designed by John Galen Howard, is completed.

• The Panama–Pacific International Exposition opens in San Francisco, commemorating the completion of the Panama Canal and promoting the rebuilding of the city's structures and culture after the 1906 earthquake. Exhibits advocate the globalization of modern American society, boast technological achievements such as the first steam locomotive, and show the art of photographers such as Edward Weston, Ansel Adams, and Paul Strand, as well as examples of Futurism and other European Expressionist movements. Alexander Calder's father, Alexander Stirling Calder, is appointed Chief of Sculpture for the Exposition.

• World War I begins in Europe.

• The British ocean liner RMS *Lusitania* is hit and sunk by a torpedo fired from a German U-boat.

• The Society of Independent Artists holds its first annual exhibition in New York. Duchamp's *Fountain* (1917) is rejected from the show.

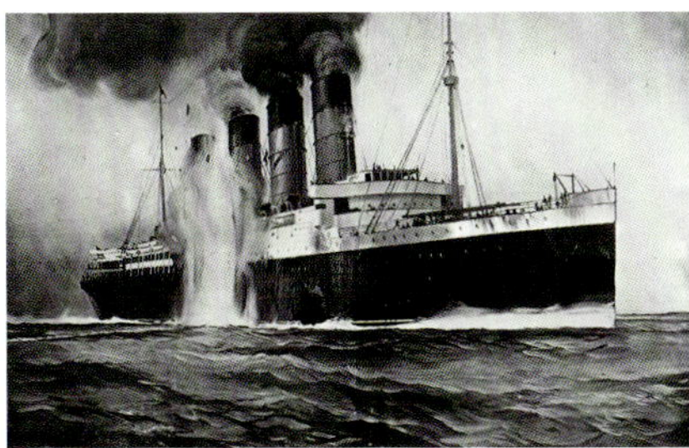

RMS *Lusitania* hit by torpedoes off Kinsale Head, Ireland, 1915.

• Robert Howard enlists in the army; the ship he boards for France is nearly sunk by a submarine attack.

• Howard graduates from Berkeley High School.

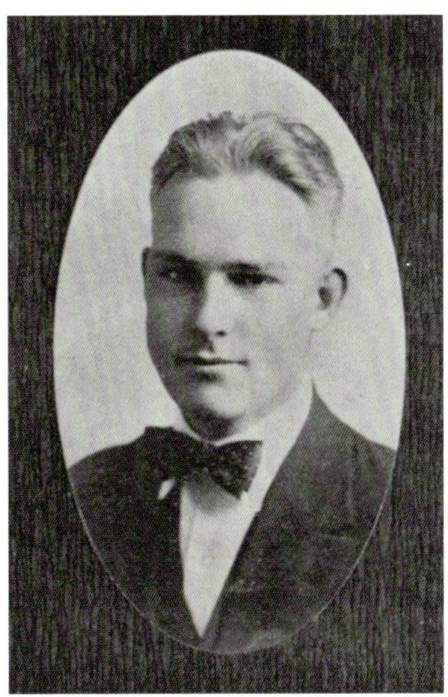

Charles Howard as editor-in-chief of *Olla Podrida*, the Berkeley High School yearbook, 1917.

• Howard enrolls as a journalism student at UC Berkeley. He leaves the university to join the Students' Army Training Corps (SATC).

• The abstract art movement De Stijl is founded by Dutch artists Piet Mondrian and Theo van Doesburg. Its defining contribution is neo-plasticism, a style of painting emphasizing horizontal and vertical lines and primary colors.

• Jackson Pollock moves to Chico, California, at the age of five.

• The interception of the Zimmerman Telegram, a communication from German Foreign Minister Arthur Zimmerman to the German Minister to Mexico, Heinrich von Eckhardt, reveals Germany's intention to initiate unrestricted submarine warfare on Britain, as well as to ally with Mexico should the US enter World War I. German U-boats begin sinking American ships soon afterward, catalyzing America's resolve to enter the war in December 1917.

• Vladimir Lenin leads the Bolshevik Revolution, overthrowing the Russian government and establishing the sovereign Soviet state that in 1922 will become the Union of Soviet Socialist Republics (USSR, or the Soviet Union).

• Arts patron and collector Gertrude Vanderbilt Whitney creates the Whitney Studio Club, a precursor to the Whitney Museum of American Art. An epicenter of modern and avant-garde art in New York, the Studio Club includes Edward Hopper, Stuart Davis, and Max Weber among its first members and becomes an important catalyst for Howard's early artistic activity in the 1920s.

• Howard spends the summer living at his family's cabin in Carmel-by-the-Sea, California.

• Germany's Kaiser Wilhelm II abdicates authority. Two days later, an armistice ends fighting between the Allied powers and Germany on the Western Front of World War I.

• The Treaty of Versailles is signed, signaling the end of World War I.

• Howard re-enrolls at UC Berkeley to study journalism.

• Howard sails to Europe on the USMS *Philadelphia* to meet his mother, sister, and brothers Robert and Henry, who are already there.

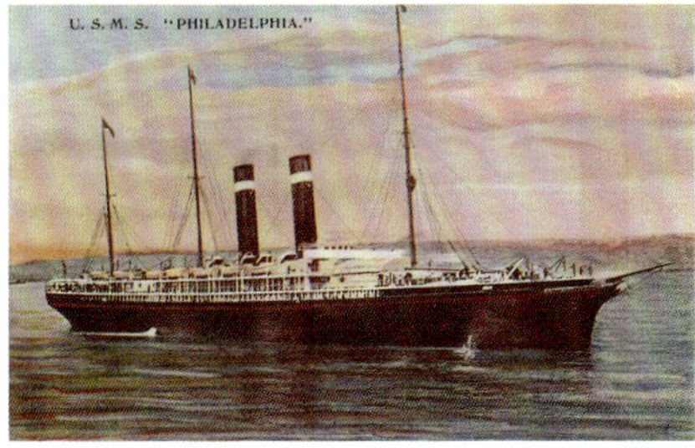

USMS *Philadelphia,* ca. 1907–14.

• Howard graduates from UC Berkeley. He becomes a common seaman and travels through the Panama Canal from New York.

• Howard enrolls in a graduate program in English at Harvard University.

1922

• Howard withdraws from Harvard. He will enroll at Columbia University in the spring.

• On July 15 Howard applies for a passport to leave for Europe, where he will travel in France, Italy, and England.

1923

• The Berkeley League of Fine Arts is founded by Bernard Maybeck, Perham Nahl, and Carol Aronovici.

• The Great Fire destroys hundreds of buildings in Berkeley, including some designed by John Galen Howard, near the north side of the UC Berkeley campus. The Howards' home on Ridge Road is also destroyed.

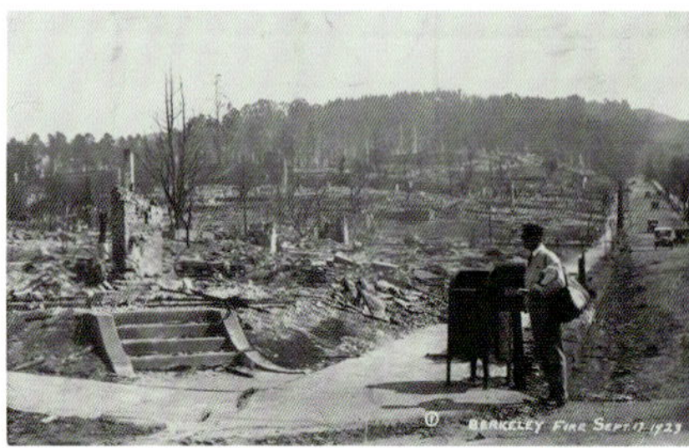

Aftermath of Berkeley's Great Fire, 1923.

• While in Europe, Howard meets Iowan artist Grant Wood and they travel throughout Italy together.

1924

• Howard returns to the US aboard the SS *France* on July 5, 1924, moves to New York, and begins painting shortly thereafter.

• Poet and critic André Breton publishes his *Manifesto of Surrealism*. Surrealism brings together writers, artists, and intellectuals influenced by Freudian theories of the unconscious. Important precursors to the movement include artists such as Duchamp and Giorgio de Chirico.

• Beatrice Judd Ryan founds the Galerie Beaux-Arts in San Francisco, the first commercial gallery on the West Coast dedicated to modern art.

• The California Palace of the Legion of Honor opens in San Francisco.

1925

• Mills College Art Gallery in Oakland opens with Roi Partridge as its first director.

1926

• Howard begins working as a journeyman painter and designer for Louis Bouché and Rudolph Guertler at their decorating firm.

• *Design,* a book written and illustrated by Howard, is published by Bridgman Publishers.

• Howard marries Hester Miller.

• The Carmel Art Association is founded in Carmel-by-the-Sea, California.

Whitney Studio Club, New York

Annual Exhibition of Paintings and Sculpture by Members of the Club, Whitney Studio Club, New York

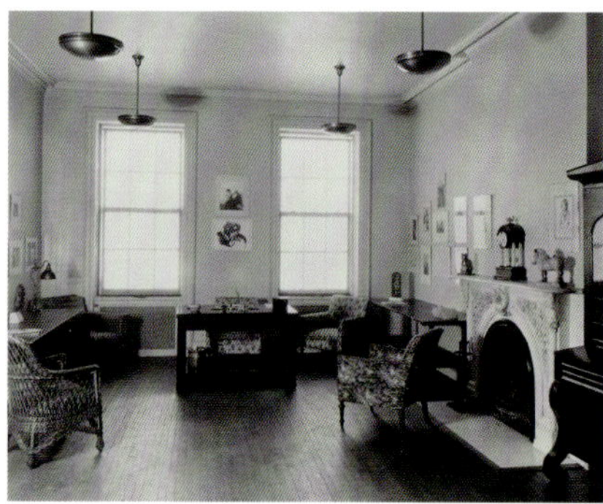

Office Interior, Whitney Studio Club, 10 West 8th Street, ca. 1928. Whitney Museum of American Art, New York, gift of Gertrude Vanderbilt Whitney. Photograph by Charles Sheeler.

1927

• *The Argus,* the first monthly journal dedicated exclusively to the arts, is established in San Francisco with Jehanne Bietry Salinger as its editor.

GROUP EXHIBITION

Playhouse Theater, Berkeley

1928

GROUP EXHIBITIONS

Annual Exhibition of Paintings and Sculpture by Members of the Club, Whitney Studio Club, New York

The Howard Brothers, Galerie Beaux-Arts, San Francisco

1929

• The Oakland Art Gallery includes works by Oskar Kokoschka, Karl Schmidt-Rottluff, Lyonel Feininger, and Emil Nolde, among others, in the exhibition *European Modernists.*

• The Museum of Modern Art (MoMA), New York, is founded by arts patrons John D. Rockefeller Jr., Cornelius Sullivan, and Lillie Bliss. Alfred H. Barr Jr. is appointed as the museum's first director, and the institution commits to being a progressive venue for the art of its time.

• More than sixteen million shares are traded on the New York Stock Exchange, an unprecedented crash that wipes out thousands of investors and ushers in the Great Depression.

1930

• The Whitney Museum of American Art opens in New York's Greenwich Village neighborhood. Gertrude Vanderbilt Whitney appoints her personal emissary, Juliana Force, as its first director. The museum focuses on modern artists including Stuart Davis, Georgia O'Keeffe, and members of the Ashcan School.

• The exhibition *Giorgio di Chirico* opens at Stendahl Galleries, Los Angeles.

• Hans Hoffman teaches a course in the Art Department at UC Berkeley at the invitation of his former student Worth Ryder.

• Diego Rivera and Frida Kahlo arrive in San Francisco. Rivera works on commissions for the California School of Fine Arts (CSFA, now the San Francisco Art Institute) and the San Francisco Stock Exchange. The Legion of Honor opens a major exhibition on Rivera's work.

1931

• Around this time, Charles and Hester Miller Howard divorce.

• John Galen Howard dies on July 3.

• The Legion of Honor presents a Hans Hoffman exhibition.

• The first major exhibition of Surrealism, *Newer Super-Realism,* is presented at the Wadsworth Atheneum Museum of Art in Hartford, Connecticut. The adapted exhibition will travel to the Julien Levy Gallery in New York the following year, just two months later.

• Construction on the Hoover Dam begins, demonstrating the prowess of American industry and technology.

1932

• *Surréalisme,* an exhibition at the Julien Levy Gallery of artists including de Chirico, Max Ernst, Joan Miró, Hans Arp, and Salvador Dalí introduces New York audiences to European Surrealism.

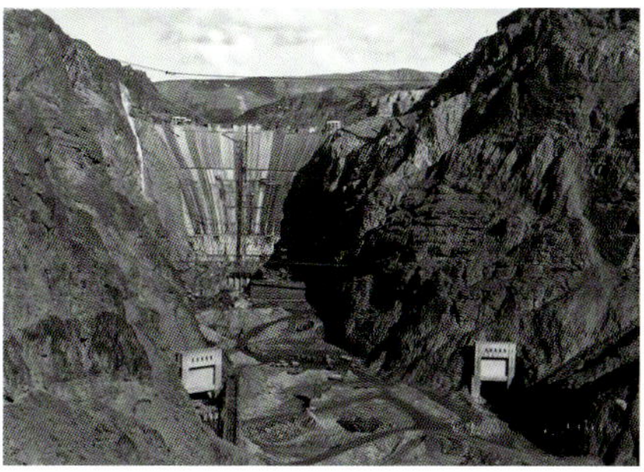

Hoover Dam under construction, Nevada, 1933.

GROUP EXHIBITIONS

Art Center, San Francisco

Salons of America, American-Anderson Galleries, New York

Surréalisme, Julien Levy Gallery, New York

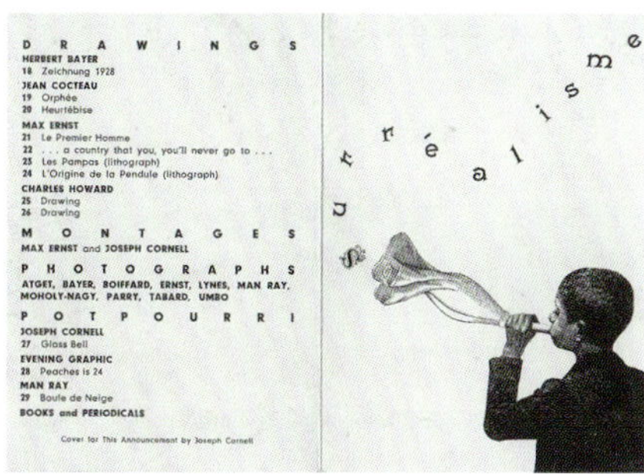

Exhibition announcement for *Surréalisme,* Julien Levy Gallery, New York, January 9–29, 1932. Designed by Joseph Cornell. Philadelphia Museum of Art Library and Archives

1933

• Howard marries English painter Madge Knight. The couple moves to London.

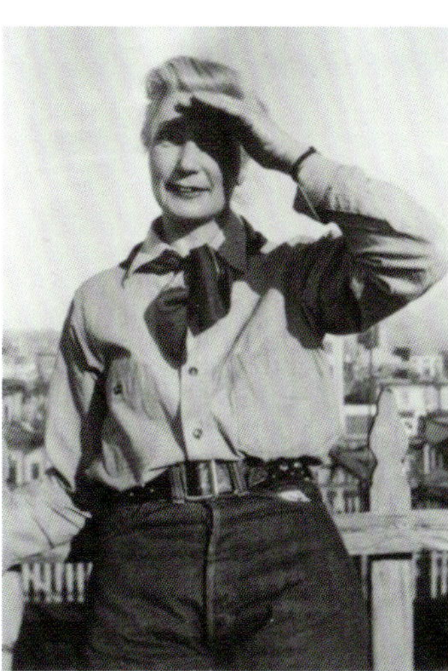

Madge Knight, n.d.

• The Public Works of Art Project, a precursor of the Works Progress Administration (WPA), is established as a New Deal work-relief program for artists. Under its auspices, Henry Temple Howard is among the team of architects that designs Coit Tower in San Francisco. Henry's wife, Jane Berlandina, and John Langley Howard are commissioned to paint some of the fresco murals inside the tower's base, all of which address leftist themes associated with Marxism, such as labor and class struggle. Robert Howard designs the phoenix above the entrance. John Langley Howard is pictured in the mural *Library* by artist Bernard B. Zakheim, reaching for Marx's *Das Kapital.* Some of the murals' controversial imagery will be painted over before the public opening of Coit Tower in 1934. That same year, a mural painted by Diego Rivera for the lobby of Rockefeller Center in New York will be destroyed for its Marxist imagery. The controversy surrounding its destruction will become emblematic of the ideological tension between art and politics in this period.

• Artist Paul Nash founds Unit One, a group of artists and architects in London that intends to reconcile the two major trends in European modernism: abstraction and Surrealism.

• Adolf Hitler is appointed Chancellor of Germany and rises to power. The Enabling Act of the Third Reich allows him to act without parliamentary consent, thereby granting him dictator status.

SOLO EXHIBITION

Paintings by Charles Howard, Julien Levy Gallery, New York

GROUP EXHIBITION

Art Center, San Francisco

1934

• London becomes a refuge for artists and intellectuals escaping fascism in Eastern Europe. Walter Gropius arrives in 1934, Naum Gabo and László Moholy-Nagy in 1935, Piet Mondrian and Oskar Kokoschka in 1938, and Kurt Schwitters in 1940.

• East West Gallery of Fine Art in San Francisco presents the exhibition *Joan Miró.*

• Alfred Frankenstein begins writing art and music reviews for the *San Francisco Chronicle.*

GROUP EXHIBITION

Progressive California Painters and Sculptors, Surrealism No. 1–2, Joseph Danysh Galleries, San Francisco

1935

• The San Francisco Museum of Art (SFMA, now the San Francisco Museum of Modern Art) opens its doors to the public in the War Memorial Veterans Building on Van Ness Avenue, with Grace L. McCann Morley as its first director.

• Art dealer Howard Putzel exhibits Ernst at his galleries in San Francisco.

SOLO EXHIBITIONS

Charles Howard, Bloomsbury Gallery, London

Charles Howard, Paul Elder Gallery, San Francisco

GROUP EXHIBITION

Paul Elder Gallery, San Francisco

1936

• Howard becomes associated with the English Surrealist Group.

• *Fantastic Art, Dada, and Surrealism,* an exhibition organized by Barr that renders a comprehensive history of Surrealism and Dada, opens at MoMA, New York. Barr receives criticism from the movements' major proponents—Éluard and Tristan Tzara—for his choice to conjoin the two concurrent European avant-gardes.

• SFMA exhibits Yves Tanguy's work.

• Duchamp visits Los Angeles and San Francisco.

• Construction of the San Francisco–Oakland Bay Bridge concludes.

GROUP EXHIBITIONS

56th Annual Exhibition, San Francisco Art Association

International Surrealist Exhibition, New Burlington Galleries, London

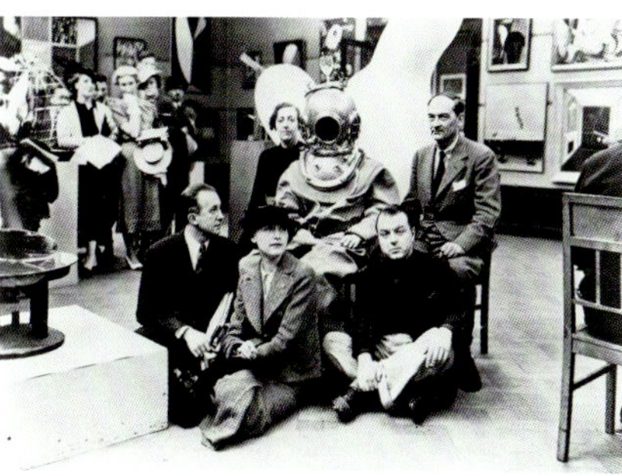

Diana Brinton-Lee, Salvador Dalí (in diving suit), Rupert Lee, Paul Éluard, Nusch Éluard, and E. L. T. Mesens at the *International Surrealist Exhibition,* New Burlington Galleries, London, June 11–July 4, 1936.

• The exhibitions *Great German Art* and *Degenerate Art* open in Munich. Organized by Adolf Ziegler and the Nazi party, *Great German Art* roots true German art in representational and idealized imagery, whereas *Degenerate Art* denigrates modernist and non-representational art as contrary to Aryan ideals. These exhibitions mark Germany's plunge into a cultural dark age.

• *Circle* magazine is founded by Gabo, Ben Nicholson, and Leslie Martin in London and releases its inaugural issue, *Circle: International Survey of Constructive Art*. Featured essays generate debates about Constructivism and abstraction.

• Pablo Picasso paints *Guernica*, a depiction of the bombing of the Basque town of Guernica during the Spanish Civil War.

• Art historical writings on California art are commissioned by the California Art Research Project under the auspices of the WPA.

• Construction of San Francisco's Golden Gate Bridge concludes.

GROUP EXHIBITIONS

57th Annual Exhibition, San Francisco Art Association

Surrealist Objects & Poems, London Gallery

1938

• The Guggenheim Jeune gallery is opened in London by Peggy Guggenheim, with the advice and help of Duchamp.

GROUP EXHIBITIONS

Exhibition of Collages, Papiers-Collés and Photo-Montages, Guggenheim Jeune, London

Il Salão de Maio, Esplanade Hotel de São Paulo, São Paulo

1939

• Artists, writers, and intellectuals including Kurt Seligmann, Tanguy, and Roberto Matta begin leaving Europe and relocating to the United States to escape the devolving political climate. Many others, including Breton, Mondrian, Fernand Léger, Ernst, and Duchamp follow in 1941–42. Although many of these European cultural figures moved to cities such as New York and Los Angeles, a number of them settled in the San Francisco Bay Area, catalyzing a period of cultural renaissance for Modernism.

• The Museum of Non-Objective Painting, the first venue and iteration of the Solomon R. Guggenheim Museum, opens in New York at the behest of curator and director Hilla Rebay.

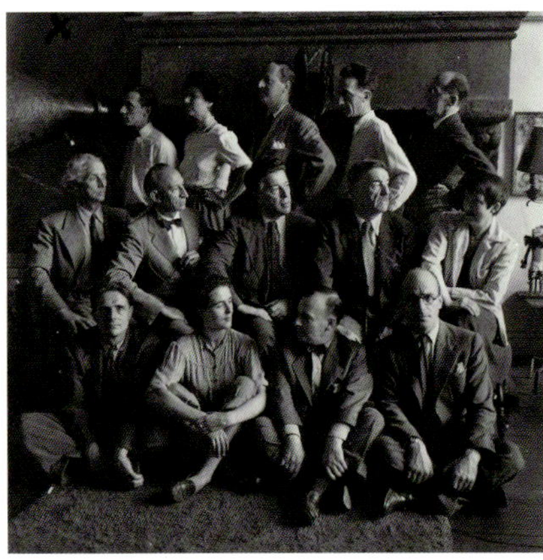

Expatriate artists in Peggy Guggenheim's apartment, New York, 1942. Front row: Stanley William Hayter, Leonora Carrington, Frederick Kiesler, Kurt Seligmann; second row: Max Ernst, Amédée Ozenfant, André Breton, Fernand Léger, Berenice Abbott; third row: Jimmy Ernst, Peggy Guggenheim, John Ferren, Marcel Duchamp, Piet Mondrian. Collection of the Münchner Stadtmuseum, Sammlung Fotografie, Archiv Landshoff.

• Art critic Clement Greenberg publishes "Avant-Garde and Kitsch" in the journal *Partisan Review*. This essay elevates abstraction and non-objective art as a response to the "kitsch" of American capitalism that Greenberg felt was co-opting art and culture. The text controversially distinguishes between high- and low-brow art and becomes a landmark in formalist interpretation of the avant-garde and of Abstract Expressionism in particular.

• The War Artists' Advisory Committee (WAAC) is established by the British government. The committee endeavors to generate pictorial reportage on the war by commissioning thousands of works by British artists.

• The Golden Gate International Exposition, held to commemorate the completion of the Golden Gate Bridge and the San Francisco–Oakland Bay Bridge, opens on Treasure Island.

• France falls to the Nazis and the balance of European power is significantly destabilized. The Nazi and Soviet regimes established by Hitler and Joseph Stalin, respectively, become the primary spheres of influence in Europe through the German-Soviet Non-Aggression Pact. Francisco Franco becomes dictator of Spain.

SOLO EXHIBITION

Charles Howard, Guggenheim Jeune, London

GROUP EXHIBITION

Living Art in England, London Gallery

1940

• Charles Howard and Madge Knight sail to San Francisco aboard the USS *George Washington* to escape the war. They arrive at Ellis Island on July 13, 1940. They move to an apartment at 91 Water Street, near Robert Howard's and Adaline Kent's studios, which were built by Henry Temple Howard.

• Stanley William Hayter marries Helen Phillips and moves to San Francisco to teach at CSFA—Helen's alma mater—for the summer.

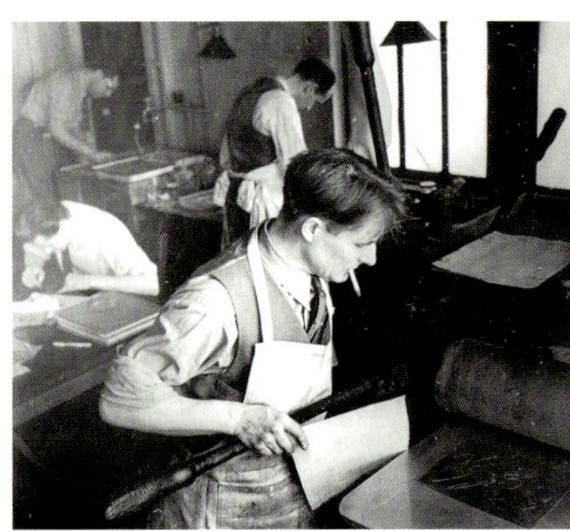

Stanley William Hayter working in the studio, 1930s–1940s.

• Atelier 17, a printmaking workshop founded by Hayter, is relocated from its original location in Paris (1927) to the New School for Social Research in New York. The atelier attracts Guggenheim, Mark Rothko, Pollock, and others, and becomes an important incubator for Abstract Expressionism.

• Man Ray flees Europe and moves to Southern California.

• Moholy-Nagy teaches at Mills College in Oakland.

• Rivera paints a mural for the Golden Gate International Exposition.

• Leon Trotsky is assassinated by one of Stalin's agents for his radical Marxist politics while living in exile in Coyoacán, Mexico.

GROUP EXHIBITIONS

60th Annual Exhibition, San Francisco Art Association

Art Association Annual, San Francisco Museum of Art

AWARD

Purchase Prize, *Art Association Annual*, San Francisco Museum of Art

• Howard works as a shipfitter at Marinship Shipyard in Sausalito, California, and as an editor in the Office of War Information in San Francisco. Under the auspices of the WPA he also designs murals for the Naval Air Station in Alameda that are ultimately not executed and becomes the Designing Supervisor in the Art Section, making posters for the Oakland Defense Council.

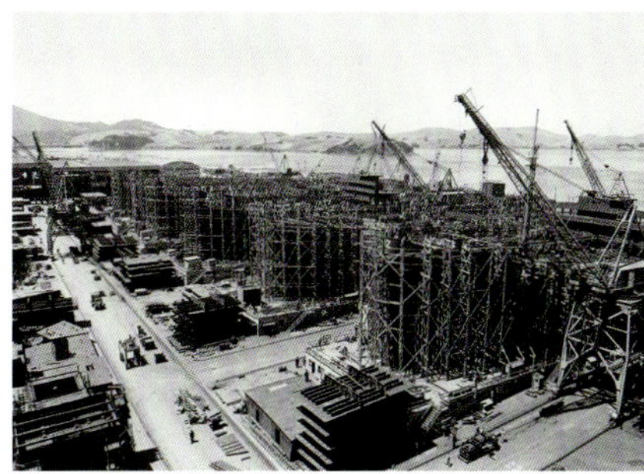

Marinship Shipyard, Sausalito, CA, 1944.

• Douglas MacAgy and his wife Jermayne move to San Francisco; he becomes a curator at SFMA and she at the Legion of Honor.

• Several major artists and their works come to the Bay Area. Man Ray exhibits at the M. H. de Young Memorial Museum. Clyfford Still moves to San Francisco. David Park becomes a teacher at CSFA. Arshile Gorky exhibits at SFMA. Léger teaches at Mills College and exhibits at SFMA.

• Patrons and artists take an interest in Los Angeles. Guggenheim, along with Ernst, searches for a gallery space there. Levy leases a gallery where he exhibits Duchamp.

• Japanese warplanes attack the American naval base at Pearl Harbor, Hawaii, provoking America to enter World War II. Nazis begin rounding up and murdering Jews by the thousands in concentration camps throughout Europe.

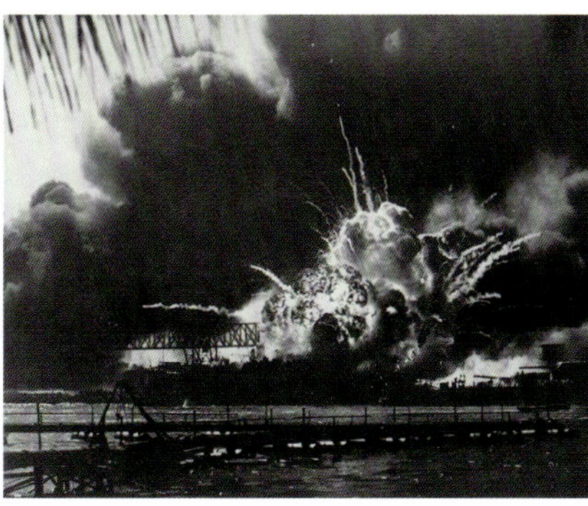

USS *Shaw* exploding during the Japanese attack at Pearl Harbor, HI, 1941.

SOLO EXHIBITIONS

Charles Howard, The Courvoisier Gallery, San Francisco

University of California Department of Art, Berkeley

GROUP EXHIBITIONS

61st Annual Exhibition, San Francisco Art Association

Annual American Exhibitions, The Art Institute of Chicago

Directions in American Painting, Carnegie Institute, Pittsburgh

1942

• *Fantastic War Machines and Guerragraphs*, an exhibition featuring works that Clay Spohn completed with Howard's encouragement, opens at SFMA.

• Howard's work is included in Guggenheim's inaugural exhibition of European and American artists at her Art of This Century in New York. The exhibition promotes surrealist, abstract, and kinetic art and includes Jean Arp, de Chirico, Wassily Kandinsky, Joseph Cornell, Hoffman, Still, and many others. Along with MoMA and the Museum of Non-Objective Painting, the gallery is located in Midtown, an area that will become a nexus for American modern artists and exiled European artists.

• The Legion of Honor features an exhibition of Dalí.

• Henry Miller moves to Los Angeles.

SOLO EXHIBITION

Charles Howard — Drawings, San Francisco Museum of Art

GROUP EXHIBITIONS

Americans 1942: 18 Artists from 9 States, The Museum of Modern Art, New York

Annual American Exhibitions, The Art Institute of Chicago

Annual Exhibition, San Francisco Art Association

Artists for Victory, The Metropolitan Museum of Art, New York

Exhibition of the Collection, Art of This Century, New York

New Rugs by American Artists, The Museum of Modern Art, New York

Sawdust and Spangles, San Francisco Museum of Art

AWARDS

Summer Exhibition Prize, San Francisco Museum of Art

Fifth Prize, *Artists for Victory* exhibition, The Metropolitan Museum of Art, New York

1943

• Madge Knight has a one-person show at SFMA.

• Still moves from the Bay Area to Virginia, where he will remain until moving to New York in 1945. He will return to San Francisco in 1946.

• *Abstract and Surrealist Art in the United States* opens at SFMA. The exhibition features the first work by Pollock, who is represented by Guggenheim's Art of This Century, to be shown on the West Coast.

GROUP EXHIBITION

Annual Exhibition, San Francisco Art Association

Abstract and Surrealist Art in the United States, San Francisco Museum of Art

1944

• Sidney Janis and Morley exhibit a survey of works by European refugee artists at SFMA.

GROUP EXHIBITIONS

Annual at the Whitney Museum of American Art, New York

Annual Exhibition, San Francisco Art Association

1945

• Howard designs the cover of *Fortune* magazine.

• Douglas MacAgy becomes director of CSFA.

• Representatives of fifty countries meet in the building housing SFMA to negotiate and sign the Charter of the United Nations. The museum relocates temporarily to Post Street as a result. The UN Charter is printed in the building that currently houses the University of California, Berkeley Art Museum and Pacific Film Archive (BAMPFA), which was formerly a university printing plant.

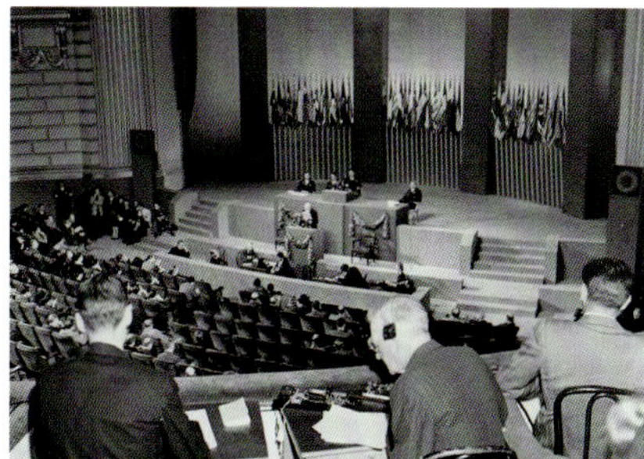

Signing of the UN Charter, San Francisco, 1945.

• Pollock has a solo exhibition at SFMA.

• CSFA presents the exhibition *Duchamp and Villon*.

• Allied powers slowly gain advantage over Axis powers. Nazi concentration camps are exposed and liberated. In the weeks that follow, Italian Prime Minister Benito Mussolini is executed, Hitler commits suicide, and German forces surrender. American President Franklin D. Roosevelt dies suddenly, and Harry S. Truman becomes President. Truman authorizes the dropping of atomic bombs on the Japanese cities of Hiroshima and Nagasaki, killing more than two hundred thousand people. World War II subsequently ends with Japan's surrender.

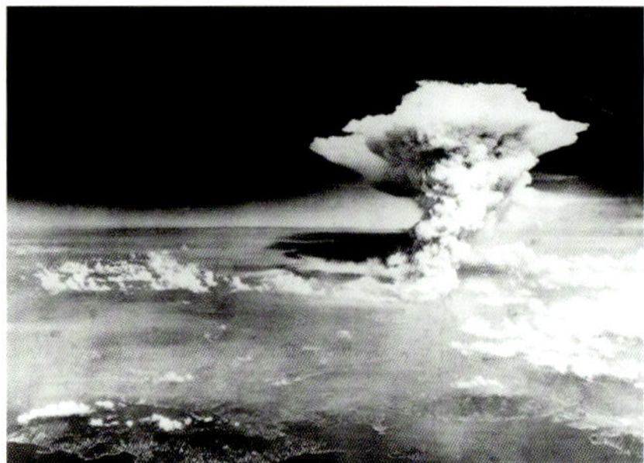

Dropping of the atomic bomb on Hiroshima, Japan, 1945. Hiroshima Peace Memorial Museum

GROUP EXHIBITIONS

American Paintings, California Palace of the Legion of Honor, San Francisco

Ninth Annual Watercolor Exhibition, San Francisco Art Association

Annual Exhibition, San Francisco Art Association

Annual at the Whitney Museum of American Art, New York

Art Gallery of Toronto, 1945

The Critics' Choice Exhibition, Cincinnati Art Museum, 1945

1946

• Charles Howard and Madge Knight return to England, where they will live until 1970.

• Still returns to San Francisco to begin teaching at CSFA, and launches Abstract Expressionism in the Bay Area.

• Experimental filmmaker Frank Stauffacher begins the Art in Cinema series in San Francisco.

• British Prime Minister Winston Churchill delivers his "Iron Curtain" speech condemning the Soviet Union's policies in Europe at Westminster College in Fulton, Missouri.

SOLO EXHIBITIONS

Charles Howard, Retrospective Exhibition 1925–1946, California Palace of the Legion of Honor, San Francisco

Works by Charles Howard, Karl Nierendorf Gallery, New York

GROUP EXHIBITIONS

Annual American Exhibitions, The Art Institute of Chicago

Annual Exhibition, San Francisco Art Association

Annual, Whitney Museum of American Art, New York

American Painting, Tate Gallery, London

Directions in American Painting, Carnegie Institute, Pittsburgh

Exhibition of Contemporary Art, Pasadena Art Institute, CA

Exposition Internationale d'Art Moderne, Musée d'Art Moderne, Paris

First Spring Annual, California Palace of the Legion of Honor, San Francisco

AWARDS

First Prize, *First Spring Annual*, California Palace of the Legion of Honor, San Francisco

Purchase Prize, *Exhibition of Contemporary Art*, Pasadena Art Institute, CA

Purchase Prize, La Tausca Competition, New York

1947

• Penrose, Herbert Read, Peter Watson, Geoffrey Grigson, and E. L. T. Mesens found the Institute of Contemporary Arts (ICA) in London. The ICA becomes a conduit for British abstract art, and later Pop art and Op art, as well as a venue for countercultural activity in the 1960s.

• Madeline Gleason, poet and founder of the San Francisco Poetry Guild, co-organizes the Festival of Modern Poetry in San Francisco with SFMA.

• Rothko begins teaching at CSFA while staying at Adaline Kent and Robert Howard's home.

• Richard Diebenkorn joins the CSFA faculty.

• Howard's *The Medusa* (1945) is included in the controversial traveling exhibition organized by the United States Information Agency (USIA) called *Advancing American Art*. Conceived as a display of diplomacy, patriotism, and democracy as the Red Scare—a fear of communists, socialists, anarchists, and other dissidents—was beginning in the US, the show positions American abstract art in pointed contrast to the Socialist Realism prevalent in the Soviet Union.

GROUP EXHIBITIONS

Abstract and Surrealist Art in America, Art Institute of Chicago, 1947, and The Museum of Modern Art, New York

Advancing American Art, United States Information Agency, Washington DC. Traveled to The Metropolitan Museum of Art, New York, and venues in Havana and Prague

Third Annual Exhibition, California Palace of the Legion of Honor, San Francisco

Third Summer Exhibition of Contemporary Art, University of Iowa, Iowa City

AWARD

Purchase Prize, *Third Annual Exhibition*, California Palace of the Legion of Honor, San Francisco

1948

• Gordon Onslow Ford has a show at SFMA.

• *The Communist Manifesto*, illustrated by Robert McChesney and Hassel Smith, is published by the International Book Store in San Francisco.

• Harry S. Truman is re-elected as President of the United States. Senator Joseph McCarthy spearheads the second Red Scare, sparking fear and paranoia of communism in the American psyche in an era following the Berlin Blockade and the Chinese Civil War.

GROUP EXHIBITION

Annual American Exhibitions, The Art Institute of Chicago

AWARDS

Honorable Mention, San Francisco Art Association

Purchase Prize, *Third Annual Exhibition*, Legion of Honor, San Francisco

1949

• Douglas MacAgy organizes "The Western Round Table on Modern Art," an international conference that includes moderator and philosopher George Boas, anthropologist Gregory Bateson, literary critic Kenneth Burke, art historian Robert Goldwater, composer Darius Milhaud, director of MoMA Andrew Ritchie, artists Mark Tobey and Duchamp, architect Frank Lloyd Wright, composer Arnold Schoenberg, and art critic Alfred Frankenstein. The conference is an important cross-disciplinary encounter and intellectual moment for modern art.

• SFMA exhibits Ernst's work.

• Park ceases to paint abstract works and returns to figurative painting.

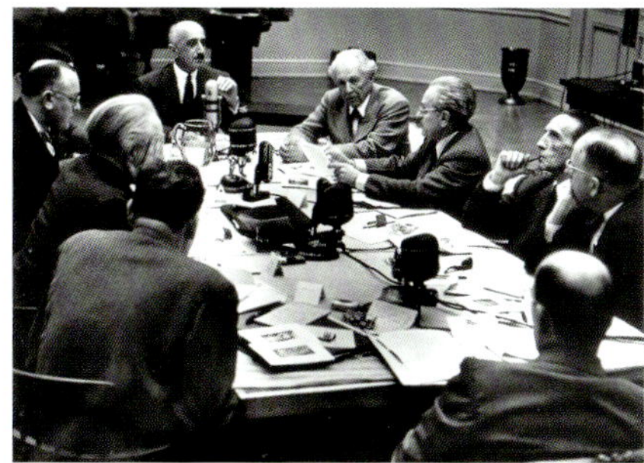

"The Western Round Table on Modern Art," California School of Fine Arts, San Francisco, April 8–10, 1949. Around table clockwise from top: George Boas, Frank Lloyd Wright, Kenneth Burke, Marcel Duchamp, Alfred Frankenstein, Robert Goldwater, Gregory Bateson, Mark Tobey, Andrew Ritchie, Darius Milhaud. San Francisco Art Institute Archives

SOLO EXHIBITION

Charles Howard, Hanover Gallery, London

GROUP EXHIBITIONS

La Collezione Guggenheim, Palazzo Strozzi, Florence, Italy

Salon des Réalités Nouvelles, Paris

Presentation of works in connection with the "Western Round Table of Modern Art," sponsored by the San Francisco Art Association, San Francisco Museum of Art

1950

• Charles Howard and Madge Knight move to Helions Bumpstead, Essex, England, where they will remain for the next twenty years.

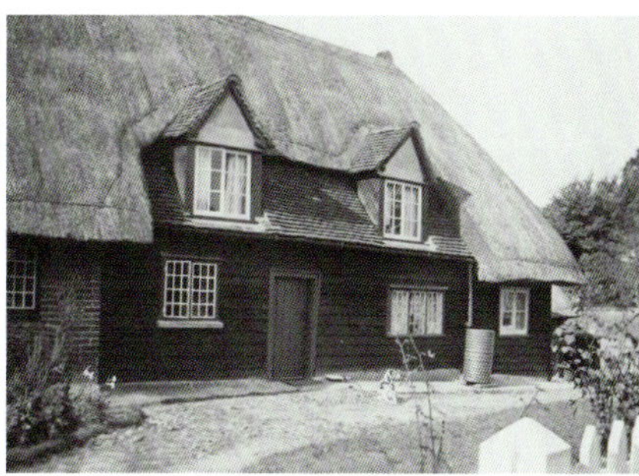

Charles Howard and Madge Knight's home in Helions Bumpstead, Essex, England, n.d.

• Wolfgang Paalen moves to Mill Valley, CA.

• Max Beckmann becomes faculty at Mills College, Oakland.

• Ad Reinhardt begins teaching at CSFA.

• North Korean troops, supported by the Soviet Union and China, cross the 38th Parallel and invade South Korea. A month later, the US allies with South Korea in the Korean War.

GROUP EXHIBITION

20th Century Painters, The Metropolitan Museum of Art, New York

1951

• Howard is included in the MoMA exhibition *Abstract Painting and Sculpture in America* as a representative of "Expressionist Biomorphic" art alongside Gorky, Pollock, and Rothko.

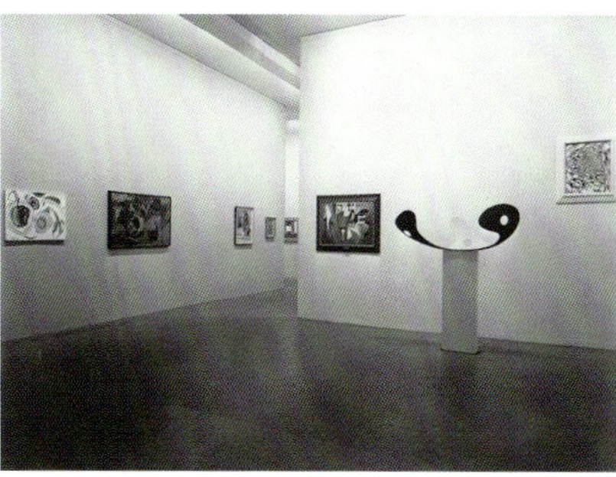

Installation view of *Abstract Painting and Sculpture in America,* The Museum of Modern Art, New York, January 23–March 25, 1951. The Museum of Modern Art Archives, New York. Howard's *Trinity* (1941) is pictured on the wall at right, to the left of the sculpture.

• The Constructionists form in England. The group, spearheaded by artist Victor Passmore, signals a return to the methods of prewar abstraction and Constructivism in response to the heavily nationalistic art of the early 1940s.

• Wolfgang Paalen, Lee Mullican, and Onslow Ford are included in the landmark exhibition "Dynaton" at the SFMA.

SOLO EXHIBITION

Recent Pictures by Charles Howard, The Heffer Gallery, Cambridge, UK

GROUP EXHIBITION

Abstract Painting and Sculpture in America, The Museum of Modern Art, New York

1952

• The Independent Group, which includes artists Eduardo Paolozzi and Richard Hamilton and critic Lawrence Alloway, meets in London to discuss the intersection of art and mass culture in an era of television, commercial advertising, and commodity production. The group stirs the beginnings of Pop art both in Europe and in the US.

GROUP EXHIBITION

Pittsburgh International Exhibition of Contemporary Painting, Carnegie Institute, Pittsburgh

1953

• Ethel and Julius Rosenberg, accused of espionage for the Soviet Union during the Cold War, are executed by electric chair in New York. Their conviction in 1951 had drawn nationwide criticism and was a climactic moment of McCarthyist hysteria during the 1950s.

SOLO EXHIBITION

Paintings and Gouaches by Charles Howard, Santa Barbara Museum of Art, CA, and the California Palace of the Legion of Honor, San Francisco

GROUP EXHIBITIONS

American Watercolors, Drawings and Prints, The Metropolitan Museum of Art, New York

British Painting and Sculpture, Whitechapel Art Gallery, London

Selection of American Paintings, Cincinnati Art Museum

Twentieth-Century Form, Whitechapel Art Gallery, London

1954

GROUP EXHIBITION

British Painting and Sculpture, Whitechapel Art Gallery, London

1955

• Painter and professor Arnold Bode founds the Society of Western Art of the 20th Century in Kassel, Germany, in an effort to bring the country back into the international art world. The group organizes an overview of major modernist movements and artists from the first half of the twentieth century, such as Expressionism, Cubism, and Futurism and the work of Kandinsky, Picasso, Moore, Ernst, Arp, and Paul Klee: all of the featured art had been labeled "degenerate" by the Nazis. Bode's exhibition attracts thousands of visitors, and due to its success the exhibition series *Documenta* is established.

• Jermayne MacAgy is appointed director of the Contemporary Arts Museum in Houston.

• The Vietnam War begins. The American government justifies the war as a necessary containment of the spread of communism, whereas the Vietnamese view it as a war of colonization.

1956

• The exhibition *Modern Art in the United States: A Selection from the Collections of the Museum of Modern Art, New York* at the Tate Gallery shows American Abstract Expressionists including Pollock, Willem de Kooning, and Rothko in London for the first time.

Charles Howard, Whitechapel Art Gallery, London

1957

• Adaline Kent dies in a car accident near Stinson Beach in Marin County, California, on March 24.

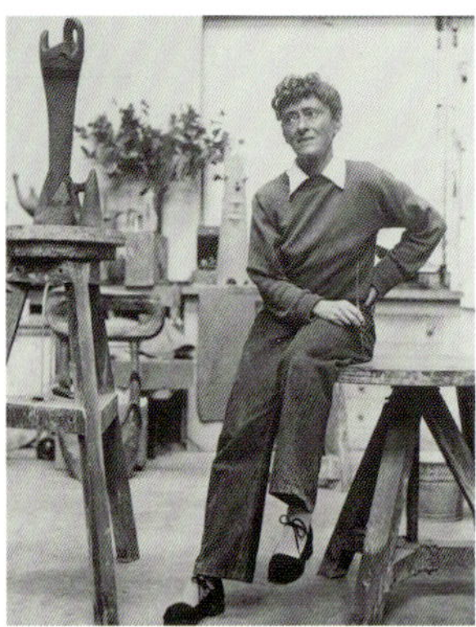

Adaline Kent, n.d.

• The Leo Castelli Gallery opens in New York and becomes a hub for postwar American art, including Pop, Minimal, and Conceptual art. Castelli champions artists such as Jasper Johns, Frank Stella, Donald Judd, Cy Twombly, Andy Warhol, and Roy Lichtenstein, among many others.

SOLO EXHIBITION

Charles Howard / Recent Drawings, St. George's Gallery, London

GROUP EXHIBITION

St. George's Gallery, London

1958

• Howard begins teaching in the Department of Painting at the Camberwell School of Arts and Crafts in London, a position he will hold until 1963.

1959

• Allan Kaprow performs *18 Happenings in 6 Parts* at the Reuben Gallery in New York. Subsequent "happenings" will be characteristic of the Fluxus movement throughout the 1960s.

• Jermayne MacAgy, along with Dominique and John de Menil, establishes the art department at the University of St. Thomas in Houston.

• The Cuban Revolution, led by Fidel Castro, ousts dictator Fulgencio Batista from Havana.

1960

• The exhibition *Situation* opens at the RBA Galleries in London. Solidifying the influence that American Abstract Expressionism and Color Field painting had in England, it includes the work of Bernard Cohen, Gordon House, William Turnbull, and Gillian Ayres. The British artists in the exhibition trace their loose painting style and pictorial flatness back to the works of Hans Hoffman and other Americans who showed in the 1956 Tate Gallery presentation of American modernists.

• The Berlin Wall is built and becomes a symbol of the Cold War between Western and Eastern Blocs in Europe.

GROUP EXHIBITIONS

Recent Acquisitions, Dallas Museum for Contemporary Arts

Painting at Camberwell, South London Art Gallery, London

1962

• *Artforum* is founded in San Francisco by John P. Irwin Jr. with an emphasis on California art. It will later shift its focus following moves to Los Angeles, then New York.

• US and Soviet leaders engage in a tense political and military standoff over the installation of nuclear-armed Soviet missiles in Cuba, ninety miles from US shores. The Cuban Missile Crisis, as this event becomes known, is ultimately quelled through a mutual nuclear disarmament plan involving missiles in Cuba and Turkey. The US imposes a trade embargo on Cuba.

GROUP EXHIBITION

British Art and the Modern Movement 1930–1940, National Museum of Wales, Cardiff, UK

1963

• Howard becomes a British citizen.

• Mary Robertson Bradbury Howard dies on June 23.

• Hoffman gifts $250,000 and forty-seven of his paintings to UC Berkeley, crediting the university as the platform from which his career as an artist and professor began in 1930. Hoffman's gift moves the university to establish the University Art Museum, now known as the University of California, Berkeley Art Museum and Pacific Film Archive (BAMPFA).

• The Green Gallery in New York opens a major group exhibition of Minimal art. The gallery will continue to exhibit the work of Minimalists Judd, Robert Morris, Dan Flavin, and others in the early 1960s.

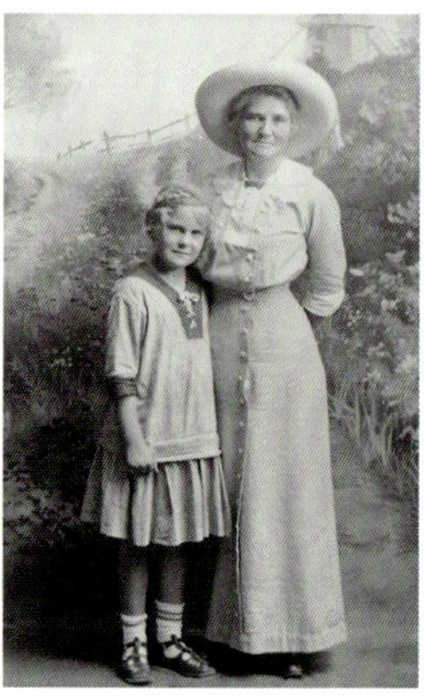

Janette and Mary Howard, 1864.

• Douglas MacAgy becomes an advisor for the Howard Wise Gallery in New York.

• Martin Luther King Jr. delivers his "I Have a Dream" speech at the March on Washington in Washington, DC.

• US President John F. Kennedy is assassinated in Dallas.

SOLO EXHIBITIONS

Charles Howard, Recent Paintings and Drawings, McRoberts & Tunnard Ltd., London

Charles Howard, Howard Wise Gallery, New York

1964

• The Civil Rights Act, the first legislation to eliminate racial segregation in public places, schools, and workplaces, is signed by US President Lyndon B. Johnson.

GROUP EXHIBITION

McRoberts & Tunnard, London

1965

• Malcolm X is assassinated during a rally in New York.

1966

• The black nationalist and socialist Black Panther Party is conceived in Oakland, California, and becomes the cornerstone of the Black Power movement.

• The Cultural Revolution led by Chairman Mao Zedong of the Communist Party begins in China, creating mass social and political upheaval.

• Betty Friedan, author of *The Feminine Mystique* (1963), becomes one of the organizers of the feminist group National Organization for Women (NOW).

1967

• Henry Temple Howard dies.

• Pollock has his first retrospective at MoMA, New York.

• Art Cologne in Germany is established as the first art fair to exhibit and sell modern and contemporary art.

1968

• North Vietnamese and Viet Cong forces launch the Tet Offensive, one of the largest and deadliest campaigns in the Vietnam War. The Offensive becomes a major turning point for the American public's perception of the conflict and protests against the war increase, leading to America's withdrawal in 1969.

• Martin Luther King Jr. is assassinated in Memphis, sparking race riots in cities across the country.

• Waves of New Left social protests occur all over Europe, with shared themes of anti-bureaucracy, civil rights, and class struggle.

• Hundreds of student anti-government demonstrators are murdered by police and military troops in Tlatelolco Square, Mexico City.

GROUP EXHIBITION

Jermayne MacAgy: A Life Illustrated by an Exhibition, University of St. Thomas, Houston

1969

• Richard Nixon is sworn in as President of the United States.

• *Apollo 11* lands on the moon and Neil Armstrong and Edwin "Buzz" Aldrin become the first men to step foot on the lunar surface.

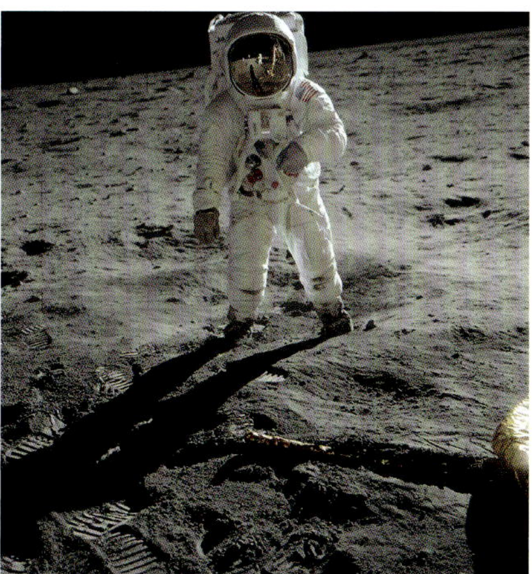

Buzz Aldrin on the moon after the *Apollo 11* landing, 1969.

• The Nuclear Nonproliferation Treaty is signed by the US, the Soviet Union, and several other nations.

• The Stonewall Riots bring the gay rights movement to the national stage.

1970

• Charles Howard and Madge Knight move to Bagni di Lucca, a small town in Tuscany, Italy.

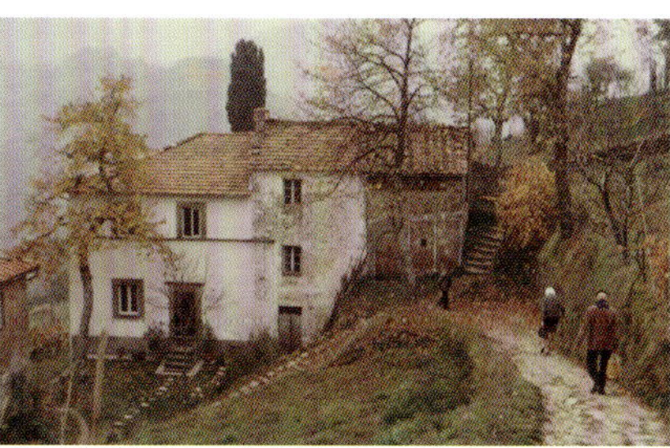

Charles Howard and Madge Knight at their home in Bagni di Lucca, Italy, 1972.

• BAMPFA opens the doors of its Bancroft Avenue building, designed by San Francisco architects Mario Ciampi, Richard L. Jorasch, and Ronald E. Wagner.

1972

• The Watergate scandal reveals the Nixon administration's wiretapping and break-in at the Democratic National Convention headquarters in Washington, DC. The scandal places heavy scrutiny on abuses of power by conservative government agencies such as the CIA, FBI, and IRS.

1973

• An oil embargo and resulting price hikes imposed by members of the Organization of Arab Petroleum Exporting Countries (OAPEC) provokes an energy crisis in the US, demonstrating the Middle East's political power.

• Augusto Pinochet leads a military coup that ousts Chilean president Salvador Allende.

GROUP EXHIBITION

A Period of Exploration, San Francisco 1945–50, The Oakland Museum, CA

1974

• Madge Knight dies of a stroke at the age of seventy-eight in Bagni di Lucca, Italy, on September 7.

• In the process of being impeached on charges related to the Watergate scandal, US President Richard Nixon resigns.

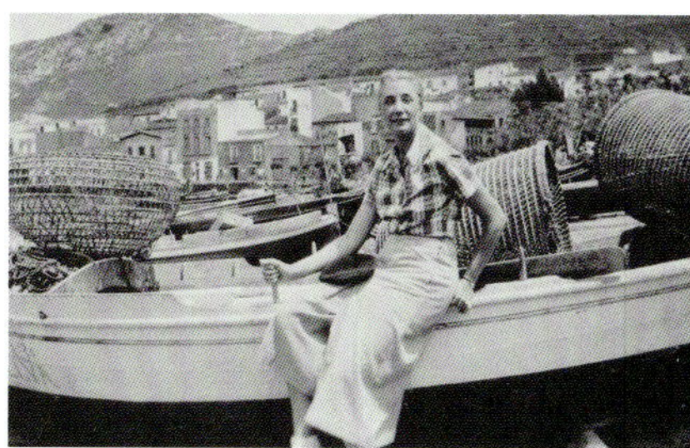

Madge Knight in Ibiza, Spain, n.d.

GROUP EXHIBITION

Painting and Sculpture in California: The Modern Era, San Francisco Museum of Art. Traveled to the National Collection of Fine Arts, Smithsonian Institution, Washington, DC

1976

• The exhibition *The Human Clay* opens at the Hayward Gallery in London. Featured School of London artists include Lucian Freud, Francis Bacon, and RB Kitaj, who revived figurative painting amid the overall European trend toward abstraction.

• The journal of art criticism and theory *October* is established by Rosalind E. Krauss and Annette Michelson. Editors include Yve-Alain Bois, Benjamin Buchloh, and Hal Foster.

1977

GROUP EXHIBITION

Queen's Jubilee Exhibition, Royal Academy of Arts, London

1978

• Charles Howard dies at the age of seventy-eight in Bagni di Lucca, Italy, on November 11.

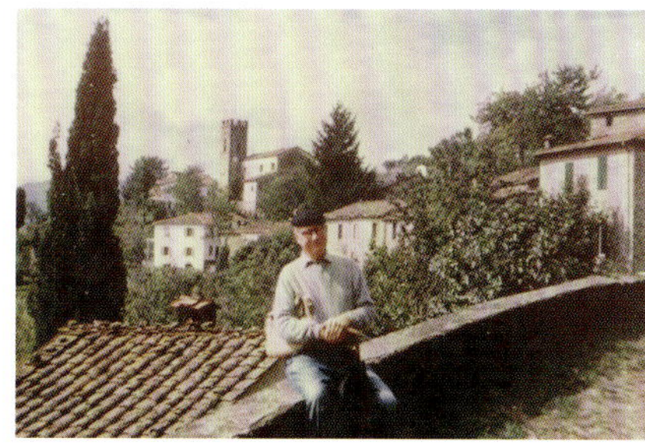

Charles Howard in Bagni di Lucca, Italy, 1966.

• Activist and San Francisco Supervisor Harvey Milk, the first openly gay person to be elected to public office in California, is assassinated at San Francisco City Hall.

• Margaret Thatcher becomes the first female prime minister of the United Kingdom.

1981

• Ronald Reagan is elected President of the United States. Along with the election of Thatcher, Reagan's victory marks a conservative backlash against the liberal politics of the 1960s and 1970s. Both the US and the UK adopt laissez-faire, neoliberal economic policies.

1982

• The US Centers for Disease Control and Prevention (CDC) begins applying the word "AIDS" (Acquired Immune Deficiency Syndrome) in relation to reported incidents of autoimmune disease outbreaks, primarily among gay men.

1983

• Robert Howard dies at the age of eighty-six on February 18.

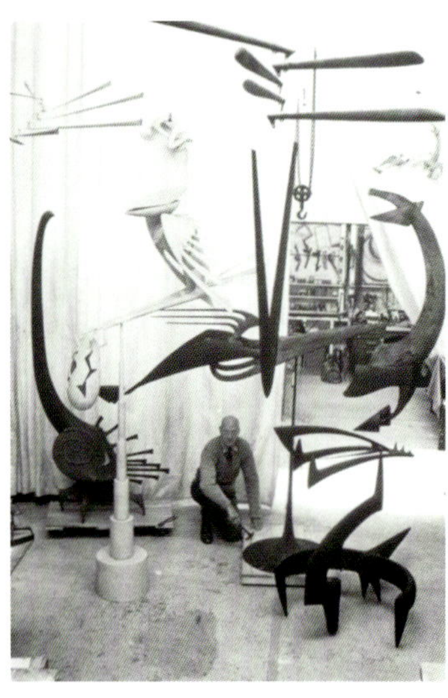

Robert Howard in his studio, ca. 1950s.

GROUP EXHIBITION

American Abstract Art, Charles Campbell Gallery, San Francisco

1984

GROUP EXHIBITION

Ceci n'est pas le surréalisme: California, idioms of surrealism, Fisher Gallery, University of Southern California, Los Angeles

1986

GROUP EXHIBITION

Surrealism in England: 1936 and After, Herbert Read Gallery, Canterbury College of Art, Cambridge, UK

1987

GROUP EXHIBITION

Surrealism in Visual Arts and Film, Retretti Art Centre, Punkaharju, Finland

1988

GROUP EXHIBITIONS

The Howards: First Family of Bay Area Modernism, The Oakland Museum, CA

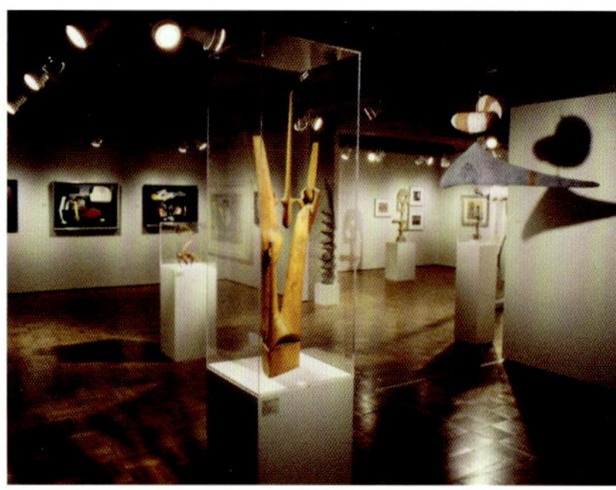

Installation view of *The Howards: First Family of Bay Area Modernism,* The Oakland Museum, CA, May 14– June 31, 1988.

The Surrealist Spirit in Britain, Whitford and Hughes, London

1989

• Social revolutions in Europe's Eastern Bloc come to a head with the fall of the Berlin Wall.

• Student protests against the communist regime turn into a massacre in China's Tiananmen Square when the country's military forces retaliate.

1990

• The first web server and internet browser are launched.

GROUP EXHIBITION

Pursuit of the Marvelous: Stanley William Hayter, Charles Howard, Gordon Onslow Ford, Laguna Art Museum, Laguna Beach, CA

1991

• The Soviet Union collapses.

GROUP EXHIBITION

Geometric Abstraction in California 1940–1960, 871 Fine Arts, San Francisco

1993

SOLO EXHIBITION

Charles Howard 1899–1978, Hirschl & Adler Galleries, New York

GROUP EXHIBITION

Michael Rosenfeld Gallery, New York

1995

GROUP EXHIBITION

Pacific Dreams: Currents of Surrealism and Fantasy in California Art, 1934–1957, Armand Hammer Museum of Art and Cultural Center, Los Angeles

1996

• Dolly the sheep becomes the first mammal to be cloned successfully. The experiment provokes both anxiety about and intrigue with the progression of biogenetics.

1997

SOLO EXHIBITION

To the Absent Friend, a Series of Drawings by American Painter Charles Howard, Rice University Art Gallery, Houston

1998

• Janette Howard Wallace dies.

GROUP EXHIBITIONS

American Surrealism, Hirschl & Adler Galleries, New York

Eccentric Orbits: Stanley William Hayter, Charles Howard, Knud Merrild, and Kay Sage, Hirschl & Adler Galleries, New York

Defining the Edge: Early American Abstraction Selections from the Collection of Dr. Peter B. Fischer, Michael Rosenfeld Gallery, New York

1999

• John Langley Howard dies at the age of ninety-seven on November 15.

2000

SOLO EXHIBITION

Charles Howard 1899–1978, Campbell-Thiebaud Gallery, San Francisco

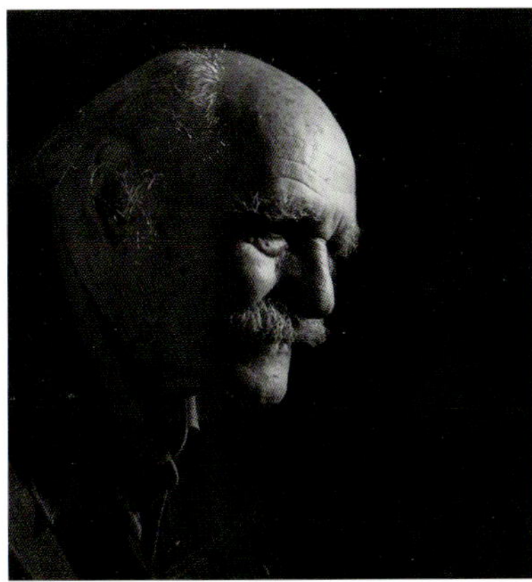

John Langley Howard, n.d.

GROUP EXHIBITION

Dreaming with Open Eyes, Museum of Israel, Jerusalem

2005

GROUP EXHIBITION

The Meat Wagon, an exhibition organized by artist Robert Gober, opens at the Menil Collection in Houston. The show includes twelve drawings from 1945 that Charles Howard had made for Douglas MacAgy. Gober presents them again in his 2007 survey exhibition at the Schaulager museum in Basel, Switzerland.

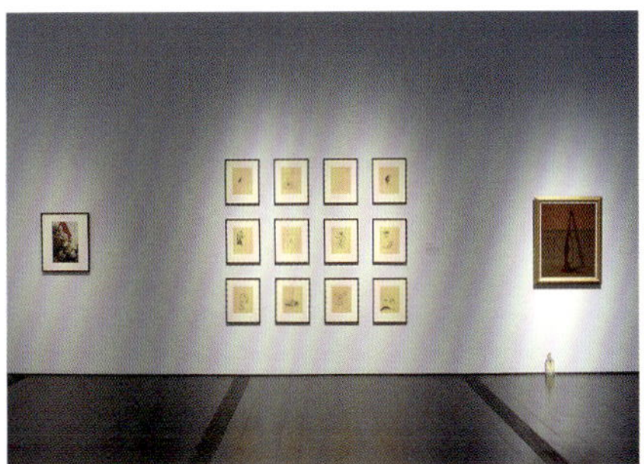

Installation view of *The Meat Wagon,* the Menil Collection, Houston, October 28, 2005–January 22, 2006.

2009

GROUP EXHIBITION

San Francisco–based sculptor Vincent Fecteau includes Charles Howard's *Banner* (1934) among his selections from the museum's collection presented at SFMOMA in his exhibition *Not New Work*.

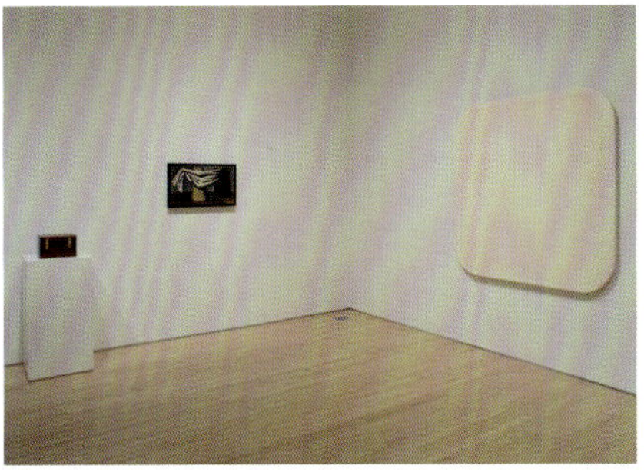

Installation view of *Not New Work,* San Francisco Museum of Modern Art, July 25–November 8, 2009.

2012

GROUP EXHIBITION

Art Interrupted: Advancing American Art and the Politics of Cultural Diplomacy, Georgia Museum of Art, University of Georgia, Athens

2017

SOLO EXHIBITION

Charles Howard: A Margin of Chaos, the first major survey of Howard's work since 1956, opens at BAMPFA.

Selected Bibliography

BOOKS AND CATALOGUES

100 American Painters of the 20th Century; Works Selected from the Collections of the Metropolitan Museum of Art. New York: Metropolitan Museum of Art, 1950.

American Abstract Art, 1909 to 1949. San Francisco: Charles Campbell Gallery, 1983.

Anderson, Susan M. *Pursuit of the Marvelous: Stanley William Hayter, Charles Howard, Gordon Onslow Ford,* exh. cat. Laguna Beach, CA: Laguna Art Museum, 1990.

Ausfeld, Margaret Lynne. *Advancing American Art: Politics and Aesthetics in the State Department Exhibition, 1946–48*. Montgomery, AL: Montgomery Museum of Fine Arts, 1984.

Baird, Joseph Armstrong. *From Exposition to Exposition, Progressive and Conservative Northern California Painting*. Sacramento: Crocker Art Museum, 1981.

Bauer, John. *Revolution and Tradition in Modern American Art*. New York: Praeger, 1967.

Beasley, David. *Douglas MacAgy and the Foundations of Modern Art Curatorship*. Simcoe, Ontario: Davus Publishing, 1998.

——. *Understanding Modern Art: The Boundless Spirit of Clay Edgar Spohn*. Ontario: Davus Publishing, 1999.

Bird, William L. and Harry R. Rubenstein. *Design for Victory: World War II Posters on the American Home Front*. New York: Princeton Architectural Press, 1998.

Bishop, Janet, Corey Keller, and Sarah Roberts, eds. *San Francisco Museum of Modern Art: 75 Years of Looking Forward*. San Francisco: San Francisco Museum of Modern Art, 2009.

Blesh, Rudi. *Modern Art USA: Men, Rebellion, Conquest, 1900–1956*. New York: Knopf, 1956.

British Abstraction of the 1930s. London: Albemarle Gallery, 1988.

Buck, Louisa. *The Surrealist Spirit in Britain,* exh. cat. London: Whitford and Hughes, 1988.

Charles Howard, 1899–1978: Drama of the Mind, exh. cat. New York: Hirschl & Adler Galleries, 1993.

Charles Howard: A Catalogue of an Exhibition of Paintings and Drawings Held at the Whitechapel Art Gallery, London, June to July, 1956. London: Whitechapel Art Gallery, 1956.

Charles Howard, Sigmund Pollitzer: 26 April to 14 May 1949: The Hanover Gallery, exh. cat. London: The Hanover Gallery, 1949.

Clisby, Roger D. *American Drawings and Watercolors from the Munson-Williams-Proctor Arts Institute*. Sacramento: Crocker Art Gallery, 1974.

Corbett, David Peters. *The Modernity of English Art, 1914–1930*. Manchester, UK: Manchester University Press, 1997.

Cummings, Paul. *Dictionary of Contemporary American Artists*. New York: St. Martin's Press, 1982.

Davidson, Susan, and Philip Rylands, eds. *Peggy Guggenheim & Frederick Kiesler: The Story of Art of This Century*. New York: The Solomon R. Guggenheim Foundation, 2004.

Defining the Edge: Early American Abstraction, Selections from the Collection of Dr. Peter B. Fischer, exh. cat. New York: Michael Rosenfeld Gallery, 1998.

Drutt, Matthew. *Robert Gober: The Meat Wagon,* exh. cat. Houston: The Menil Foundation, 2005.

Du Pont, Diana C, ed. *San Francisco Museum of Modern Art: The Painting and Sculpture Collection*. San Francisco: San Francisco Museum of Modern Art, 1985.

Eccentric Orbits: Stanley William Hayter, Charles Howard, Knud Merrild, Kay Sage: April 9– May 29, 1998. New York: Hirschl & Adler Modern, 1998.

Ehrlich, Susan, ed. *Pacific Dreams: Currents of Surrealism and Fantasy in California Art, 1934–1957,* exh. cat. Los Angeles: Armand Hammer Museum of Art and Cultural Center, University of California, Los Angeles, 1995.

Falk, Peter, ed. *Who Was Who in American Art*. Madison, CT: Sound View Press, 1985.

Fort, Ilene Susan, and Tere Arcq, eds. *In Wonderland: The Surrealist Adventures of Women Artists in Mexico and the United States*. New York: Prestel Publishers, 2012.

Frost, Rosamund. *Contemporary Art, the March of Art from Cézanne Until Now*. New York: Crown Publishers, 1942.

Genauer, Emily. *Best of Art*. Garden City, NY: Doubleday, 1948.

Goodway, David. *Herbert Read Reassessed*. Liverpool: Liverpool University Press, 1998.

Guggenheim, Peggy, ed. *Art of This Century*. New York: Arno Press, 1942.

Hailey, Gene, ed. *California Art Research: John Galen Howard, Robert Boardman Howard, Charles Houghton Howard, Adaline Kent, Jane Berlandina*. San Francisco: Works Progress Administration California Art Research Project, vol. 17, 1936–37.

Hale, Robert. *100 American Painters of the 20th Century*. New York: Metropolitan Museum of Art, 1950.

Hopkins, Henry T. *Painting and Sculpture in California: The Modern Era*. San Francisco: San Francisco Museum of Modern Art, 1976.

Howard, Charles. *Design*. Pelham, NY: Bridgman Publishers, 1926.

John Galen Howard Papers, BANC MSS 67/35 c. The Bancroft Library, University of California, Berkeley.

Janis, Sidney. *Abstract and Surrealist Art in the United States*. 1st ed. San Francisco: San Francisco Museum of Art, 1944.

Karlstrom, Paul J. *On the Edge of America: California Modernist Art, 1900–1950*. Berkeley: University of California Press, 1996.

Landauer, Susan. *The San Francisco School of Expressionism*. Laguna Beach, CA: Laguna Art Museum, 1996.

Levy, Julien, ed. *Surrealism*. New York: The Black Sun Press, 1936.

——. *Memoir of an Art Gallery*. New York: Putnam, 1977.

Lucie-Smith, Edward. *Art of the '30s, The Art of Anxiety*. New York: Rizzoli International Publications, Inc., 1985.

Mayor, A. Hyatt, ed. *Artists for Victory: An Exhibition of Contemporary American Art,* exh. cat. New York: The Metropolitan Museum of Art, 1942.

McChesney, Mary Fuller. *A Period of Exploration, San Francisco 1945–1950,* exh. cat. Oakland, CA: The Oakland Museum, 1973.

McCurdy, Charles. *Modern Art: A Pictorial Anthology*. New York: MacMillan, 1942.

Miller, Dorothy C. *Americans 1942: 18 Artists from 9 States,* exh. cat. New York: The Museum of Modern Art, 1942.

Morris, Lynda, and Robert Radford. *AIA, The Story of the Artists International Association 1933–1953*. New York: The Museum of Modern Art, 1983.

Moss, Stacey. *The Howards, First Family of Bay Area Modernism*. Oakland, CA: The Oakland Museum, 1988.

Moure, Nancy Dustin Wall. *California Art: 450 Years of Painting & Other Media*. Los Angeles: Dustin Publications, 1942.

Orr-Cahall, Christina. *The Art of California: Selected Works from the Collection of the Oakland Museum*. Oakland, CA: The Oakland Museum, 1984.

Ray, Paul C. *The Surrealist Movement in England*. Ithaca, NY: Cornell University Press, 1971.

Read, Herbert. *Art Now: An Introduction to the Theory of Modern Painting and Sculpture*. 1st ed., New York: Harcourt, Brace & Company, 1933; 2nd ed., New York: Pitman Publishing Corporation, 1948.

——. *Surrealist Objects & Poems*. London: London Gallery Ltd., 1937.

——. *A Concise History of Modern Painting*. New York: Praeger, 1959.

Remy, Michel. *Surrealism in Britain*. Brookfield, VT: Ashgate Publishing Company, 1999.

Richardson, E. P. *A Short History of Painting in America: The Story of 450 Years*. New York: Thomas Cowell, 1956.

Ritchie, Andrew Carnduff. *Abstract Painting and Sculpture in America*. New York: The Museum of Modern Art, 1951.

Robertson, Bryan, ed. *Charles Howard: A Catalogue of an Exhibition of Paintings and Drawings Held at the Whitechapel Art Gallery, London, June to July, 1956,* exh. cat. London: Whitechapel Art Gallery, 1956.

——. *Charles Howard: Paintings and Drawings,* exh. cat. London: McRoberts and Tunnard, 1963.

Schaffner, Ingrid, and Lisa Jacobs, eds. *Julien Levy: Portrait of an Art Gallery*. Cambridge, MA: MIT Press, 1998.

Sims, Patterson. *Alexander Calder. A Concentration of Works from the Permanent Collection of the Whitney Museum of American Art*. New York: Whitney Museum of American Art, 1981.

Sweet, Frederick, and Katherine Kuh, eds. *Abstract and Surrealist American Art: Fifty-Eighth Annual Exhibition of American Painting and Sculpture*. Chicago: Art Institute of Chicago, 1947.

Vail, Karole P. B., ed. *Peggy Guggenheim, A Celebration*. New York: Solomon R. Guggenheim Foundation, 1998.

Wechsler, Jeffrey. *Surrealism and American Art 1931–1947,* exh. cat. New Brunswick, NH: Rutgers University Art Gallery, 1977.

Woodbridge, Sally B. *John Galen Howard and the University of California: The Design of a Great Public University Campus*. Berkeley: University of California Press, 2002.

ARTICLES, REVIEWS, AND EPHEMERA

"Abstract Canvases, Levy Gallery." *Art News* 31, no. 15 (January 7, 1933): 9.

"Abstraction by C. Howard Wins San Francisco Honor." *Art Digest* 15, no. 7 (January 1, 1941): 21.

"Acquisitions from the Third Annual Exhibition." *Bulletin of the California Palace of the Legion of Honor Museum* 6, no. 8 (December 1948): 70.

"Art: San Francisco Notes." *Arts and Architecture* 63, no. 6 (June 1946): 8.

Alloway, Lawrence. "Art News from London." *Art News* 55, no. 3 (May 1956): 14.

"Art Roster: New Exhibitions." *New York Times*. January 1, 1933.

Baer, Kurt. "Charles Howard Abstractions Are Essentially Intellectual." *Santa Barbara News-Press*. April 15, 1953.

Bouché, Louis. *Paintings by Charles Howard,* brochure. New York: Julien Levy Gallery, 1932.

Bulliet, C. J. "Modern Art Not Divorced from Modern Life." *Art Digest* 23, no. 7 (January 1, 1949): 16.

Charles Howard / Recent Drawings, brochure. London: St. George's Gallery, 1958.

"Charles Howard." *Art News* 45, no. 8 (October 1946): 56-57.

"Charles Howard Has Queer Exhibit." *San Francisco Chronicle*. July 2, 1933.

Church, Robert M. "Sixty-Seventh Annual." *San Francisco Art Association Bulletin* 14, no. 2 (February 1948).

Colodny, Dorothy N., ed. "Charles Howard Exhibit." *San Francisco Art Association Bulletin* 12, no. 11 (November 1946).

——. "Charles Howard Exhibition." *San Francisco Art Association Bulletin* 12, no. 5 (May 1946).

Cravens, Junius. "Charles Houghton Howard," *San Francisco News*, May 4, 1935.

Danysh, Joseph. "The Art World." *Argonaut*, June 30, 1933.

Duncan, Michael. "West Coast Surrealism." *Art in America* 84, no. 1 (January 1996): 39–45.

Ehrlich, Susan. "Pacific Dreams: Currents of Surreal." *American Art Review* 7, no. 4 (August–September 1995): 130–35.

"Exhibition at Whitechapel Art Gallery." *Art News* 55, no. 3 (May 1956): 14.

"Exhibition, Julien Levy Galleries." *Art Digest* 7, no. 7 (January 15, 1933): 15.

"Exhibition of Oils and Gouaches at the Santa Barbara Museum of Art." *Art News* 52, no. 2 (April 1953): 44.

Frankenstein, Alfred. "Around the Art Galleries: This Is Very Good for You Though Not for Us." *San Francisco Chronicle*. May 10, 1942.

——. "Howard Wins First Prize for Painting." *San Francisco Chronicle*. March 25, 1946.

——. "Art Galleries." *San Francisco Chronicle*. May 12, 1946.

——. "Public Art and The Abstracts in The Modern Era." *San Francisco Sunday Examiner and Chronicle*. September 19, 1976.

——. "The Local Galleries: Charles Howard Described as One of Most Important U.S. Painters." *San Francisco Chronicle*. May 12, 1946.

Frankfurter, Alfred M. "The Artists for Victory Exhibition: The Paintings." *Art News* 41, no. 16 (January 1, 1943): 8–18.

Hoene, Anne. "Exhibition at Howard Wise Gallery." *Arts Magazine* 39, no. 10 (March 1965): 66.

——. "In the Galleries." *Arts Magazine* 39, no. 10 (October 1965): 66.

Holland, Katherine Church. *From the Collection: The Gifts of Jermayne MacAgy,* brochure. San Francisco: San Francisco Museum of Modern Art, 1983.

Howard, Charles. "What Concerns Me." *Magazine of Art* 39, no. 2 (February 1946): 63–65.

——. "Charles Howard Writes from England." *San Francisco Art Association Bulletin* 17, no. 1 (January 1951): 3.

Langsner, Jules. "Art News from Los Angeles." *Art News* 52, no. 2 (April 1953): 44-56.

MacAgy, Douglas. "The Art of Charles Howard" *Critique* 1, no. 3 (February 1947): 36–38.

——."A Margin of Chaos." *Circle* 10 (Summer 1948): 39–42.

——. "Charles Howard." *Magazine of Art* 47, no. 4 (April 1953): 155–59.

MacAgy, Jermayne. "Acquisitions from the Third Annual Exhibition." *California Legion of Honor Bulletin* 6, no. 8 (December 1948).

——. *Charles Howard, Retrospective Exhibit 1925–1946,* brochure. San Francisco: California Palace of the Legion of Honor, 1946.

——. *Second Annual Exhibition of Painting*. San Francisco: California Palace of the Legion of Honor, 1948.

Millier, Arthur. "Enriched by Hearst." *Art Digest* 21, no. 12 (March 15, 1947): 20.

"Mr. Charles Howard's New Exhibition." *The Times,* April 30, 1963.

Mullins, E. "Exhibition at McRoberts and Tunnard Gallery, London." *Apollo* 77 (May 1963): 416.

"One Man Show for Experimentalists." *Art News* 45, no. 7 (September 1946): 8.

"Progenitors Acquired by Museum." *Bulletin of the California Palace of the Legion of Honor Museum* 6, no. 8 (December 1948).

Putzel, Howard. "The Art Galleries." *The Monitor*. March 31, 1928.

Reavey, George. "Charles Howard." *London Bulletin,* no. 13 (April 1939): 13–15.

"Recent Pictures by Charles Howard." *The Heffer Gallery*, 1951.

Salinger, Jehanne Biétry. "In San Francisco Galleries." *The Argus* 3, no. 1 (April 1928): 5–6.

Santiago, Chiori. "The Howard Family: Creators of Bay Area Landmarks." *The Museum of California*, June 1988.

Smith, Roberta. "Filling in the Many Gaps in American Surrealism." *New York Times*. March 31, 2005.

"The Summer in London." *Arts Magazine*, May 1963.

"Surrealism and 'Emptiness.'" *Art Digest* 7, no. 7 (January 15, 1933): 15.

Three One-Man Shows: Herbert Bayer, Charles Howard, and Charmion von Wiegand, brochure. New York: Howard Wise Gallery, 1965.

"Ten Year Tenure of the Moderns in San Francisco." *Art News*, February 1, 1945.

"Two California Artists Picked for National Exhibit." *Star-News*. February 24, 1946.

"Variety Included in Howard Exhibition." *San Francisco Chronicle*. March 18, 1928.

Vere, Bernard. "Enigma Variation: Edward Wadsworth's 'Marine Still-Lifes' and Giorgio de Chirico." *Visual Culture in Britain* 7, no. 1 (June 2006): 39–58.

Wallace, Janette Howard. "Reminiscences of Janette Howard Wallace, Daughter of John Galen Howard and Mary Robertson Howard." Unpublished manuscript, 1986. BANC MSS 87/89 c. The Bancroft Library, University of California, Berkeley.

"War and Exhibitions." *San Francisco Art Association Bulletin* 8, no. 9–10 (May 1942): 5.

Wessels, Glen. "The Art World." *Argonaut*. September 20, 1935.

Wolf, Ben. "Charles Howard, Veteran Abstractionist." *Art Digest* 21, no. 1 (October 1, 1946): 13.

Works in the Exhibition

This listing reflects the information available at the time of publication.

Charles Houghton Howard
United States, 1899–1978

PAINTINGS

Excavation, 1932
Oil on canvas, 24 × 34 in. (61 × 86.4 cm)
Courtesy of Hirschl & Adler Galleries, New York
(plate 7)

Grotto, 1932
Oil on canvas, 24 × 34 in. (61 × 86.4 cm)
Collection of William and Carol Achenbaum
(plate 8)

Banner, 1934
Oil on canvas, 15 × 26¾ in (38.1 × 68 cm)
San Francisco Museum of Modern Art, gift from the family of Robert B. Howard and Adaline Kent, acquired 2009, 2009.140
(plate 12)

The Dove, 1939
Oil on canvas, 11¹⁵⁄₁₆ × 13¹⁵⁄₁₆ in. (32.4 × 51.8 cm)
Norton Museum of Art, West Palm Beach, Florida, purchase, R. H. Norton Trust, 2001.7
(plate 26)

First War Winter, 1939–40
Oil on canvas, 24¼ × 34 in. (61.6 × 86.4 cm)
San Francisco Museum of Modern Art, purchase, acquired 1940, 40.5313
(plate 27)

Bivouac, 1940
Oil on board, 16 × 20 in. (40.6 × 50.8 cm)
Anonymous
(plate 28)

Generation, 1940
Oil on canvas, 22¾ × 25¾ in. (57.8 × 65.4 cm)
Collection of the Oakland Museum of California, Museum Donors Acquisition Fund, A75.110 (plate 29)

Trinity, 1941
Oil on canvas, 24 × 34 in. (61 × 86.4 cm)
The Art Institute of Chicago, Wilson L. Mead Fund, 1945.292
(plate 32)

Prescience, 1942
Oil on canvas, 28¼ × 40½ in. (52.4 × 102.9 cm)
The Metropolitan Museum of Art, New York, Arthur Hoppock Hearn Fund, 1942, 42.163
(plate 33)

Departure, ca. 1943
Oil on canvas, 13¹⁵⁄₁₆ × 17¹⁵⁄₁₆ in. (35.4 × 45.6 cm)
Private collection, New York
(plate 34)

Glyptic, 1943
Oil on canvas board, 9 × 12 in. (22.9 × 30.5 cm)
Collection of Kim and Todd Crockett
(plate 35)

Untitled, 1944
Oil on canvas, 12 × 15⅞ in. (30.5 × 40.3 cm)
Smithsonian American Art Museum, Washington, DC, bequest of Edith S. and Arthur J. Levin, 2005.5.41
(plate 36)

Wild Park, 1944
Oil on canvas mounted on board, 13⅞ × 17⅞ in. (35.3 × 45.4 cm)
Munson-Williams-Proctor Arts Institute, Utica, NY, Edward W. Root Bequest, 57.163

Dove Love, 1945
Oil on canvas, 18 × 24⅛ in. (45.7 × 61.3 cm)
The Menil Collection, Houston, Bequest of Jermayne MacAgy, 1964-154 McA
(plate 37)

The Medusa, 1945
Oil on canvas, 14⅛ × 18³⁄₁₆ in. (35.9 × 48.3 cm)
Fred Jones Jr. Museum of Art, The University of Oklahoma, Norman; Purchase, U.S. State Department Collection, 1948, 1721
(plate 38)

The Chain of Circumstance, 1946
Oil on canvas, 12⅛ × 24⅛ in. (30.8 × 61.3 cm)
Collection of Dan and Claire Carlevaro
(plate 40)

The First Hypothesis, 1946
Oil on canvas, 16¼ × 22⅛ in. (41.3 × 56.2 cm)
The Menil Collection, Houston, Bequest of Jermayne MacAgy, 1964-155 McA
(plate 41)

The Progenitors, 1947
Oil on canvas, 24⅜ × 34½ in. (61.9 × 87.6 cm)
Fine Arts Museums of San Francisco, de Young Museum, museum purchase, Mildred Anna Williams Collection, 1948.13
(plate 45)

The Aimant, 1949
Oil on canvas mounted on board, 12 × 16 in. (30.5 × 40.6 cm)
University of California, Berkeley Art Museum and Pacific Film Archive, purchase made possible through a bequest of Phoebe Apperson Hearst, by exchange, and funds provided by the Norma H. Schlesinger, Andrew & Paul Spiegel Fund, the Marcia Simon Weisman Foundation Fund, the Jan Boyce Fund for Contemporary Art, the Friends and Trustees Acquisitions Endowment Fund, and Sally B. Woodbridge, 2016.25
(plate 48)

The Ascending Aperture, 1949
Oil on canvas mounted on board, 12 × 16 in. (30.5 × 40.6 cm)
Private collection
(plate 49)

The Cumulative Emblem, 1949
Oil on canvas, 10 × 13¹⁵⁄₁₆ in. (25.4 × 35.6 cm)
Collection of David and Linda Supino
(plate 50)

Double Circle, 1950
Oil on canvas, 32 × 41½ in. (81.3 × 105.4 cm)
Los Angeles County Museum of Art, Los Angeles, M.2006.73.2

Binary Armature, 1951
Oil on canvas, 10 × 17 in. (25.4 × 43.2 cm)
Courtesy of Michael Rosenfeld Gallery, LLC, New York
(plate 51)

Night Painting, 1955
Oil on canvas, 40¼ × 57¼ in. (102.2 × 145.4 cm)
Collection of Joel and Nancy Hart
(plate 52)

Painting (I), 1962
Oil on canvas, 24⅛ × 34¾ in. (61.3 × 88.3 cm)
Blanton Museum of Art, The University of Texas at Austin, gift of the artist, 1976, G1976.17.6
(plate 55)

Painting (VI), 1962
Oil on canvas, 33¹⁄₁₆ × 46¹⁄₁₆ in. (83.8 × 116.8 cm)
Blanton Museum of Art, The University of Texas at Austin, Michener Acquisitions Fund, 1969, P1969.14.1
(plate 56)

Painting (VI), 1964
Oil on canvas, 33¼ × 46¼ in. (84.5 × 117.5 cm)
Blanton Museum of Art, The University of Texas at Austin, gift of the artist, 1976, G1976.17.11
(plate 57)

DRAWINGS AND GOUACHES

Untitled, ca. 1927–29
Gouache and graphite on drafting paper, 19 × 14³⁄₁₆ in. (48.3 × 35.6 cm)
Collection of the Howard Family
(plate 2)

1826 into 1926, 1927
Watercolor and graphite on paper, 13½ × 13¼ in. (34.3 × 33.7 cm)
Fine Arts Museums of San Francisco, gift of the Family of Robert B. Howard and Adaline Kent, 2010.67.1
(plate 1)

Untitled, 1931
Ink on paper, 22 × 15 in. (55.9 × 38.1 cm)
Fine Arts Museums of San Francisco, gift of the Family of Robert B. Howard and Adaline Kent, 2010.67.3
(plate 3)

Untitled, 1931
Ink on paper, 15 × 21½ in. (38.1 × 54.6 cm)
Fine Arts Museums of San Francisco, gift of the Family of Robert B. Howard and Adaline Kent, 2010.67.4
(plate 4)

Untitled, 1931
Gouache and watercolor on paper, 14 × 20 in. (35.6 × 50.8 cm)
Los Angeles County Museum of Art, Los Angeles, Bequest of Fannie and Alan Leslie, M.2006.73.8
(plate 5)

Untitled Abstract Landscape, ca. 1931–32
Watercolor on paper, 13¾ × 21⅛ in. (34.9 × 53.3 cm)
Fine Arts Museums of San Francisco, Gift of Walter and Josephine Landor, 2001.97.8
(plate 6)

Untitled, 1932
Gouache and graphite on paper, 14½ × 21¾ in. (36.8 × 55.3 cm)
Collection of the Howard Family
(plate 9)

Untitled (#1), 1932
Gouache and graphite on paper, 18½ × 13½ in. (47 × 34.3 cm)
Collection of Dr. Alexandra Lajoie and Mr. W. Ulysses Fowler
(plate 10)

Untitled (#2), 1932
Gouache and graphite on paper, 18⅜ × 13⅜ in. (46.7 × 34 cm)
Collection of Dr. Alexandra Lajoie and Mr. W. Ulysses Fowler
(plate 11)

Untitled, ca. 1935
Ink on paper, 15¼ × 22¼ in. (38.7 × 56.5 cm)
Fine Arts Museums of San Francisco, gift of the Family of Robert B. Howard and Adaline Kent, 2010.67.5
(plate 14)

Untitled, 1935
Gouache and graphite on paper, 13 × 21 in. (33 × 53.3 cm)
Courtesy of Hirschl & Adler Galleries, New York
(plate 13)

Untitled, 1935
Gouache and graphite on paper, 13³⁄₁₆ × 20¼ in. (33.5 × 51.4 cm)
Collection of the Howard Family
(plate 15)

Concretion, 1936
Gouache and graphite on paper, 10 × 14 in. (25.4 × 35.6 cm)
Private collection
(plate 16)

Sketch for an Abstract Painting, 1936
Gouache and graphite on paper, 9¼ × 13 in. (23.5 × 33 cm)
Private collection
(plate 17)

Untitled, 1936
Gouache and graphite on paper, 9⅞ × 14⅛ in. (25.1 × 35.9 cm)
Collection of the Howard Family

Untitled, ca. 1937
Graphite, ink, and watercolor on paper, 12⁷⁄₁₆ × 18½ in. (31.8 × 47 cm)
University of California, Berkeley Art Museum and Pacific Film Archive, gift of Galen Howard Hilgard in memory of her parents, Robert B. Howard and Adaline Kent, 2016.93
(plate 20)

The Mother (Makes the Son) Plants the Seed, 1937
Gouache and graphite on paper, 10⅜ × 14⅝ in. (26.4 × 37.2 cm)
Courtesy of Hirschl & Adler Galleries, New York
(plate 18)

The Sons Await Tradition, 1937
Gouache on paper, 9¼ × 16 in. (23.5 × 40.6 cm)
Courtesy of Hirschl & Adler Galleries, New York
(plate 19)

The Cage, 1938
Tempera and watercolor on paper, 21⅝ × 29⅝ in. (54.9 × 75.3 cm)
Solomon R. Guggenheim Museum, New York, Solomon R. Guggenheim Founding Collection, 46.1032
(plate 23)

Precinct, 1938
Gouache and watercolor on paper, 18½ × 27 in. (47 × 68.6 cm)
Collection of the Oakland Museum of California, Museum Donors Acquisition Fund, A83.44
(plate 21)

Presage, 1938
Gouache, watercolor, ink, and graphite on paper,
14⅞ × 22 in. (37.8 × 55.9 cm)
Arkansas Arts Center Foundation Collection, Little Rock,
purchase, Tabriz Fund, 2015.006
(plate 22)

Elevation, 1939
Gouache and graphite on paper, 21⅜ × 29½ in.
(54.3 × 74.9 cm)
Collection of the Howard Family
(plate 24)

Hare Corner, 1939
Gouache and graphite on paper, 26⅝ × 35⅞ in.
(67.6 × 90.9 cm)
Whitney Museum of American Art, New York, purchase, with funds from the Katherine Schmidt Shubert
Purchase Fund, 93.66
(plate 25)

Esplanade, 1941
Gouache on paper, 20⅝ × 27 in. (52.4 × 68.6 cm)
Collection of Richard Blacher
(plate 30)

Hieroglyph, 1941
Gouache on paper, 15½ × 22⅝ in. (39.4 × 57.5 cm)
Private collection
(plate 31)

Selections from a series of 54 untitled drawings
sent to Douglas MacAgy, December 31, 1944–
February 22, 1945
Ink on paper, each 11 × 8½ in. (27.9 × 21.6 cm)
The Menil Collection, Houston, Bequest of Jermayne
MacAgy, 1964–282 McA
(pp. 35–42)

Untitled, ca. 1946
Ink, graphite, and gouache on paper, 15 × 21¼ in.
(38.1 × 54 cm)
Fine Arts Museums of San Francisco, gift of the Family of
Robert B. Howard and Adaline Kent
(plate 44)

California, from the *United States Series,* 1946
Gouache on paperboard, 13 × 10⅜ in. (33 ×
26.4 cm)
Smithsonian American Art Museum, Washington, DC,
gift of Container Corporation of America, 1984.124.121
(plate 39)

Nasty 7: VII: 46, 1946
Gouache, pen and ink, and graphite on paper, 15 ×
21¹⁵⁄₁₆ in. (38.1 × 55.9 cm)
Collection of Adaline J. Hilgard
(plate 42)

Nasty 8: VIII: 46, 1946
Gouache and graphite on paper, 15 × 22 in. (38.1 ×
55.9 cm)
Collection of the Howard Family
(plate 43)

The Gift, 1948
Gouache on paper, 13¾ × 20³⁄₁₆ in. (34.9 × 51.3 cm)
Collection of Jack Propp Heller
(plate 46)

Untitled, 1948
Watercolor and ink on paper, 15⅜ × 21⅞ in.
(39 × 55.6 cm)
Collection of Alvin and Susan Marr
(plate 47)

Untitled, 1956
Pen, ink, and graphite on paper, 17¾ × 25¹⁵⁄₁₆ in.
(45 × 65.9 cm)
Collection of John Raimondi and Ralph Cantin
(plate 53)

Untitled, 1956
Pen and ink on paper, 17¾ × 25⅞ in. (45 × 65.7 cm)
Collection of Galen Rohrs Roll
(plate 54)

Untitled, 1958
Ink on paper, 17¼ × 25¾ in. (43.82 × 65.41 cm)
Collection of the Howard Family

Lenders to the Exhibition

William and Carol Achenbaum

Anonymous

Arkansas Arts Center Foundation, Little Rock

The Art Institute of Chicago

University of California, Berkeley Art Museum and Pacific
Film Archive

Richard Blacher

Blanton Museum of Art, The University of Texas at Austin

Dan and Claire Carlevaro

Kim and Todd Crockett

The Fred Jones Jr. Museum of Art, University of Oklahoma,
Norman

Adaline J. Hilgard

Hirschl & Adler Galleries, New York

The Howard Family

Fine Arts Museums of San Francisco

Joel and Nancy Hart

Jack Propp Heller

Dr. Alexandra Lajoie and Mr. W. Ulysses Fowler

Los Angeles County Museum of Art, Los Angeles

Alvin and Susan Marr

The Menil Collection, Houston

The Metropolitan Museum of Art, New York

Michael Rosenfeld Gallery, LLC, New York

Munson-Williams-Proctor Arts Institute, Utica

Norton Museum of Art, West Palm Beach

Oakland Museum of California

Private collections

John Raimondi and Ralph Cantin

Galen Rohrs Roll

San Francisco Museum of Modern Art

Smithsonian American Art Museum, Washington, DC

Solomon R. Guggenheim Museum, New York

David and Linda Supino

Whitney Museum of American Art, New York

Index

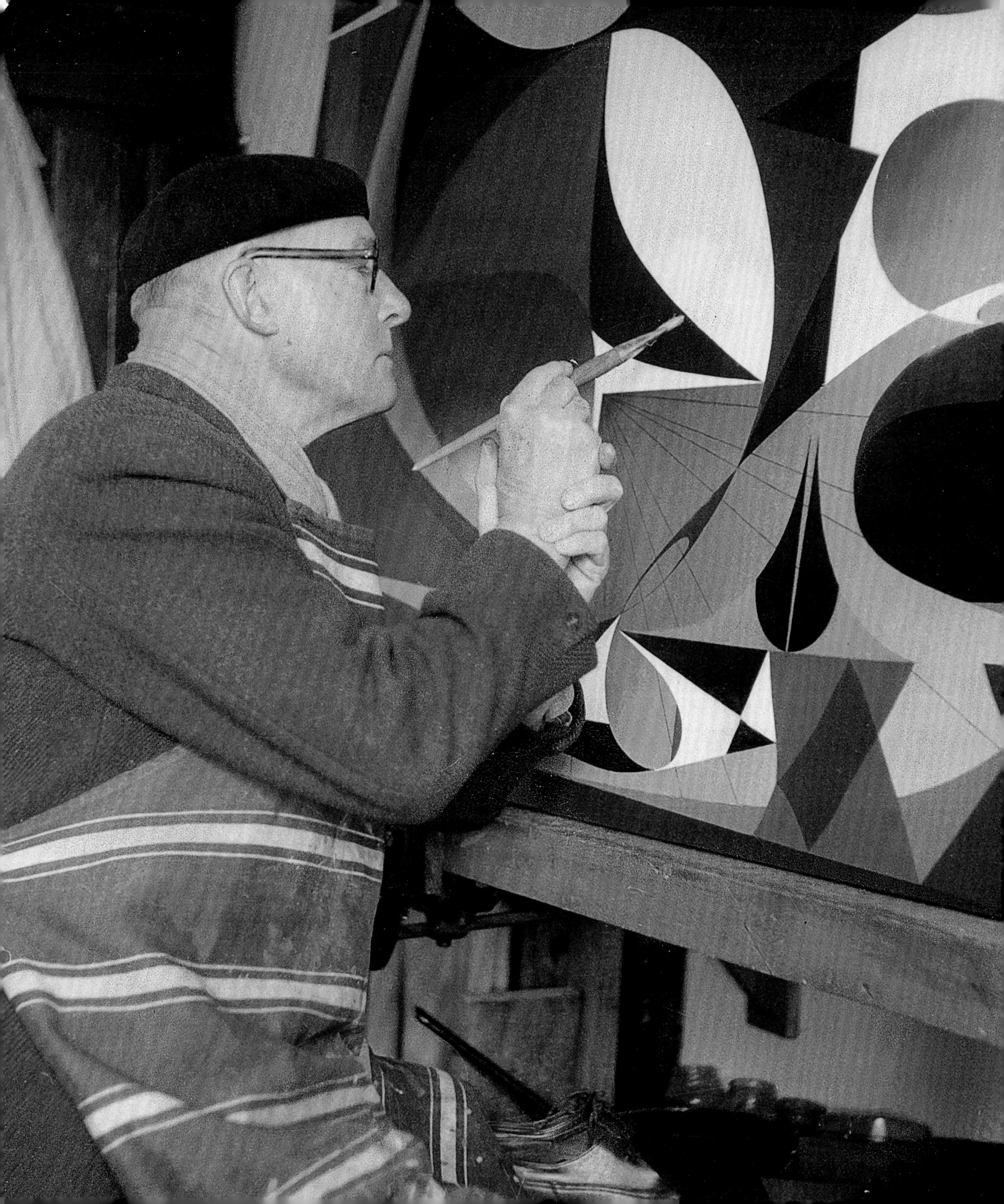

Image Credits

All artworks by Charles Howard are © copyright the estate of Charles Howard and are reproduced by permission of the estate and the owners of the artworks named below. Additional image credits are noted where applicable.

PLATES

2, 10, 11, 15, 24, 35: images © 2016 Bonhams & Butterfields Auctioneers Corp. All Rights Reserved. **6, 14, 45**: Fine Arts Museum of San Francisco. **7, 13, 18, 20**: Photo: Eric W. Baumgartner, Hirschl & Adler Modern, New York. **8**: Photo: Joshua Nefsky. **12, 13**: Photo: Don Ross. San Francisco Museum of Modern Art. **16, 17, 31**: Private collection. Photo: Tom Little. **19, 48**: Photo: Sibila Savage. **21, 29**: Oakland Museum of California. **22**: Arkansas Art Center Foundation Collection. **23**: Solomon R. Guggenheim Museum, New York **25**: Whitney Museum of American Art, New York. **26**: Norton Museum of Art, West Palm Beach, Florida. **32**: Art Institute of Chicago. **33**: The Metropolitan Museum of Art. Image source: Art Resource, NY. **34**: photo: Calder Foundation, New York / Art Resource, New York, © 2016 Calder Foundation, New York / Artists Rights Society (ARS), New York;. **36, 39**: Smithsonian American Art Museum. **38**: The Fred Jones Jr. Museum of Art, University of Oklahoma, Norman. **37, 41**: Photo: Paul Hester, Courtesy of the Menil Collection, Houston. **40**: Photo: Johnna Arnold. **47**: Photo: Aidan Fitzpatrick. **51**: Photo: Michael Rosenfeld Gallery, LLC. **52**: Photo: Jacek Gancarz. **55, 56, 57**: Blanton Museum of Art, The University of Texas at Austin.

FIGURES

Copyright to the illustrated works is held by the artists or their representatives as named in the image captions or noted below. All images are reproduced by permission of the rights holders and the institutions and individuals identified here.

DiQuinzio: **1, 22**: Photo: Berenice Abbott / Getty Images. **2, 4, 16, 18, 25, 31**: The Howard Family. **3**: BANC PIC 19xx.552—PIC. The Bancroft Library, University of California, Berkeley. **5**: BANC MSS 67/35 c. The Bancroft Library, University of California, Berkeley. **6**: Courtesy of the Ufficio Diocesano per l'arte sacra e I beni culturali. **7**: Courtesy of the Ministero dei beni e delle attività culturali del turismo, Gallerie dell'Accademia di Venezia. **8, 12, 14**: Photo: Sibila Savage **9**: Digital Image © Whitney Museum, N.Y. © 2016 Calder Foundation, New York / Artists Rights Society (ARS), New York. **13**: © Succession Marcel Duchamp / ADAGP, Paris / Artists Rights Society (ARS), New York 1910. **15**: © Salvador Dalí, Fundació Gala-Salvador Dalí, Artists Rights Society (ARS), New York 1931. Photo: The Museum of Modern Art / Licensed by SCALA / Art Resource, NY. **17**: Giorgio de Chirico "Souvenir of Italy" 1913 © 2016 Artists Rights Society (ARS), New York / SIAE, Rome. **20**: © 1925 Estate of Pablo Picasso / Artists Rights Society (ARS), New York. **23**: © Estate of Adaline Kent. San Francisco Museum of Modern Art. **24**: Photo: Don Myer. San Francisco Museum of Modern Art. **26**: © Man Ray Trust / Artists Rights Society (ARS), NY / ADAGP, Paris 1936. **27**: San Francisco Museum of Modern Art. **28**: © The Museum of Modern Art / Licensed by SCALA / Art Resource, NY. **29**: Artist Ephemera Files. Courtesy SFMOMA Research Library.
Gober: **1**: Photo: Ellen Bransten. San Francisco Art Institute Archives. **Kroiz**: **1**: © 2016 Artists Rights Society (ARS), New York / ADAGP, Paris. **2**: Photo: Ken Howie. Courtesy of Phoenix Art Museum. All rights reserved. **3**: © 2016 Angela Verren Taunt / All rights reserved / ARS, NY / DACS, London. **4**: Henry Moore Archive. Reproduced by permission of the Henry Moore Foundation. **6**: De La Warr Pavilion Charitable Trust. **7**: Estate of Madge Knight. San Francisco Museum of Modern Art. **8**: Photo: Sibila Savage. **9, 10**: © 2016 Bonhams &

Butterfields Auctioneers Corp. All Rights Reserved. **Chronology: 1899, 1902a, 1902b, 1902c, 1933, 1950, 1957, 1963, 1970, 1974, 1978, 1983, 1999:** The Howard Family. **1906:** Photo: Harry Smith. Copyright 1981 Stephen White Gallery / Los Angeles, California. BANC PIC 2001.198, The Bancroft Library, University of California, Berkeley. **1917a:** The Library of Congress Prints and Photographs Division, Washington, DC. **1917b:** Berkeley High School. **1920:** Photo: Francis Godolphin Osbourne Stuart. Courtesy of the Watkinson Library, Trinity College, Hartford, Connecticut. **1923:** BANC PIC 1999.080—PIC, The Bancroft Library, University of California, Berkeley. **1926:** Photo: Charles Sheeler. Whitney Museum of American Art, New York. **1932a:** Photo: Glen Davis. Davis Collection 0020 0064, UNLV Libraries Special Collections. **1932b:** Julien Levy Gallery records, Philadelphia Museum of Art, Archives. **1936:** © Tate, London 2016. **1939:** Collection of the Münchner Stadtmuseum, Sammlung Fotografie, Archiv Landshoff. Image courtesy of the Philadelphia Museum of Art Library and Archives. **1940:** © Tate, London 2016. **1941a:** Photo no. P79-141.265x. San Francisco Maritime National Historical Park. **1941b:** Photo no. 80-G-16871. The National Archives, Washington DC. **1945a:** Photo no. AAD-8877, San Francisco Historical Photograph Collection. San Francisco History Center, San Francisco Public Library. **1945b:** Photo: US Army. The Hiroshima Peace Memorial Museum. **1949:** Photo: © William Heick. San Francisco Art Institute Archives. **1951:** Digital Image © The Museum of Modern Art / Licensed by SCALA / Art Resource, NY. **1969:** Courtesy of the National Aeronautics and Space Administration, NASA History Office and the NASA JSC Media Services Center. **1988:** Oakland Museum of California. **2005:** Photo: George Hixson. Courtesy of Menil Archives, The Menil Collection, Houston. **2009:** Photo: Ian Reeves. San Francisco Museum of Modern Art.

This book is published in conjunction with the exhibition *Charles Howard: A Margin of Chaos*, presented at the University of California, Berkeley Art Museum and Pacific Film Archive from June 21 to October 1, 2017.

Charles Howard: A Margin of Chaos is organized by Apsara DiQuinzio, curator of modern and contemporary art and Phyllis C. Wattis MATRIX Curator, with Valerie Moon, curatorial assistant. The exhibition is made possible through major support from the Terra Foundation for American Art. Additional support is provided by Michael Rosenfeld Gallery, Galen Howard Hilgard, Bonhams, and Claire and Dan Carlevaro.

TERRA
FOUNDATION FOR AMERICAN ART

Published by University of California, Berkeley Art Museum and Pacific Film Archive

Available through:
ARTBOOK | D.A.P.
75 Broad Street, Suite 630
New York, NY 10004
www.artbook.com

Produced by Lucia | Marquand, Seattle
www.luciamarquand.com

Edited by Amanda Glesmann
Designed by Ryan Polich
Typeset in Mercury Text by Maggie Lee
Proofread by Elissa Greisz
Indexed by Enid L. Zafran
Color management by iocolor, Seattle
Printed and bound in Italy by Graphicom

Library of Congress Cataloging-in-Publication Data
Names: Container of (work): Howard, Charles, 1899–1978. Works. Selections. | Berkeley Art Museum and Pacific Film Archive, host institution, organizer.
Title: Charles Howard: a margin of chaos.
Description: Berkeley: University of California, Berkeley Art Museum and Pacific Film Archive, 2017. | Published in conjunction with the exhibition held at the Berkeley Art Museum and Pacific Film Archive, June 21–October 1, 2017. | Includes bibliographical references and index.
Identifiers: LCCN 2017005893 | ISBN 9780983881322 (hardcover: alk. paper)
Subjects: LCSH: Howard, Charles, 1899–1978—Exhibitions. | Art, Abstract—United States—Exhibitions.
Classification: LCC N6537.H658 A4 2017 | DDC 759.13—dc23
LC record available at https://lccn.loc.gov/2017005893

Endsheets: *Untitled* (sketchbook drawing), n.d. (details). Graphite on paper, 16 × 20 in. (40.6 × 50.8 cm). Courtesy the Howard Family.
pp. 2–3: *Banner*, 1934. Oil on canvas, 15 × 263 in. (38.1 × 68 cm). San Francisco Museum of Modern Art, gift from the family of Robert B. Howard and Adaline Kent, acquired 2009. Photo: Don Ross. San Francisco Museum of Modern Art.
p. 4: *Hare Corner*, 1939 (detail). Gouache and graphite on paper, 26⅝ × 35⅞ in. (67.6 × 90.9 cm). Whitney Museum of American Art, New York, purchase, with funds from the Katherine Schmidt Shubert Purchase Fund. Digital Image © The Whitney Museum of American Art, New York.
p. 6: *The Cage*, 1938 (detail). Tempera and watercolor on paper, 21⅝ × 29⅝ in. (54.9 × 75.3 cm). Solomon R. Guggenheim Museum, New York. Image courtesy the Howard family.
p. 10: *The Aimant*, 1949 (detail). Oil on canvas mounted on board, 12 × 16 in. (30.5 × 40.6 cm). University of California, Berkeley Art Museum and Pacific Film Archive, purchase made possible through a bequest of Phoebe Apperson Hearst, by exchange, and funds provided by the Norma H. Schlesinger, Andrew & Paul Spiegel Fund, the Marcia Simon Weisman Foundation Fund, the Jan Boyce Fund for Contemporary Art, the Friends and Trustees Acquisitions Endowment Fund, and Sally B. Woodbridge. Photo: Sibila Savage.
p. 44: *First War Winter*, 1939–40 (detail). Oil on canvas, 24¼ × 34 in. (61.6 × 86.4 cm). San Francisco Museum of Modern Art. Photo: Don Ross. San Francisco Museum of Modern Art.
p. 56: *The Chain of Circumstance*, 1946 (detail). Oil on canvas, 12⅛ × 24⅛ in. (30.8 × 61.3 cm). Photo: Johnna Arnold.
pp. 60–61: *Untitled*, 1935. Gouache and graphite on paper, 13³⁄₁₆ × 201 in. (33.5 × 51.4 cm). Collection of the Howard Family. Image © 2016 Bonhams & Butterfields Auctioneers Corp. All Rights Reserved.
p. 126: Charles Howard at work on *Winter Painting*, 1956. Image courtesy the Howard Family.
See page 127 for additional image credits.

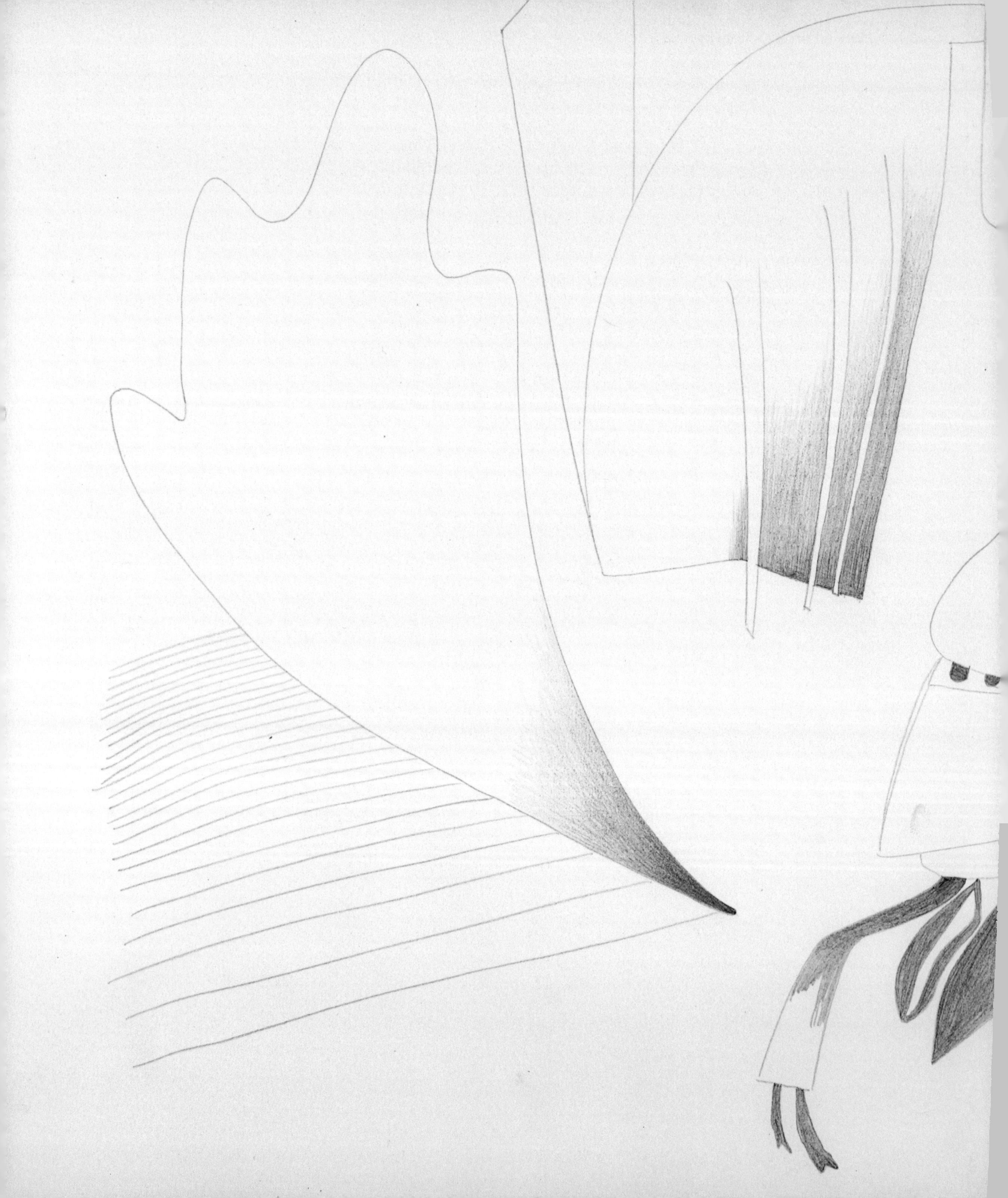